Anxious Men

For Ellie, Edward, Max, Polly and Ruby

Anxious Men

Masculinity in American Fiction of the Mid-Twentieth Century

Clive Baldwin

EDINBURGH
University Press

Edinburgh University Press is one of the leading university presses in the UK. We publish academic books and journals in our selected subject areas across the humanities and social sciences, combining cutting-edge scholarship with high editorial and production values to produce academic works of lasting importance. For more information visit our website: edinburghuniversitypress.com

© Clive Baldwin, 2020, 2022

Edinburgh University Press Ltd
The Tun – Holyrood Road,
12(2f) Jackson's Entry,
Edinburgh EH8 8PJ

First published in hardback by Edinburgh University Press 2020

Typeset in 11/13 Adobe Sabon by
IDSUK (DataConnection) Ltd

A CIP record for this book is available from the British Library

ISBN 978 1 4744 2387 8 (hardback)
ISBN 978 1 4744 9489 2 (paperback)
ISBN 978 1 4744 2388 5 (webready PDF)
ISBN 978 1 4744 2389 2 (epub)

The right of Clive Baldwin to be identified as the author of this work has been asserted in accordance with the Copyright, Designs and Patents Act 1988, and the Copyright and Related Rights Regulations 2003 (SI No. 2498).

Contents

Acknowledgements	vi
Introduction: Anxiety, Conformity and Masculinity	1
1. 'Organization Man', Domestic Ideology and Manhood	30
2. 'Everything in him had come undone': Violent Aggression, Courage and Masculine Identity	72
3. Representing Sexualities and Gender	111
4. Identity and Assimilation in Jewish American Fiction	160
5. African American Identity and Masculinity	196
Afterword	235
Works Cited and Consulted	239
Index	260

Acknowledgements

First, I must thank my family and friends who have supported me through the years of research and writing that have culminated in this book, and who have made me feel that it was a worthwhile and interesting project.

During those years, when I was studying at Birkbeck College and working at the Open University, fellow students and colleagues at those institutions engaged me in a stimulating intellectual environment while giving me the encouragement to keep going. As my doctoral supervisor at Birkbeck, Lynne Segal gave me perceptive comments and suggestions – as well as showing great patience with my tortoise-like progress. Richard Allen, as Dean of Arts at the Open University, gave me support and space to work on my research. Throughout the period, Catherine King has been a source of inspiration and invaluable wise advice. Richard Danson Brown has read carefully and commented thoughtfully on the various drafts of this writing – knowing that I could call on his friendship and depend on the acuity of his reading has been absolutely essential to completing this book.

Finally, to Kiki Olympios-Clark, who not only read the complete draft of the book and discussed it with me, but is my enduring source of loving support.

Introduction

Anxiety, Conformity and Masculinity

Chester Himes, *If He Hollers Let Him Go*, 1945:
    All the tightness that had been in my body, making my motions jerky, keeping my muscles taut, left me and I felt relaxed, confident, strong. I felt just like I thought a white boy oughta feel; I had never felt so strong in all my life. (45)

Jim Thompson, *The Killer Inside Me*, 1952:
    I killed Amy Stanton on Saturday night on the fifth of April, 1952, at a few minutes before nine o'clock. [. . .]
    She smiled and came towards me with her arms held out. 'I won't darling. I won't ever say anything like that again. But I want to tell you how much –'
    'Sure,' I said. 'You want to pour your heart out to me.'
    And I hit her in the guts as hard as I could.
    My fist went back against her spine, and the flesh closed around it to the wrist. I jerked back on it, I had to jerk, and she flopped forward from the waist, like she was hinged. (152, 164–5)

Norman Mailer, *The Naked and the Dead*, 1948:
    Their love-making is fantastic for a time:
    He must subdue her, absorb her, rip her apart and consume her. [. . .]
    I'll take you apart, I'll eat you, oh, I'll make you mine, I'll make you mine, you bitch. (419)

John Horne Burns, *The Gallery*, 1947:
    I caught on fast, with the lessons she gimme [the corporal said]. These babes know something . . . She taught me to kiss slow, to take my time. I useta close my eyes an just jab, hoping for the best . . . Rosetta kisses sleepy like. Sometimes she puts her tongue in my ear. Or just brushes her lips along my throat. Gee . . . (305)

James Baldwin, *Giovanni's Room*, 1956:
    I was not suggesting for a moment that you jeopardize, even for a moment, that [. . .] immaculate manhood. (33)

> J. D. Salinger, *The Catcher in the Rye*, 1951:
>> But I'd plug him anyway. Six shots right through his fat, hairy belly. [. . .] Then I'd [. . .] call up Jane and have her come over and bandage up my guts. I pictured her holding a cigarette for me to smoke while I was bleeding and all.
>> The goddam movies. They can ruin you. I'm not kidding.
>> [. . .] Then I got back into bed. It took me quite a while to get to sleep – I wasn't even tired – but finally I did. What I really felt like, though, was committing suicide. I felt like jumping out the window. (94)
>
> Jack Kerouac, *On the Road*, 1957:
>> You have absolutely no regard for anybody but yourself and your damned kicks. All you think about is what's hanging between your legs and how much money or fun you can get out of people and then you just throw them aside. [. . .] It never occurs to you that life is serious [. . .] (176)

These quotations serve to open up a number of central themes relating to masculinity in this period that will be explored further as I consider the representation of masculinity in American fiction published in the middle of the twentieth century. The quotation from Chester Himes's novel emphasises the importance of the body and its strength to a sense of manliness. Thompson's description of the murder of a woman by Lou Ford, his first-person narrator, might be seen as typifying certain aspects of 'masculinity' in its misogyny and violence and in the projection of emotion onto the feminine. Thompson's novel links sexuality with violence and such a connection can similarly be seen in the quotation from *The Naked and the Dead*, in which 'fantastic' heterosexual sex is about male domination and subjection of the woman. In contrast, John Horne Burns in *The Gallery* describes a more sensual male sexuality. Yet Holden Caulfield's fantasy of retribution and sexual reward in the face of humiliation warns against assuming any natural or essential attributes of manliness. He perceives that his fantasy is based on a model of masculinity that is constructed in the representations of the movie industry. Moreover, this image of manhood is a hollow construct that only temporarily distracts him from his actual despair, and Caulfield's vulnerability implies that idealised notions of manliness can be damaging to men.

The quotations also suggest how this idealised masculinity depends on the way it is constructed in relation to other identities. The narrator in the quote from Chester Himes's novel is an African American whose notions of manhood are embedded in an ideology of white superiority. Similarly, David, a principal character in Baldwin's *Giovanni's Room*, seeks to protect his 'immaculate manhood' by clinging to a heterosexual identity. Heterosexuality, whiteness, strength, aggression (and the willingness to commit violence) are all present in these few quotations and indicate attributes that were central to American notions of masculinity in this period. Yet the quotations also represent the diversity of American manhood and alert us to the pitfalls of expecting to identify a singular masculine experience. While certain attributes might have been expected of men, their lived experience was that of multiple and hierarchical masculinities. The diversity of men's experiences suggests the possibility of the transformation of dominant versions of masculinity over time. Moreover, the final quotation, from *On the Road*, indicates that women, who were subordinated and restricted by a masculinity that energised patriarchal structures of power, could be resistant.

These novels were published during a significant period in American culture, marked by the legacy of the Depression and the Second World War, with atomic weapons, fear of communism and the Soviet Union, and unease relating to the Holocaust causing anxiety despite it also being a period of economic expansion and greater affluence. Cultural disquiet in the period had significant implications for gender and sexuality, with anxious debate about sex roles and a particular concern about American masculinity, as large corporations and mass consumerism came to dominate economic activity. The publication of *The Decline of the American Male* by *Look* magazine in 1958 encapsulated a general feeling of a crisis in American masculinity. Such circumstances make this a fertile period for considering the representation of masculinity in novels. Indeed, the quotation above from *The Catcher in the Rye* speaks to the importance of understanding how fictional and imaginative texts might contribute to the construction of notions of masculinity, or indeed be subversive of such notions. This book therefore considers fictional representations of masculinity in this period of 'crisis' and anxiety while relating them to other discourses about gender. The focus is on novels published in the ten years after the war and so avoids being drawn into the cultural transformations emerging later in the Fifties.[1] The examination of the novels within their historical context, and the exploration of the relationship between masculinity and issues of race, sexuality, class and violence, contribute to a complex and nuanced analysis of the expectations of men in the period. My approach is broadly informed by feminist theories of gender identity and the politics of gender. I therefore intend the book to make a contribution to the project of understanding, challenging and removing inequalities between men and women. Within such a context, the book contributes to an understanding of the ways in which gender may be constructed and reinscribed within relationships of authority and power.

The choice of fiction provides a wide range of perspectives, comprising a mixture of the canonical with the now less well known, and the mainstream with the more experimental. Although other writers have analysed some of this fiction through the lens of gender, the extensive range and variety of novels considered in this book allows for a much broader and deeper understanding of the complexities and contradictions of manhood in the period. Theories about the construction of gender provide interpretative tools for analysing the novels, but this book also keeps in focus the historical context in which the fiction was produced. Without making claims for straightforward causative relationships, the book shows the consistency in the themes and ideas relating to gender that preoccupied writers, journalists and intellectuals in this period. The following section of the Introduction therefore provides a preliminary perspective on gender identity and roles in what was a significant period in the development of the relations of power and gender in the United States.

Gender Roles and Conformity in Mid-century United States

The post-war years in the United States have typically been seen as ones in which traditional views of the centrality of the family and gender roles were in the ascendant, but a strong case can be made that the immediate post-war period was one of ferment, with a number of aspects of society highly contested. For example, while the American form of Freudian psychoanalytical theory was broadly conservative and oriented to the notion of 'conformity' – strikingly in its hostility to homosexuality – at the same time the work of Alfred C. Kinsey and the emergence of other texts supportive of varieties of human sexual activity challenged conservative views. The African American population suffered under Jim Crow and racist oppression and segregation, but new factors, such as the emergence of significant sociological analyses of their condition and the publication of widely read fictional representations of their experience, opened up new debates about these divisions in American society.

In the periodisation of America in the mid-twentieth century, the Second World War itself is generally represented as a historical caesura, with conceptualisations of the 'Fifties' and the 'Sixties' used to structure analysis of subsequent history. Within such historical generalisation there has been a consensus that the period immediately following the Second World War was one of anxiety, despite victory over the Axis powers. The sources of this anxiety were diverse, but it has been argued that a consistent response was a broad conservative impulse in American society in the Fifties. A significant element of this was an attempt to enforce sharply differentiated gender roles, whose demarcations had been blurred during the war. This emphasis on separate gender roles has been seen as connected with other social developments in relation to work and styles of living and leisure. In *Homeward Bound*, Elaine Tyler May traces the contours of this trajectory, arguing that the dominant metaphor of the Fifties was 'containment' and that, as a cultural impulse, it connected the Cold War world view with an ideology of the family. Containment was the 'key to security' at a time when the security of Americans seemed threatened by new and powerful forces, such as the Soviet Union, the atomic bomb and internal subversion (May 1999: xxiv). Although May acknowledges that there were those who did not conform to the ideal of the nuclear family and political quietism, *Homeward Bound* argues that 'containment' and conformity was the dominant ethos of the period, enforced through powerful ideological forces which played on strongly felt anxieties.

This perception of the Fifties fits together with a corresponding view of the Sixties as a period in which Americans broke with the static and repressive elements of Fifties culture, entering a new period in which society became more equal and individuals were allowed greater powers of self-expression. May, for example, supports such a view, arguing that containment 'held sway well into the 1960s, on the diplomatic and domestic levels, when it collapsed in disarray' (1999: xxv–xxvi). Such generalisations tend to homogenise and simplify the complexities of American society, for example in privileging the experience of the white middle classes over other social groups.[2] Historians writing more recently have tended to point to the complexities of American society in the post-war years and consider the continuities as well as the changes.[3] For example, while there was undoubtedly an emphasis on the role of woman as mother and housewife as men returned to work after military service, in fact, women constituted one of the fastest growing sectors of the workforce in the period after 1945 (Gerhard 2001: 54). As Bill Osgerby writes in *Playboys in Paradise*, 'Contradictions were germane to constructions of gender throughout the post-war period. Rather than being marked by straightforward conservative retrenchment, the Cold War was a time of tensions and transformations' (2001: 75). Perhaps the most notable source of tension was the discursive anxiety about conformity that coexisted with a powerful impulse towards the regulation and marginalisation of any behaviour that was perceived as unconventional. As Michael Kimmel puts it in *Manhood in America*, 'In the 1950s American men strained against two negative poles – the overconformist, a faceless selfless nonentity, and the unpredictable, unreliable nonconformist' (2006: 155).

The historian James Gilbert in *Men in the Middle* argues that the Fifties saw a 'public dialogue of stunning complexity' around the issue of masculinity (2005: 220). Gilbert also questions the way in which 'the basic account of the history of masculinity in the twentieth century has become one of crisis and response, rapid change, problematic compromise, and shifting definitions of manliness with the 1890s and the 1950s as key moments of transition' (21). Gilbert is sceptical about the 'reality and pervasiveness of a mood of masculinity crisis' (21) and he is cautious about generalising about masculinity, 'particularly about the 1950s, which was a period of remarkable cultural transition, growth, and development, as well as an era of appalling political conformity' (21–2). He maintains that for 'many men there was no crisis at all': 'They happily moved to the suburbs, consumed from the cornucopia of new products around them, and delighted in the new mass culture without registering worry about their masculinity' (221). Such men provide an example of change that involved an 'opportunity for a new fluidity in gender roles, for new forms of self-expression, not the sorry end of individualism or a chilling menace to American manhood' (221). From a historical perspective, then, there is considerable debate about both the representation and experience of masculinity after the Second World War.

Not surprisingly, such debate is echoed in contemporary accounts of gender and difference. Many of the issues relating to the roles of men and women were considered by Margaret Mead in *Male and Female: A Study of the Sexes in a Changing World*, which was first published in 1949. Mead was a cultural anthropologist whose book *Coming of Age in Somoa* (1928) established both her academic reputation and her public visibility in American cultural discourse. *Male and Female* may therefore be read as a conscious and deliberate intervention in a set of discourses through which American culture was struggling to articulate and control the representation of femininity and masculinity in relation to gender roles and sexuality.

Mead frames this debate in a set of questions that are being 'asked in a hundred different ways in contemporary America': 'How are men and women to think about their maleness and femaleness in this twentieth century [. . .]?'; 'Have we over-domesticated men [. . .]?'; Have we cut women off from their natural closeness to their children [. . .]?'; In educating women like men, have we done something disastrous to both men and women alike [. . .]?' (Mead 1949: 3). Mead then goes on to rework these questions from the perspective of heterosexual lovers: 'When he is insistent, should she yield, and how much? When she is demanding, should he resist, and how firmly? Who takes the next step forward or the next step back? What is it to be a man? What is it to be a woman?' (4). And such questions are evidently generated out of considerable anxiety: 'Polls and tracts and magazine-articles speculate and fulminate and worry about the relationship between the sexes' (3). Later in the book, she refers to current 'raucous and angry writing' and a 'spate of books that claim that women are being masculinized' and 'another spate [. . .] that insist that men are being feminized' (300).

From Mead's account, there can be no doubt that there was a great deal of concern about gender roles, and masculinity and femininity. The cause of this may have been the result of changes in American culture that were disrupting traditional expectations. The Second World War undoubtedly had a significant effect, but researchers and writers such as David Riesman, William H. Whyte and C. Wright Mills also identified longer-term trends that were changing American society. Such writers expressed an anxiety that American society was becoming conformist and homogenised in ways that constituted an undermining of individual autonomy. Given that the 'individual' was predominantly assumed to be a white, middle-class male, such changes were seen as threatening to American masculinity. Indeed, an element of these discourses was a fear that America was becoming feminised, and these anxieties influenced views about America's position in the world, the performance of American men in the war, the viability of the family, sexuality, mass culture, the organisation of work and the consequent effects on male and female roles. These key themes are an essential context for consideration of the fiction of the period and are considered in depth in the following chapters.

Mead's text, however, also reflects an optimistic belief in the analytical powers of the social sciences: only through 'greater understanding of man himself can we build a world in which human beings can realize more of their potentialities and live in greater harmony one with another' (431–2). The period is certainly notable for the emergence into public discourse at a heightened level of new modes of theoretical analysis. Perhaps most pervasive and influential was psychoanalytic theory, which combined with sociological and anthropological approaches in the work of Mead and other public academics such as Erich Fromm, Riesman, Whyte and Mills. For example, at the beginning of *White Collar* (1953), Mills argues that the liberalism of the early part of the century and the Marxian view of the 1930s is now 'often inadequate' (Mills 1953: xx). He continues: 'We need to characterize American society of the mid-twentieth century in more psychological terms, for now the problems that concern us most border on the psychiatric' (xx). Similarly, writing in 1940 on 'Freud and literature', Lionel Trilling claims that 'with the acclimatization of psychoanalysis and the increased sense of its refinements and complexity, criticism has derived from the Freudian system much that is of great value, most notably the license and the injunction to read the work of literature with a lively sense of its latent and ambiguous meanings [. . .]' (Trilling [1940] 1951: 39)

In his account of the history of psychoanalysis in the United States, Nathan Hale argues that there was an optimistic rhetoric around psychoanalysis in the period, citing both the medical and popular writings of psychoanalysts such as William Menninger and Franz Alexander, who 'created a strong impression of the efficacy of psychotherapy and the scientific status of psychoanalytic theory and practice' (Hale 1995: 277). Mead's analysis is strongly flavoured with psychoanalytic insights, although some of her views are unconventional.[4] Yet as Hale concludes, the terms of the popularisation of psychoanalysis after the war identified it with established social authorities and downplayed the 'iconoclastic, rebellious aspects' of psychoanalysis. He argues further that it tended 'to reconcile psychoanalysis with morality, religion, and received social values, particularly in its treatment of sexual roles and the issue of homosexuality' (299).

The Freudian elements in Mead's work thus contribute to her broadly conservative views, although she does challenge the 'fashionable' identification of America as a 'matriarchy', and argues that 'In our legal forms, we are a patrinominal, patrilineal, patrilocal, and legally, for the most part, a patriarchal society' (Mead 1949: 302). Her conservatism derives from her ultimately essentialist views about biological difference. These views overwhelm the elements of cultural relativism in her approach that she espouses as a cultural anthropologist.[5] Early in the book she seems concerned to emphasise the crucial importance of the cultural shaping of notions of masculinity and femininity:

> In every known society, mankind has elaborated the biological division of labour into forms often very remotely related to the original biological differences that provided the original clues. Upon the contrast in bodily form and function, men have built analogies between sun and moon, night and day, goodness and evil, strength and tenderness, steadfastness and fickleness, endurance and vulnerability. Sometimes one quality has been assigned to one sex, sometimes to the other. (7–8)

Yet her notion of a 'biological division of labour' locates the issue of 'male and female' inescapably in the body.

> Because we are mammals, and male and female mammals at that, we have limitations [. . .] All through our lives the fact that we are creatures who are made not only to be individuals but to continue the human race, is a persistent, unavoidable condition that we must meet. (20)

Mead's views have been quoted here at some length because they are typical of many of her contemporaries in their discussion of sex roles and masculinity and femininity. In the face of social change, the impulse is to cling on to bodily difference as an essential signifier of difference between men and women; from this premise is constructed a case for differentiation in social roles. One example is Talcott Parsons and Robert F. Bales's *Family: Socialization and Interaction Process* (1956). Parsons' functionalist approach was widely influential and the essays in the book explore functional role differentiation within the American white, middle-class nuclear family. The book generally upholds the view that biological differences between men and women determine their social and familial roles.

The essays in *Family: Socialization and Interaction Process* approach socialisation and role within the nuclear family in the light of Bales's studies of the structure of small task-oriented groups. When Morris Zelditch applies Bales's analysis in his chapter, 'Role differentiation in the nuclear family', he inserts a biological determinism to the perception of appropriate roles. He asserts that there is a key 'division of organisms into lactating and nonlactating classes' (Zelditch 1956: 313). This is despite the acknowledgement that with the 'successful' development of bottle-feeding, such division is no longer a requirement for the survival of human babies.[6] Nevertheless, the 'mother-child attachment' is seen as 'the core relation of a family with children' (313). The conclusion is therefore that the mother will be the 'likely expressive focus of the system as a whole' (314). The corresponding role of the father is that of 'instrumental leadership' – his function is 'managerial' and also contains responsibilities for 'discipline and control' (314). As a consequence:

> The American male, by definition, *must* 'provide' for his family. He is *responsible* for the support of his wife and children. His primary area of performance is the occupational role, in which his status fundamentally inheres; and his *primary* function in the family is to supply an 'income', to be the 'breadwinner'. There is simply something wrong with the American adult male who doesn't have a 'job'. (339)

In their conclusion to the volume, Parsons and Bales argue that the power position of the husband/father is also articulated in relation to his public role:

> [. . .] our evidence suggests the near if not complete universality of the proposition that the extrafamilial participations of the masculine role are, in any given society, both more complex and weigh more heavily in the personality structure than is the case with the feminine personality in the same society. (Parsons and Bales 1956: 356–7)

Ultimately these differentiated roles are inscribed on the body through biological difference:

> We believe sex to constitute in a developmental sense the most 'primitive' of the differentiations of generic personality type to which we have referred. [. . .] Motivationally it means the acceptance of the set of goals ascribed to one's own sex-role, and correspondingly renunciation of those ascribed to the other. (Parsons and Bales 1956: 387)

That the linkage between power, masculinity and heterosexuality is expressed through the male body is made explicit by Zelditch:

> The cult of the warm, giving 'Mom' stands in contrast to the 'capable', 'competent, 'go-getting' male. The more expressive type of male, as a matter of fact, is regarded as 'effeminate', and has too much fat on the inner side of his thigh. (Zelditch 1956: 339)

The appropriate form of American democratic masculinity is here represented through a set of binary oppositions in which it is not simply the different biology of the male and female sex that leads to the appropriate differentiated roles. Masculinity does not just reside in the form and presence of male genitalia but in other bodily significations that may create an effeminate subject identity.[7]

This approach is echoed in Carl C. Seltzer's article, 'The Relationship between the Masculine Component and Personality', published in 1949. Seltzer draws on the Grant Study for the notion of the 'masculine component' (1949: 84), the notion that the male body can be assessed on a continuum from strong to weak masculine component.[8] At one extreme is the 'angular, rough-surfaced, narrow-hipped, well-muscled, masculine type', at the other the 'rounder, softer, broader-hipped, less-well-muscled feminine type' (Seltzer 1949: 85). Seltzer analyses the Grant Study of the masculinity component in relation to the Study's personality evaluations of the same group of young men. He concludes that the individuals with 'weakness of the masculine component are more inclined to possess such traits as shyness, sensitivity, self-consciousness, inhibition, creativeness, and the like' (91). On the other hand, those with a strong masculine component have 'the stronger and more vital personality traits such as the humanistic, the sociable, the pragmatic, the vital affect' (91). Again, in a circular logic, different forms of the male body manifest forms of gendered identity, with dominant notions of masculinity connected with a particular bodily form.

This blending of bodily difference into the cultural signifiers of masculinity and femininity is explicit in Mead's discussion of sexuality. She argues that 'whatever the elaborations during learning, the adult sex act itself remains a complementary act; the male enters, the female is entered, however much these anatomical fundamentals may be overlaid and distorted' (74).

I want to emphasise the recurrent linkages between the supposed attributes of the body and the mechanics of heterosexual coitus, to an inevitable distribution of social roles. The circularity of these arguments is evident in Parsons and Bales's insistence on men and women accepting their pre-ordained roles and renouncing what is deemed as inappropriate. Mead warns of the 'perils' of inappropriate bodily performance and later concludes that for women, 'it is only necessary that they be permitted by the given social arrangements to fulfil their biological rôle, to attain this sense of irreversible achievement' (Mead 1949: 160). It is 'through education' that they are made 'restless and questing' (160).

This emphasis on the body in the writers considered so far may be seen to have a variety of interlocking imperatives. In the first place there is a reiteration of the notion that 'anatomy is destiny' and that ultimately women's potential for reproduction makes them fit primarily to be mothers. While the biology of difference determines social roles, there is additionally a need for the performative. The male or female body must act out these roles in order to fix an individual's masculinity or femininity in an unambiguous way. Any ambiguity of bodily performance undermines the necessary distinctions between men and women. This expectation that men and women occupy roles appropriate to a biological essentialism contributed to the pressure to conform in the period.

These expectations of a straightforward connection between biology, sexuality and social roles made heterosexuality in this period a key attribute of conventional masculinity. A correspondingly strong cultural hostility towards male homosexuality was reflected in the politics of the Cold War. The post-war period was marked by the emergence of a deep antagonism towards the Soviet Union and a related anxiety about the threat of communists within the American body politic. The Cold War generated another discourse relating to masculinity and sexuality that deployed the metaphors of 'hard' and 'soft'. Cold War politics incubated a hard, aggressive and 'masculine' stance in relation to communism and the Soviet Union, while those who were 'soft' were feminised. While a combative attitude to the Soviet Union and communism was to be expected from the right of American politics, in the post-war period such an attitude became common amongst former Trotskyists and Liberal centrists.[9] The metaphor of softness was articulated in terms of the predominance of the feminine in American society and the emasculation of the male – a combination that was perceived as undermining American resilience and power in foreign policy. For example, in an article in 1940 – before the United States had joined the Second World War – Roy Helton wrote of the way 'modern Western democracies have become state matriarchies' and argues that 'the only way democracies can survive' is through 'male purpose' (Helton 1940: 338, 342).

Mid-century anxieties about social change and the erosion of white male individualism thus fed into wider concerns about the international position of the nation. Such worries were evident in Arthur Schlesinger's book *The Vital Center*, first published in 1949. In the book's preface, Schlesinger makes clear that his purpose is to make a case for American liberalism, in particular the necessity of taking a strong stance against communism (Schlesinger [1949] 1998: xxi). In his critique, Schlesinger's metaphorical language is consistently gendered. For example, the 'dynamism of capitalism is trickling out in a world where the passion for security breeds merger and monopoly', and capitalism loses 'its bold, creative vigor' (26).

However, Schlesinger's scorn is strongest in attacking the 'doughface progressives' who are marked by 'sentimentality' and are 'soft not hard', and thus open to 'Communist permeation and conquest' (36). In contrast, the political leaders of democratic socialism (for example, Franklin D. Roosevelt and Aneurin Bevan) have 'brought a new virility into public life' (147).

In her book *Manhood and American Political Culture in the Cold War*, K. A. Cuordileone argues that Schlesinger's book is a defence against a perceived crisis in American masculinity. She maintains that Schlesinger contributed 'to the notion that became commonplace in the 1950s of a nexus between political and sexual subversion' (Cuordileone 2005: 28). For example, Schlesinger asserts that communism 'perverts politics into something secret, sweaty and furtive like nothing so much [. . .] as homosexuality in a boys' school' ([1949] 1998: 151). Similarly, he associates the clandestine recognitions of American Communist Party members with the 'famous scene in Proust where the Baron de Charlus and the tailor Jupien suddenly recognize their common corruption' (127). Such linkages between internal subversion and homosexual perversion were manifested politically in McCarthyism. In *In the Name of National Security*, Robert J. Corber shows how the connection of homosexuals and lesbians to issues of national security was through medical discourses that suggested they were maladjusted and emotionally unstable and therefore open to blackmail by Soviet agents. As a result, 'more homosexuals and lesbians were expelled from the federal government in the 1950s than were suspected Communists and fellow travelers' (Corber 1993: 8). The pervasiveness of such attitudes can be seen in 1946, when Henry Wallace – then Commerce Secretary – made a speech sympathetic to the Soviet Union's strategic priorities and claimed that he was representing the government's position. President Truman reacted furiously. He criticised Wallace privately and said that 'All the "Artists" with a Capital A, the parlor pinks and the soprano voiced men are banded together . . . I am afraid they are a sabotage front for Uncle Joe Stalin' (quoted in Patterson 1997: 125).

Cultural anxiety about American masculinity was frequently focused on the need for men to resist the pressure to conform, and both Schlesinger's article on 'The crisis of American masculinity' (1958) and *The Decline of the American Male* (Attwood, Leonard and Moskin 1958) argue that men must resist group conformity and reassert their individuality. Yet the authors of *The Decline of the American Male* make clear that the American middle-class male negotiating the boundaries between conformity and individuality is faced by contradictory demands. The American male has to 'grow up emotionally', but the authors recognise that it is not 'easy' to 'adjust to society without surrendering to its dictates; to be considerate of a wife without abdicating domestic authority to her; to work without undue strain, and to tolerate the massive insecurity of the mid-twentieth century without undue fear' (Attwood, Leonard and Moskin 1958: 66).

Norman Mailer presents a more radical critique of contemporary conformist society in 'The white Negro: superficial reflections on the hipster' (1957), arguing that the new cultural phenomenon of the hipster is a response to this. Mailer maintains that the effect of the concentration camps and the atom bomb has been to create an anxiety about human society and its murderous nature that led to 'years of conformity and depression' (Mailer [1959] 1961: 283).

> It is on this bleak scene that a phenomenon has appeared: the American existentialist – the hipster, the man who knows that if our collective condition is to live with instant death by atomic war, relatively quick death by the State as *l'univers concentrationnaire*, or with a slow death by conformity with every creative and rebellious instinct stifled [. . .], why then the only life-giving answer is to accept the terms of death, to live with death as immediate danger, to divorce oneself from immediate society, to exist without roots, to set out on that uncharted journey into the rebellious imperatives of the self. (283)

Mailer's account of the dichotomy between the Hip and the Square, the rebel and the conformist, brings together gender and race. To be the hip rebel takes courage and this is indeed what it takes 'to be a man' (284). The articulation of hip identity is seen particularly through violence and sexuality, although Mailer's discussion of expressing self through violence is uneasy and his principal focus is the orgasm.[10] This is 'Not love as the search for a mate, but love as the search for an orgasm more apocalyptic than the one that preceded it' (291). This search is gendered in that it is expressed as the hipster finding a 'little more between his woman and himself, or indeed between his mate and himself (since many hipsters are bisexual)' (295). Moreover, the converse of being hip – to 'goof' – is to lose your control, reveal the buried weaker more feminine part of your nature' (295). Weakness is to be despised because 'the sweet goes only to the victor, the best, the most, the man who knows the most about how to find his energy and how not to lose it' (293). Despite the apparent openness about sexual diversity, in fact the perspective is homophobic: weakness can lead to a situation in which 'one is impotent in the world of action and so closer to the demeaning flip of becoming queer' (296). The importance of virile heterosexuality to Mailer's thesis is emphasised in sociologist Ned Polsky's response to Mailer, in which he claims that many Hip men are sadistic in their sexual relationships, whereas others are 'so narcissistic that inevitably their orgasms are premature and puny' (Mailer [1959] 1961: 311).

For Mailer 'the source of Hip is the Negro' and the explanation for 'the presence of Hip as a working philosophy in the sub-worlds of American life is probably due to jazz, and its knife-like entrance into culture, its subtle but so penetrating influence on an avant-garde generation' (Mailer [1959] 1961: 284). It is noticeable that Mailer's deployment of metaphor again valorises the sexual and the violent. His explanation of the influential power of 'the Negro' is because 'he has been living on the margin between totalitarianism and democracy for two centuries' (284). Although such an assertion links with Mailer's main thesis about the hipster, his rhetorical enthusiasm lies elsewhere in the supposed lifestyle of African American men. His view that the 'Negro has the simplest of alternatives: live a life of constant humility or ever-threatening danger' (285) is one element of the fictional representation of the experience of African Americans discussed in Chapter 4. However, Mailer also indulges in a rehearsal of racist clichés:

> [T]he Negro (all exceptions admitted) could rarely afford the sophisticated inhibitions of civilization, and so he kept for his survival the art of the primitive, he lived in the enormous present, he subsisted for the Saturday night kicks, relinquishing the pleasures of the mind for the more obligatory pleasures of the body, and in his music he gave voice to the character and quality of his existence, to his rage and the infinite variations of joy, lust, languor, growl, cramp, pinch, scream and despair of his orgasm. For jazz is orgasm, it is the music of orgasm, good orgasm and bad, and so it spoke across a nation [. . .] (285)

The effect of jazz and the 'black man's code' suggests to Mailer that the hipster has 'absorbed the existential synopses of the Negro, and for practical purposes could be considered a white Negro' (285).

Although Mailer can be criticised for his superficial generalisations about the experience of African Americans, his introduction of race as an issue is notably different from other writers who simply make an assumption that 'America' is 'white' America. However, for Mailer, like the other writers discussed in this section, questions of politics, society and culture can never be far removed from questions of gender. Sometimes investigation of these questions assumes the white male as the universal subject, at other times the white male appears as threatened by the feminine. Mailer's essay is unusual in its introduction of race; more often the assertion or testing of masculine identity is against the feminine Other, who provides both a threat and a benchmark for differentiation.

The contemporary debates around sex roles and gender provide a vital context for a consideration of mid-century fiction, and further aspects of it are discussed in the following chapters. However, ideas about gender and identity are also an important perspective for analysis of the novels, and it is to this element that I now turn.

Masculinity, Feminism and the Study of Gender and Identity

In the Foreword to Judith Kegan Gardiner's collection of essays, *Masculinity Studies and Feminist Theory* (2002), Michael Kimmel argues that the study of masculinity is 'not necessarily the reactionary defensive rage of the men's rights groups' but 'is a significant outgrowth of feminist studies', which 'can be informed by a feminist project to interrogate different masculinities, whether real (as in corporeal) or imagined (as in representations and texts)' (Kimmel 2002: viii). Gardiner in her Introduction traces the relationship between feminism and Western discussion of 'masculinity', both in academic and popular discourses. Much of the debate has been expressed in antagonistic terms, with feminist thought often associating 'masculinity with institutional practices, attitudes, and personality traits of men – like aggression and competitiveness – that uphold male dominance and oppress women' (Gardiner 2002: 3). At the same time, the response of men has been defensive, with a 'masculinist' men's movement reasserting male dominance and identifying feminism as victimising men. The rhetoric of a 'crisis in masculinity' has emerged as a widespread obsession in Western culture (Gardiner 2002: 6–7). In *Why Feminism?* Lynne Segal notes that in this discourse men are the disadvantaged sex, with boys failing at school, adolescent males more miserable than adolescent girls and men having 'far higher incidences of suicide, alcoholism, drug addiction, serious accidents, cardio-vascular disease and significantly lower life expectancies than women' (1999: 160). However, such disenfranchisement apparently coexists with structures of power, wealth and authority that still favour men over women. As Gardiner puts it, 'feminists note that men retain social power, progressive change has been capped, glass ceilings and frozen attitudes inhibit women's gains, and male violence still threatens households and nations' (2002: 8). Segal points out that a significant explanation for the apparent contradiction lies in the assumption that men are a homogeneous group: 'Compared with women, in all parts of the world, men still have overwhelmingly greater access to cultural prestige, political authority, corporate power and individual wealth [. . . b]ut of course, it is only particular groups of men in any society who will occupy positions of public power and influence' (Segal 1999: 161). Indeed, in Britain it is 'particular groups of men, especially unemployed, unskilled and unmarried men who have far higher mortality and illness rates compared with other groups of men. Class, ethnicity and "race", not gender, are the major predictors of educational failure, unemployment and crime' (162).

The debate around the 'crisis in masculinity' continues and indeed divisions have hardened in recent years. Issues relating to masculinity in the United States are framed within the 'culture wars' – that split between conservatives and liberals focused on hot points such as abortion, gun control, feminism, family values, gay marriage, transgender rights and religion. On one side, the development of 'fourth-wave' feminism has set a context for the Women's Marches and the #MeToo campaign on Twitter against sexual violence.[11] At the same time, the idea that masculinity can be 'toxic' – characterised by misogyny, male violence against women, men's expectations of sexual entitlement and so on – has gained traction. On the other side are defenders of 'traditional' masculinity. For example, Gad Saad, writing for *Psychology Today*, argues in favour of traditional masculine virtues from the perspective of human evolution:

> There has been a relentless ideological attack on masculinity, stemming from radical feminism, the most recent example of which is the bogus term 'toxic masculinity.' It literally seeks to pathologize masculinity in ways that are profoundly harmful to the existential sense of self of young men. [. . . M]ost of the traits and behaviors that are likely found under the rubric of 'toxic masculinity' are precisely those that most women find attractive in an ideal mate! (Saad 2018)

Similarly, Peggy Noonan, writing in the *The Wall Street Journal* in the aftermath of the traumatic attacks on New York in September 2001, praises the 'manly men' who responded to those events. She argues that there is 'a new respect for physical courage, for strength and for the willingness to use both for the good of others'. Noonan rehearses conservative hostility to liberals in claiming that John

Wayne – Duke – embodied such virtues, but he was killed 'by a thousand cuts', not only by 'feminists but peaceniks, leftists, intellectuals, others' (Noonan 2001).

The continuing fractiousness over gender issues is personified by Jordan Peterson, an academic and clinical psychologist whose involvement in a legal dispute about 'free speech' in Canada has earned him favour with conservatives. Peterson draws on an evolutionary perspective at the beginning of his book *12 Rules for Life* when he describes the competitive fight for survival of the lobster. The example of the lobster is pertinent to humans as it represents the 'ever-present dominance hierarchy' (Peterson 2018a: 13). Evolutionary theory is then transmuted into individualist precepts for everyday social interaction in the title of the chapter – 'Stand up straight with your shoulders back'. Peterson's advice seems generalised, but is addressed primarily to men. For example, standing up straight means standing up for yourself and being willing to be aggressive: 'the ability to respond with aggression and violence decreases rather than increases the probability that actual aggression will become necessary' (24–5). Peterson argues that order is symbolically associated with the masculine while chaos is associated with the feminine (40–1). Order is God the Father and the men who have built the world throughout history (40). The book's sub-title is 'An Antidote to Chaos', which implies a primer for men. Certainly Peterson's view of chaos and order is an element of his view that gendered archetypes based in biology set a behavioural pattern for men and women. Peterson's views correlate with conservative views about gender roles, marriage and parenting and are presented alongside a strong hostility to feminism. He maintains that feminism is an ideology linked with Marxism and is irrational. This positioning leads him to such provocative statements as advocating 'enforced monogamy' in an interview with Nellie Bowles in the *New York Times*, and the assertion that feminism is 'a murderous equity doctrine' on Twitter in response to Justin Trudeau's support for women's rights (Peterson 2018b).

The implication in conservative discourse is that there is an authentic, natural masculinity that has been attacked by 'radical feminism'. Such concerns correspond with Gardiner's view that masculinity is a 'nostalgic formation, always missing, lost, or about to be lost, its ideal form located in a past that advances with each generation in order to recede just beyond its grasp' (Gardiner 2002: 10). Most feminist interrogations of gender and identity differ from conservative views in emphasising the constructedness of identity as opposed to its naturalness. The key signifiers of masculinity – heterosexuality, fatherhood, family governance, soldiery, citizenry – can be 'viewed as a set of prescriptive norms that contain potential contradictions within and between men' (Wiegman 2002: 43). Wiegman also points out that the motivation for much feminist work in masculinity studies has been 'to intervene in the practices of patriarchal domination while locating the possibilities for men to challenge their constitution as men' (43). It is the ongoing debate around gender and power that makes this work of understanding the construction and representation of masculinity of continuing importance, and to which this book contributes.

Making such a contribution has generally been pertinent for workers in the academic field of masculinity studies and it is to the work of one of the pioneering and most influential theorists of masculinity, the Australian sociologist R. W. Connell, that I now turn, considering in particular the notion of 'hegemonic masculinity'. In *Masculinities*, Connell reviewed and critiqued past approaches to the concept of 'masculinity' before moving on to articulate masculinity, 'not as an isolated object, but as an aspect of a larger structure' (Connell 1995: 67). In doing so, Connell proposed some key ideas about the concept. First, that masculinity is 'inherently relational' – it has no meaning except in contrast to 'femininity' (68). Secondly, Connell challenges essentialist ideas about male and female identity, locating 'masculinity' as an element in gender relations, defining gender as a 'structure of social practice' (71). For Connell, gender refers to the body, but as a social process it cannot be reduced to a fixed set of biological determinants (71). Connell's approach to gender – significantly for a study of masculinity – foregrounds issues of power, of the organisation of systems of production, and of desire (72–3). Connell's model also emphasises the relationship of masculinity to other social structures such as class and 'race', and from this comes the recognition of 'multiple masculinities', structured in a hierarchy of dominant and subordinate masculinities (75–8). Masculine identity therefore intersects with other markers of identity such as class, race and sexuality.

Connell draws on Gramsci's theorisation of hegemony to propose the concept of 'hegemonic masculinity', which is constituted through ideological social formations that legitimate and naturalise the interests of the powerful (77). Hegemonic masculinity is primarily constituted through the subordination of women and other forms of masculinity, in particular the effeminacy associated with male homosexuality (78–9). If gender identity is constituted through historical social practices, then there can be no *fixed* form of hegemonic masculinity. As a consequence, hegemonic masculinity is continuously contested. Indeed, if hegemonic masculinity is constituted in the interests of the powerful, then men without power or authority occupy an ambiguous relationship to the signifiers of dominant masculinity. Heterosexual men, unlike women or gay men, seemingly possess core attributes of dominant masculinity and may express their association with it through misogyny or homophobia. Yet they may themselves remain oppressed by particular social formations, although, as Connell argues, all men are likely to benefit from what is described as the 'patriarchal dividend' (79).

Connell's theoretical approach has been widely influential, but also subject to some criticism, aspects of which she has answered in an article written in 2005 with James Messerschmidt, 'Hegemonic Masculinity: Rethinking the Concept'.[12] This article is useful in its re-emphasis and clarification of aspects of hegemonic masculinity. In particular, the origins of the concept in Gramscian thinking require attention to the dynamics of historical change – this opens the possibility of the displacement of older forms of masculinity and introduces an 'element of optimism in an otherwise rather bleak theory' (Connell and Messerschmidt 2005: 833). Hegemony means 'ascendancy achieved through culture, institutions, and persuasion', not necessarily through violence (832), which implies an element of complicity or compliance. Some men, who benefit from patriarchy without occupying a dominant position in a masculine hierarchy – and some heterosexual women – may be regarded as compliant. One might also add that the Gramscian idea that cultural hegemony produces 'common sense' ideas that are deployed in everyday life is also relevant to the formation and circulation of popular notions of roles and behaviours supposedly appropriate for men and women.

Freudian psychoanalytic theory has also been influential in accounts of gender identity and suggests a provisionality and instability in the inscription of 'femininity' and 'masculinity' in the subject. For example, Jacqueline Rose emphasises Freud's 'stress on the division and precariousness of human subjectivity itself' (Rose 1982: 29). Toril Moi refers to the arguments of both Jacqueline Rose and Juliet Mitchell in writing that 'Freud does not take sexual identity to be an inborn, biological essence, and that Freudian psychoanalysis in fact sees sexual identity as an unstable subject position which is socially and culturally constructed in the process of the child's insertion into human society' (Moi 2002: 28). Jacques Lacan's 'return to Freud' in the middle years of the twentieth century and his post-structuralist account of our entry into sexual identity have prompted further debate about gender, sexuality and identity.[13] Neither the Freudian nor the Lacanian account of our acquisition of sexual identity suggest that it is anything other than fraught. For men, the Freudian and Lacanian narratives both associate potency and mastery with masculinity but also imbue the male with a psychic anxiety of castration. For Frosh, 'living up to [the phallus] becomes the necessary condition of masculinity, which is therefore always in danger of being betrayed and undermined' (Frosh 1994: 78). Two conclusions may be drawn from such an explanation of difference. One is that a masculinity produced from this narrative is forever embattled, seeking to prove its dominance by identifying supposedly lesser forms of identity and asserting itself against them. The second is that men in their lives are bound to fail to measure up to such impossible demands. Men who fall behind the ideal in terms of cultural significations of power and authority may be more likely to assert an extreme version of a dominant masculinity, for example in marking their bodily 'strength' by inflicting violence on others or themselves.

Masculinity is commonly expressed through the body, and in his book *Masculinity in the West*, Christopher Forth focuses on the male body. Forth begins with the 'time-honored assumption that bodily difference is what undergirds and authorizes male supremacy' and proceeds to develop an argument that the male body is, however, 'subject to environmental conditions that diminish its capacity to generate properly "masculine" practices and habits' (Forth 2008: 4). Forth particularly associates such conditions with the development of modernity (from the sixteenth century), in that the changes generated by modernisation are 'attended by resistance and ambiguity'. Such dislocations in the field of gender and masculinity provide an explanation for crisis as a 'recurring component of modern life' (4). The focus on the body raises some questions for the reading of literary texts. For example, in the quotation from Michael Kimmel cited above, he claims a significant distinction between masculinities that are 'real (as in corporeal) or imagined (as in representations and texts)'. Similarly, in a review of Forth's book, published in *Social History of Medicine*, Sean Brady refers to the debates raging between those scholars who 'emphasise historical representations of masculinity, and those who emphasise alterity, experience and agency' (Brady 2010: 203). Of course fiction is undoubtedly representational and constructed from literary linguistic codes and therefore not 'real'. However, instead of the dichotomy proposed by Kimmel, my approach through this book is to maintain that fiction generates a connection between imagined manliness and men's lived experience. It is for this reason that the fiction is situated in relation to other historical discourses that prescribe appropriate gendered behaviour.

As Forth argues, the body plays a critical role in relation to notions of gender identity, even if binary discourses about the male and the female often associate men with rationality and the mind, and women with emotion and the body. Yet this division is far from straightforward. For example, men from origins other than European have been represented in the West in ways that bend gender through the distorting refractions of 'racism'. There has, for example, been the 'wily oriental' whose intellectual powers are acknowledged but seen as corrupted by a feminising unreliability; the identity of African men, in contrast, has been constructed through an emphasis on their supposed heightened bodily strength and sexuality. Moreover, despite the hierarchical ordering of mind over body, the male body may also be valorised as a source of power, strength and authority – in protecting the family, in productive labour, in heterosexual athleticism and reproductive plenitude, in heroic war exploits and in sport (see for example the quotation from Peggy Noonan above). Representation of the male body can then be seen as a key locus on and through which the discourses of patriarchy negotiate, shape and assert forms of masculinity.

An example of this can be seen in Jean Grimshaw's discussion of how Simone de Beauvoir's survey of the repression of the female body involves a counter-idealisation of the male body and male movement (Grimshaw 1999: 106). This is starkly demonstrated in de Beauvoir's description of sexual initiation: 'man imparts to [the male organ] a movement that is voluntary; it goes back and forth, stops, moves again while the woman takes it submissively' (quoted by Grimshaw 1999: 106). De Beauvoir here seems unquestioningly to incorporate essentialising representations of male and female sexuality. Will Self's and David Gamble's *Perfidious Man*, which contains Stephen Whittle's narrative of his transition from female to male, also suggests that assumptions about masculinity and the sexed body remain deeply embedded. This is most tellingly demonstrated in Self's comparison between his father and Stephen Whittle. While his father's masculinity seems embodied in his physiology, both in his phallic mastery ('he pissed like a horse'; Self and Gamble 2000: 3) and in his heterosexual prowess ('a Lothario'; 4), Self argues that Stephen Whittle's masculinity is separate from 'what kind of genitals he has' (14). And yet, for Whittle himself, there is the sense that he is struggling with the idea that to have a 'large penis' may be the vital final stage of his transition: 'the idea of being able to do that ['having intimate sexual intercourse with Sarah'] is what I've always wanted; it's a thing I've always missed' (95). While Whittle does not himself use the word 'penetration', his aspirations echo de Beauvoir's characterisation of male–female sex.

From a post-structuralist perspective, such discourses in fact produce culturally mediated male and female bodies, circumscribing their potential physical actions, while simultaneously fixing their biological 'essence'. Grimshaw goes on to argue that de Beauvoir's attitude to the male body both ignores how such male bodily movements may be oppressive to women and suggests a false notion of a 'free' and 'unrepressed' male body. While the actions of the female subject are always encumbered by representations of her body, discourses naturalise and universalise the masculine in ways that veil male embodiment. The male body is idealised as 'free' and 'unrepressed' – a body whose activity is able to resist scrutiny. In reality, however, to exercise power in the world requires the subject to be able to move and act in material space. Consequently, as Jean Grimshaw suggests, there is the possibility of subjecting the male body to scrutiny. These ideas suggest that attending to representation of male physicality in literary texts will be a rewarding way of considering their relationship to the cultural processes involved in the structuring of gender.

This brief summary of certain aspects of debates around gender and masculinity sets a theoretical context for the consideration of literary texts in this book. What is not available is a single methodological tool for approaching issues of masculinity in relation to literary texts. Indeed, as Whitehead and Barrett have suggested in their introduction to *The Masculinities Reader*, the growing influence of post-structuralist theories on feminist thinking and the increasingly pluralistic character of scholarship and research produced by the sociology of masculinity makes 'distinct answers' and 'single "solutions"' distant hopes (Whitehead and Barrett 2001: 13).

Moreover, to write as a man about masculinity from a critical perspective is fraught with potential difficulties. 'Masculinity' is itself irredeemably constituted in 'patriarchal' discourses, so there is a risk that analysis of 'masculinity' may drift into a recuperation of dominant structures of power. Indeed, some feminists have strongly resisted male involvement in the feminist project of challenging men's privileges and power. However, there has also been recognition that while it might have served feminism as a political project to categorise men as a single oppressive group, recognition of the reality of 'multiple masculinities' opens up a different perspective in which 'the politics of masculinity can be seen as a contested field of power moves and resistances, rather than being constructed as a fixed set of power relations' (Hooper, quoted in Hebert 2007: 37). My approach in this book is to keep in mind a feminist perspective and to be alert to relations of power and privilege. In exploring the construction of an ideology of masculinity and the representation of multiple masculinities that emerge from the perspectives of race, class and sexuality, the book can contribute to a greater understanding of masculinity and the possibility of change.[14] In 'Gosh, Boy George, you must be awfully secure in your masculinity', Eve Sedgwick provided a salutary reminder that masculinity can and should be untethered from men: '[W]hen something is about masculinity, it is not always "about men"' (Sedgwick 1995: 12). Sedgwick questioned the value of an inquiry that 'begins with the presupposition that everything pertaining to men can be classified as masculinity, and everything that can be said about masculinity pertains in the first place to men' (12).[15] To remember that the biological male does not equate to the masculine in the same way that the biological female does not equate to the feminine is to keep in mind the complexities of the hierarchies of relations of power between men and women.[16]

Literature and Gender

What is striking about the historical context for the fiction discussed in the following chapters is the consistency with which there is contestation around masculine identity and the male body. How might literary works be read in relation to such a context? In explanations of gender difference, symbolic representations of masculinity and femininity in forms of art may be seen to play an important role in constructing and negotiating gender identity (see for example the quotation from *The Catcher in the Rye* at the beginning of the Introduction). On the one hand, cultural products such as novels may be seen as reinforcing the dominant schema of gender difference or of providing normative accounts of the systemic organisation of gendered practices and relationships within a particular society. Yet, the novel has also become a means of representing, exploring and interrogating the interiority of the subject. Insofar as gender identity is conceived of as fragile, provisional and unstable, a literary text may in its narrative, and perhaps in particular, in the silences within that narrative, reveal and open for revision the instabilities of dominant gender identities. Moreover, in their employment of tropes, literary texts are both reflective of and constitutive of the metaphorical application of notions of femininity and masculinity. Indeed, the very form of the text, as a genre or at the level of the sentence, may be seen as symbolically related to gender. So, for example, Virginia Woolf could write that Dorothy Richardson had 'invented a sentence we might call the psychological sentence of the feminine gender' (quoted in Gillespie 1990: 396). Correspondingly, the terse literary style of Thompson's *The Killer Inside Me* might be connected with a certain type of masculine identity.

While literary texts may be revealing of the ambiguity, provisionality and anxiety of a dominant ideology such as masculinity, embedded in the approach, however, are distinct difficulties. Literary texts may also be produced as interlocking elements in sets of discourses that authorise, shape and focus structures of power and knowledge. In this way they may be viewed as important sites for the assertion of dominant notions of masculinity. Theoretical approaches to the production of power within such linguistic discourses may further suggest a determinist inevitability in existing structures as much as opportunities for change. Furthermore, optimistic revelations of the anxieties and gaps in the symbolic discourses of power often seem to be belied by the lived experience of subordinated groups.

Sally Robinson's *Marked Men* – an analysis of the white male response in the United States to the identity politics of the Sixties – is an instructive example of how literary texts may respond to particular historical circumstances in relation to gender and power. She suggests that a 'crisis' in masculinity may be a rhetorical stratagem used by 'white men to negotiate shifts in understandings of white masculinity' (Robinson 2000: 10). She argues, moreover, that 'crisis need not signify a loss of belief in male power or privilege' (10). In that period minority groups marked as other and subordinate by normative cultural values turned such a marking back on itself by a positive claiming of these identities and subjectivities. One element of this self-identification as a subordinated subject was a claim to speak for and represent oneself and to bring into discourse narratives of exclusion, victimisation and injury. Robinson argues that in responding to this development, 'white masculinity most fully represents itself as victimized by inhabiting a wounded body' (6). She describes this as performing 'the cultural work of *re*centering white masculinity by *de*centering it' (12).

Literary representation of the male body is therefore a discursive field in which complex and contradictory significations are manifested. It is through the body that identity is constructed and represented and, as dominant forms of masculinity are brought into representation, so, too, the male body is, inevitably, brought into visibility and opened to scrutiny. If, in Robinson's terms, the body is 'marked' in its representation, how then is the mythical, universal, unmarked man recuperated? In negotiating such contradictions, literary texts expose significant fractures and silences. This book examines literary texts from such a perspective, seeking to further an understanding of the discursive processes of masculinity and its relationship to the assertion and exercise of power. While the notion of a fixed and singular 'masculinity' is an ideological construct, it is within the symbolic representations of texts such as novels that this construct is constituted and asserted in relation to subordinated forms of identity. However, attention to fractures and silences may also reveal subversive glimpses of the male body as an object of desire and source of sensuality.

My readings of the novels discussed in this book aspire to such a critical reading. A close critical reading is combined with a historicisation of the selected fictional texts in relation to relevant discourses of the period. This approach is intended to develop a closer understanding of the ways in which the expectations of men were constructed, reproduced, circulated and – sometimes – challenged.

Selection of the Fiction

The book explores a selection of American novels, published after 1945 up to the mid-1950s, bringing into consideration a number of novels that have received little attention from literary scholars. The novels cannot be read without some understanding of their context, but as complex pieces of imaginative writing the stories they tell do not fit neatly into sociological or historical perspectives. This approach conditioned the selection of novels for analysis. To locate the analysis historically and to make comparison possible, most texts that have been chosen had both literary significance and were widely read. Using such criteria, it is justifiable to regard the texts as providing evidence of current and resonant discourses about gender and identity. In addition, the book considers some literary texts that were not widely read at the time but which contain different or counter-representations of gender identity.

I begin discussion of the novels in detail in Chapter 1. Unlike later chapters, which are thematically organised, Chapter 1 selects four significant novels through which to begin to test how far the representation of masculinity conforms to contemporary views of gender roles. In their diverse representations of masculinity these novels serve to exemplify the complexities and anxieties associated with male identity in the period. It compares the aspiration to a metropolitan masculinity in J. D. Salinger's *The Catcher in the Rye* (1952) with the exploration of conformity and suburban masculinity in Sloan Wilson's *The Man in the Gray Flannel Suit* (1955). I then argue that Jack Kerouac's *On the Road* (1957) seeks to reinvigorate an adventurous male identity with its rejection of a feminising domesticity. Edna Ferber's *Giant* (1952) was widely read in the 1950s and offers a counter-perspective on masculinity from its primary female character Leslie Lynnton/Benedict. It is read as a critique of traditional white Texan masculinity – personified as the cowboy – in relation to gender and race.

Chapter 2 examines the assumption that male identity is inextricable from violent behaviour. The chapter begins with an analysis of Jim Thompson's *The Killer Inside Me* (1952), showing how male violence in personal relationships can be related to wider cultural hostility to women. The chapter proceeds to extended analysis of two major novels – Norman Mailer's *The Naked and the Dead* (1948) and James Jones's *From Here to Eternity* (1951) – in relation to debates that took place in America after the war about the masculine performance of American servicemen and the implications for American national identity. Mailer's novel ultimately valorises a notion of masculinity that is decisive, authoritarian and violent. Jones's novel represents army life on Hawaii in the months leading up to the Pearl Harbor attack, and the chapter explores how the army as an institution reinforces hegemonic codes of masculinity relating to physical resilience and violence, and the consequences for ordinary soldiers.

The third chapter, which considers the representation of male sexuality, is framed in relation to the publication of the first Kinsey report in 1948 – *Sexual Behavior in the Human Male*. The Kinsey report exposed contradictions in expectations of male sexual behaviour and these are discussed in relation to Robie Macauley's *The Disguises of Love* (1952). One defining characteristic of normative masculine identity was heterosexuality, and the chapter considers the queer challenge to that assumption found in Gore Vidal's *The City and the Pillar*, Truman Capote's *Other Voices, Other Rooms* and Patricia Highsmith's *The Talented Mr Ripley* (1955). Finally, the chapter considers the sensuous sexuality represented in John Horne Burns's *The Gallery*.

Chapter 4, 'Identity and Assimilation in Jewish American Fiction', analyses Arthur Miller's *Focus* (1945), Irwin Shaw's *The Young Lions* (1948), Saul Bellow's *The Adventures of Augie March* (1953) and Jo Sinclair's *The Wasteland* (1946), considering how far representations of Jewish American masculinity can be read as adapting to dominant codes of American masculinity. The authors explore Jewish American masculine identity, and issues relating to assimilation and anti-Semitism. The novels were written in the circumstances of the post-war period, which was overshadowed by the legacy of the Holocaust, at the same time as shifting notions of 'whiteness' moderated overt anti-Semitism in American society and allowed Jews to claim a legitimate American identity.

Chapter 5 considers fiction written from the perspective of African Americans whose identity is perceived as 'other' to the ideals of white American male identity. The chapter reprises themes discussed earlier in the book, for example in considering the relationship between black identity and sexuality in Chester Himes's *If He Hollers Let Him Go* (1945). In Ralph Ellison's *Invisible Man* (1952) the narrator explores various aspects of the dilemma of black masculinity, concluding that his blackness ironically renders him invisible. These male writers seek to articulate a coherent black masculinity, but in *The Street* (1946) Ann Petry offers a critique of the way African American male identity conformed to dominant forms of masculinity. In *Giovanni's Room* (1956), James Baldwin seeks to deconstruct the conventional expectations of masculinity and sexuality that appear to be required of American male identity.

Notes

1. Hutchinson in *Facing the Abyss* (2018) argues that the Forties have been unduly neglected.
2. May (1999) is careful to emphasise that the familial ideology of the Fifties excluded African Americans; see for example xviii–xix.
3. See for example Buhle 1998; Corber 1993 and 1997; Gerhard 2001.
4. One example is her adoption of Karen Horney's notion of 'womb envy'.
5. Writing in 1950, Diana Trilling points out the contradiction between Mead's analysis of 'primitive cultures', which emphasises the social construction of masculine and feminine characteristics, and her later 'assumption of what amounts to an inherency of certain female traits' (Trilling 1950: 370).
6. Mary McCarthy engages with the debate about breastfeeding through the character of Priss Hartshorn Crockett in *The Group* ([1954] 1991: 286ff).
7. Complementary views on the role of women can be found in Johnson E. Fairchild's collection of essays, *Women: Society and Sex* (1952), while William G. Niederland maintains that women who 'do not want to become homemakers, [or . . .] mothers' 'lack warmth, tenderness, delicacy, and sweetness [. . .]' (Niederland 1952: 124–5).

8. See Heath et al. (1946) for the Grant Study, in which Seltzer was a participant. Heath's work is discussed further in Chapter 2 below.
9. On the New York Jewish Trotskyists, see Bloom, *Prodigal Sons: The New York intellectuals and their world*; see also Chapter 4.
10. Mailer maintains that murder takes courage but also acknowledges that it can be argued that the murder of 'a candy store keeper' by 'two strong eighteen-year-old hoodlums' takes little courage (Mailer [1959] 1961: 291).
11. The *Guardian*'s article on patriarchy in summer 2018 is an example of how feminist ideas have re-entered the mainstream (Higgins 2018).
12. There is not space to discuss in detail critiques of Connell's concept of hegemonic masculinity, but see for example Beasley 2008; Demetriou 2001; Moller 2007; Wetherell and Edley 1999.
13. See Eagleton 1983; Frosh 1994; Moi 2002; and Rose 1982 for exposition of Lacan's theories.
14. In his book *Recreating Men* (2000), Bob Pease explores such issues for 'profeminist' men.
15. Jack (Judith) Halberstam also challenges the association of masculinity with men; see *Female Masculinity* (1998).
16. This very useful point is made by Hebert (2007: 37).

Chapter 1

'Organization Man', Domestic Ideology and Manhood

This chapter focuses on four significant novels published in the post-war period: Sloan Wilson's *The Man in the Gray Flannel Suit* (1955); J. D. Salinger's *The Catcher in the Rye* (1951); Jack Kerouac's *On the Road* (1957); and Edna Ferber's *Giant* (1952). Analysis of the novels provides a test of how far the representation of masculinity conforms to contemporary perspectives on gender described in the Introduction. The chapter begins with Sloan Wilson's *The Man in the Gray Flannel Suit* and contemporary sociological interest in the 'Organization' and in the suburban family. While the 'man in the gray flannel suit' has become an icon of post-war American conformity, the novel opens up the complex demands on men at work in the Organization and at home in the suburbs. The other three novels represent other dimensions of male experience in the period. Jack Kerouac's *On the Road* represents a resurgent, mobile masculinity in the unconfined space of the 'Road'. J. D. Salinger's *The Catcher in the Rye* focuses on adolescent masculinity in the urban spaces of New York, and opens up questions about the nature of modern manhood. Finally, Edna Ferber's *Giant* is read as a critique of traditional Texan masculinity, which was constructed in relation to the feminine and a racialised Other. In their diverse representations of masculinity, these novels serve to exemplify the complexities and anxieties associated with male identity in the period. In the novels masculinity is expressed, worried over or questioned, in a variety of circumstances.

Sloan Wilson, *The Man in the Gray Flannel Suit*

Wilson's popular novel, which was turned into a major film starring Gregory Peck and Jennifer Jones in 1956, has generally been seen as fictionalising many of the aspects of corporate life and suburban culture written about by contemporary sociologists. The novel may also be read in relation to May's historical analysis, which identifies historical and cultural factors in post-war America that combined to create a 'domestic ideology' (May 1999: xxi). This ideology constructed egalitarian marriage and the nuclear family as the foundation of democracy, with the suburbs idealised as the space in which aspirational middle-class values and the ideology of the nuclear family could be expressed (May 1999: 65). As May puts it, 'The most tangible symbol of [the post-war American] dream was the suburban home – the locale of the good life, the evidence of democratic abundance' (143). However, there were tensions for American men between the ideal of the suburban life and the feminising threat of conformity, and Wilson's novel can be seen as exploring the complexities and contradictions of these tensions.

To provide a context for the novel, it is necessary to consider contemporary sociological interest in the Organization and in the family in the suburbs. Significant contemporary sociological texts include David Riesman's *The Lonely Crowd*, first published in 1950, C. Wright Mills's *White Collar: The American Middle Classes* (1953) and William H. Whyte's *The Organization Man* (1956). These books were widely influential on publication and each of these texts is diagnostic in the sense that the authors are seeking to explain and suggest remedies for aspects of American culture that are causing concern. For example, Riesman identifies the 'passivity and joylessness of Americans, their obedience to unsatisfying values' (Riesman 1950: xxxii) and in this he refers to the contemporary perception of Americans as conformist. His analysis seeks to explain this conformity and in so doing considers other contemporary concerns, such as the influence of the mass media and consumerism. Mills claims that white-collar workers are alienated and suffering from a malaise both in their work and their leisure; he sees them as politically 'impotent' and concludes that '[. . . W]hite-collar man has no culture to lean upon except the contents of a mass society that has shaped him and seeks to manipulate him to its alien ends' (Mills 1953: xvi).[1]

At the beginning of *The Lonely Crowd*, Riesman proposes three social character types, which he calls 'tradition-directed', 'inner-directed' and 'other-directed' (1950: 9). The latter two types are the key ones for mid-twentieth-century America: 'inner-directed' people internalise a set of goals, while 'other-directed' people are sensitised to the expectations and preferences of others. Riesman indicates the sort of occupational categories that distinguish inner-direction from other-direction. The former is the 'old' middle class – 'the banker, the tradesman, the small entrepreneur, the technically oriented engineer, etc' (21). The latter typically is the 'bureaucrat, the salaried employees in business, etc' (21). Broadly this is the consequence of growth in economic activity requiring white-collar work and employees in the service industries. The expansion of the service industries, education and leisure goes hand in hand with a new 'torrent' of information from the mass media of communications (21). Riesman argues that such changes require 'more "socialized" behaviour' (22). Individuals derive a source of direction from their contemporaries, from friends or indirectly from peers and the mass media. Contemporary 'behavioral conformity' is imbued 'through an exceptional sensitivity to the actions and wishes of others' (22). In the Preface of 1960, Riesman contrasts the 'considerateness, sensitivity and tolerance that are among the positive qualities of other-direction' with the rugged individualism and 'toughness and invulnerability' of inner-directedness (xx) – the former traits conventionally associated with the feminine and the latter with masculinity. This sort of language suggests that the analysis in *The Lonely Crowd* traces an undermining of traditional masculine traits in work, politics and consumption.

The effect of other-directedness in the world of work is significant: 'the other-directed man tends to think of work in terms of people – people seen as something more than the sum of their workmanlike skills and qualities' (115). Attention is directed at the '"softness" of men rather than the "hardness" of material' (131). In these circumstances self-advancement 'depends less on what one is and what one does than on what others think of one – and how competent one is manipulating others and being oneself manipulated' (46). This requires the individual to produce a 'personality' through which one can differentiate oneself from others (47).

Whyte's analysis corresponds to Riesman's. He identifies the insidious and dangerous attractions of the Organization and its erosion of individualism. Although he professes not to advocate a return to 'rugged individualism', Whyte argues that the individual 'must *fight* The Organization' and 'turn the future away from the dehumanized collective that so haunts our thoughts' (Whyte 1956: 13–15, 24, 448). He is scathing about the ideologies of 'belongingness' and 'togetherness' that for him typify modern American culture. Like Riesman he sees producing a 'personality' as a key marker of the period. However, he sees personality more in terms of conformism than in differentiating oneself. Whyte identifies conformism in the widespread deployment of personality tests in American corporate culture (189–222). Such tests draw heavily on psychoanalytic theory, but as Whyte points out, they embody the values of the Organization (201), and it is most important to appear average in relation to these values (449). In a parallel with Whyte's diagnosis, Mills quotes Harold Taylor, the president of Sarah Lawrence College in New York: 'The ideal graduate in the present employment market of industrial executives is a fraternity man with a declared disinterest in political or social affairs, gentile, white, a member of the football team, a student with a record of A in each course, a man popular with everyone and well-known on campus, with many memberships in social clubs' (Mills 1953: 267).

Taylor's definition of the character required by the corporations reveals the exclusion of large elements of the population on grounds of gender and race. Beyond that, he reveals the careful balance between demonstrating the traditional signifiers of masculinity – sports and rationality – and the new requirement to be personable. In this he provides a description of how the traits of traditional hegemonic masculinity might be changing. Significantly, Taylor makes no mention of any achievements in the artistic field and in this exclusion concurs with Whyte's advice to score weakly in the fields of art and aesthetics in personality tests (Whyte 1956: 214). This illuminates a point made by Margaret Mead, who concluded that American society's teaching of masculinity rests on the 'simple device' of teaching boys not to be women, 'but there is an inevitable loss in such an education, for it teaches a man to fear that he will lose what he has, and to be forever haunted by this fear' (1949: 315). She also sees this sharp distinction between male and female and the corresponding denial of the overlapping potentialities for all men and women as resulting in 'the terrible tragedies of wrong definition of one's own sex in the man who becomes a homosexual because of the way in which society defines his desire to paint or to dance' (1949: 375–6). The boundaries between an acceptable conformity to new norms of behaviour for men and the signification of a dangerous effeminacy are tightly drawn.

Lewis Mumford's *The City in History* painted a negative view of the suburbs that contrasted with the perspective of 'domestic ideology':

> a multitude of uniform, unidentifiable houses, lined up inflexibly, at uniform distances, on uniform roads, in a treeless communal waste, inhabited by people of the same class, the same income, the same age group, witnessing the same television performances, eating the same tasteless prefabricated foods, from the same freezers, conforming in

> every outward and inward respect to a common mold, manufactured in the central metropolis. [. . .] Those who accept this existence might as well be encased in a rocket hurtling through space, so narrow are their choices, so limited and deficient their permitted responses. Here indeed we find 'The Lonely Crowd'. (Mumford 1961: 486, 512)

With its reference to Riesman's text, Mumford's summary echoes the anxieties about conformity discussed above. Mumford describes the closures involved in living in the suburbs, but these were also closed spaces in that they were inaccessible to African American families as a result of segregation and the Federal Housing Authority's 'redlining' policies (see May 1999: 152). The suburbs were thus occupied by white, heterosexual middle-class families.

Underlying the arguments of Riesman, Whyte and Mills is a dominant discursive anxiety about the nature of post-industrial America and the contradictions between the ideology of American individualism and the reality of a mass society dominated by powerful government organisations and corporations. Key to this analysis is the view that an idealised individualism, embodied in the white, male body, is being eroded along with a consequent feminisation of American culture.

Although the suburban middle-class home was a space where the wife was expected to support the family in her role as homemaker, it was also an important space for the husband. Men in the postwar period wanted 'the good life', which included security at work (a vital aim following the experience of depression and war). The trade-off was loss of autonomy and the need to get along in organisations that did not value aggressive, manly individualism. These men therefore made compromises at work but looked for 'happiness' in their families (see May 1999: 76). Contemporaries saw an active role in fathering as essential to counteract the excessive mothering that was thought to create 'sissies', who supposedly were likely to become homosexuals or victims of the communists.[2] It was a father's duty to make sure this did not happen to their sons, and it was vital that weak fathers were not overshadowed by strong women: 'Many fathers are not fully grown up and selfreliant themselves [. . .] Too often the early years of a boy's life are dominated by women' (Andre Fontaine, *Better Homes and Gardens*, December 1950; quoted by May 1999: 130).[3]

William Whyte devotes a significant proportion of *The Organization Man* to analysis of suburban life. Like Riesman, Whyte makes connections between the worlds of work and of home and leisure and this is echoed in Wilson's novel. Whyte emphasises the transient nature of suburban life, which paradoxically, given the view implied by Mumford that it is characterised by stasis, is full of change and movement. This is generated by two related factors: people's ambitions for advancement and the corporations' requirement that their young executives move from job to job and location to location. Whyte argues that most families adapt to these circumstances, but in *The Man in the Gray Flannel Suit* Wilson suggests that a sense of dislocation is common. The novel opens in suburbia with a description of the alienation of 'Thomas R. Rath and his family' from their home (S. Wilson [1955] 1983: 1). In particular, the interior space of the house is marked by conflict between Tom Rath and his wife Betsy in the crack shaped like a huge question mark embedded in the wall of the living room, a crack caused by Tom throwing a vase at the wall. Tom and Betsy feel trapped in their house, but Betsy asks why they feel 'discontented all the time' (3). She analyses this discontentment later in relation to the social interactions of the locality and the constant pressure to advance oneself (108–9) – in these circumstances, 'contentment was an object of contempt' (109).[4]

The connection between sociological analysis and fiction in this case is made explicit in Whyte's discussion of *The Man in the Gray Flannel Suit* in *The Organization Man*. Whyte's perspective is sarcastic as he describes Tom Rath as typical of the new 'organization' men, who are bland, 'sanctimonious' materialists (1956: 146, 278). Catherine Jurca draws on Whyte's criticism of Rath in her essay on the novel, 'The sanctimonious suburbanite'. Jurca focuses on the representation of class and suburbia in the novel and she argues that the trajectory of the narrative of Tom Rath and his wife Betsy is about asserting their difference from the conformity of suburban life. In this she challenges Barbara Ehrenreich's view in *The Hearts of Men* that these issues are gendered. Jurca writes, 'In postwar suburban literature, discontent knows no gender because it is not directed against male and female roles but is conceived as a self-serving resistance to one's class' (1999: 94). Here I want to challenge Jurca's view on gender while accepting much of her analysis. Ehrenreich's thesis in *The Hearts of Men* concerns the changing expectations of men contained in what she calls the 'breadwinner ethic' (1983: 11). She argues that there was resistance to the role of men in relation to work and the family in the post-war period, amongst what she calls the 'gray flannel dissidents' (29). This resistance was about a finely tuned and ironic recognition of their entrapment in conformity (40–1). However, neither Jurca nor Ehrenreich take into account two key elements of Wilson's novel that are essential to an understanding of representations of masculinity in the period. These are the effects of men's experience of the war and male sexuality, themes that are taken up respectively in Chapters 2 and 3 below, but which are introduced here.

I will begin by considering sexuality and the workspaces of the Organization, drawing on Graham Thompson's *Male Sexuality under Surveillance*. In his analysis of *The Man in the Gray Flannel Suit*, Thompson identifies certain anxieties prevalent in the discourses of post-war America (see G. Thompson 2003: ch. 5). There is the concern that in the bureaucracies of the corporate state there is little space for the individual and a marked similarity to the collectivisation of the Soviet Union – a worry rehearsed by Whyte. Secondly, there was a profound anxiety about homosexuality, marked by the corporate world's repudiation of any effeminate interest in the arts. This was reinforced by the psychoanalytic theory of latency – the suggestion that any man could potentially turn out to be homosexual. These fears were brought together in the red scares around McCarthyism. Thompson sums up these linkages: 'Sovietized and feminized, the Organization had become treacherous and queer' (2003: 85). In relation to Wilson's novel, Thompson discusses the performance of masculinity in the corporate office space, concentrating in particular on Tom Rath's relationship with his boss, Ralph Hopkins, the head of the United Broadcasting Corporation (UBC) and a public figure in corporate America. As Thompson's chapter title suggests, he sees the opacity of the glass used in the offices at UBC as symbolic of the operations of the corporation, arguing that 'the narrative purpose served by the opaque glass bricks and Tom's determination to demolish and penetrate them is to allow, respectively, the accusation of secrecy to be levelled against the Organization and a process of inscription to be undertaken against those men who dwell in that secrecy, men like Hopkins' (85).

Thompson emphasises the issue of sexuality in the office, arguing that it is a site where 'the scripting and de-scripting of male identity and sexuality is an ongoing process' (2003: 65). He draws particular attention to Rath's relationship with Ralph Hopkins, whose sexuality is open to question. Office rumour suggests that amongst other things Hopkins may be 'queer' (S. Wilson [1955] 1983: 29).[5] As the novel develops, other aspects of Hopkins's character reinforce his 'queerness' – his distant relationship with his wife (155), the conclusion of his psychoanalysis that he had a fear of homosexuality (156) and his effeminate style and physique (150–1). The story of the novel has Rath first moving to a new job at UBC, which involves writing a speech about mental health for Hopkins, and then moving closer to Hopkins as his personal assistant, and finally being offered a senior post in UBC – it is Rath's refusal of this offer that Whyte mocks. In all this Rath has to negotiate a fine line in attempting to sustain his masculinity. Rath must not only resist the queer secrecy that Thompson identifies, but assert his masculinity in the feminine spaces of the office. His vulnerability is most noticeable when he becomes Hopkins's assistant and is moved into an office with female workers – the move seems 'more like a demotion than a promotion' (233). In all this, the novel reflects the perception that the Organization is threatening to men's individuality and masculinity.

Rath also needs to reconcile himself to his wartime experiences, and here the novel reflects contemporary concerns about how well ex-servicemen could reintegrate into civilian life. Rath's wartime experiences represent an alterity, in a complex relationship with the present. The novel represents both the space of combat and the sexual spaces of his relationship in Rome with Maria, who became pregnant. In comparison with his unsatisfactory marriage, the relationship with Maria is idealised. This is made most explicit in an episode when Rath and Maria drive out of Rome and picnic in an abandoned and partially destroyed villa. In this space, marked by the destruction of war, far from the apparent security of suburbia, Rath effortlessly asserts his male heterosexuality. His memory of the preciousness with which he valued time in his limited period with Maria is contrasted with his perception that he and Betsy are wasting their time (181).

The second wartime memory that troubles Rath's present is a haunting of the dead, and there are two particular deaths that disturb him. The first is the killing of a young German soldier. After a disastrous parachute drop, Rath and his buddy, Hank Mahoney, are separated from other American soldiers and behind German lines. They kill two German guards and take their leather jackets, which are still warm. It is the sight of a similar jacket in New York that brings to the surface a series of memories for Rath. Crucially, it reminds him that the lift operator at the UBC building who has seemed familiar was a corporal in his company, and privy to Rath's affair with Maria. He was also witness to an attack on the Japanese during which Rath inadvertently blew up Mahoney with a grenade. Rath responds with a period of madness – one soldier refers to him as 'psycho' (93) – during which he suicidally assaults a Japanese position and then seeks medical attention for Mahoney, who is dead.

After this madness has subsided he decides that 'the final truth of war' was that it was 'simply incomprehensible and had to be forgotten' (95). Later he elaborates on this, thinking that at the end of wars there should be 'a course in basic forgetting' (98). He sees himself as living in 'a disconnected world, a lunatic world, where what is true now was not true then'. Whatever has happened in the past, he is now 'just a man in a gray flannel suit', who has a duty: 'I will go to my new job, and I will be cheerful, and I will be industrious, and I will be matter-of-fact. I will keep my gray flannel suit spotless' (98). When he is first back from the war, he admits to himself that 'he didn't believe in the dream any more' (173). Rath clearly suffers from guilt and anger and Wilson himself has pointed out that Rath's name was supposed to signify his anger. Rath's war experiences haunt the present and Betsy perceives 'something hanging over us, something that makes it hard to be happy' (129).

Rath's resistance to these threats to his masculinity lies in his heterosexuality, which is manifested in his marriage and children, and his family is a key reason why he turns down Hopkins's offer of an executive post (251–2). Yet the novel also shows that his sexual relationship with Betsy is in a crisis. In reflecting on her discontent, Betsy compares the three months of marriage she experienced before Tom went to war with their current situation. They have moved from fun to tiredness, and the implication is that this is a change from sexual fulfilment to impotence in Tom's lack of 'enthusiasm' (112–13). However, there is a change towards the end of the novel when they are going to bed the night before Tom has to fly to California with Hopkins. Betsy remarks that they still have eight hours before he has to go – 'quite a lot of time' – and Tom thinks that 'time had become precious again' (248). It is on this trip to California that Hopkins makes the offer of advancement to Rath that he refuses, and it seems that this refusal is an assertion of masculinity that takes strength from a renewal of his heterosexuality. The trajectory of the novel might then be seen as Rath's successful negotiation of the tricky requirements of contemporary masculinity in the spaces of work and home.

Yet Rath's rediscovery of his sexuality and masculinity is only one aspect of the novel's resolution of his dilemmas, and here he is shown to be dependent on values that are seen as associated with the feminine in American culture. Margaret Mead, for example, believes that both culture and morality in America are associated with the feminine. She sees this as a consequence of the experience and ideology of the frontier that permeate American culture. As the frontier became more settled, women were expected to play a public role: 'The finer things of life – moral and aesthetic values – were delegated to women in a new and more active form' (Mead 1949: 303). The consequence is that in contemporary America those occupations which are concerned with 'good works' cannot be occupied by men without 'peril of accusations of effeminacy' (Mead 1949: 304). Writing in *The American People*, Geoffrey Gorer shares this view in claiming that that 'moral precepts and rules [are] inculcated by the mother and the schoolteacher' (Gorer 1948: 46).[6] In conformity with this, it is Betsy who acts as Tom Rath's conscience, challenging his cynical view of the conventions of corporation work. Rath has shown Betsy the draft speech, and she judges it as both 'boring' and 'silly' (S. Wilson [1955] 1983: 185). She asks him what he really thinks of it, and he says it is 'terrible' (186). However, he says that it is standard practice not to say what you think but to sound out your boss and then tell him 'exactly what he wants to hear' – thus mirroring Riesman's description of the behaviour of the 'other-directed' (185). Betsy rebukes him for becoming 'The guy who has no respect for himself or anyone else' (186). Rath's virtue in telling the truth therefore comes from Betsy rather than as an attribute of his manhood. He finally makes a decision to be honest with Hopkins and tell him that the speech that he has been working on is unsatisfactory. Ironically, although Rath thinks that he is taking a risk and breaching the conventions of corporate culture, in fact his honesty is rewarded with the offer of promotion. Rath then moves on to talk to Betsy about his affair with Maria, and his wish to provide financial support for his son in Italy. Rath's actions recuperate a masculinity rooted in integrity that restores his self-esteem and wins back Betsy.

The novel therefore represents a variety of contradictions around post-war masculinity. The legacy of war is not a patriotic record of courage but of psychopathic rage, ambiguous homosocial connections, adultery and an illegitimate son. In the post-war suburbs, fulfilling the regimes of domestic ideology – Rath cooking breakfast for his children in his shoes, socks and underpants, for example (38) – does not prevent marital and sexual trouble. In the Organization, the demands of other-directedness shade into a queering that threatens the masculine values of inner-directedness. In the end, the novel attempts to resolve the contradictions and complexities around masculinity by fusing Rath's heterosexuality with a display of patriarchal integrity that is intended to bolster male individualism against the threats of conformity.

Jack Kerouac, *On the Road*

Jack Kerouac's novel *On the Road* was first published in 1957 and taken then as symptomatic of youthful resistance to the prevalent conformism of American culture.[7] In contrast to Wilson's novel, which attempts to work through the contradictions of conformity and masculinity, *On the Road* can be seen as a challenging assertion of masculinity.

On the Road is open to multiple interpretations, particularly in relation to its status as a critique of conformist America. Malcolm Cowley, in his survey *The Literary Situation*, described the 'beat generation' as the one group that 'refused to conform and waged a dogged sort of rebellion [which was] individual and nihilistic' (1954: 241).[8] Cowley identifies Kerouac as having coined the term the 'beat generation'. In *The Hearts of Men*, Barbara Ehrenreich positions the Beats in a rebellious posture, but frames their resistance in relation to a developing male refusal to agree to the 'breadwinner ethic':

> In the Beat, the two strands of male protest – one directed against the white-collar work world and the other against the suburbanized family life that work was supposed to support – come together into the first all-out critique of American consumer culture. (1983: 52)

In contrast, Manuel Martinez argues in *Countering the Counterculture* that although the Beats appeared to resist corporate America, in fact the terms of their resistance had much in common with conformism and corporatism:

> both [. . .] were manifestations of a fear of the growing visibility and demands of women and minorities, and the restrictions inherent in organized life. [. . .] Ultimately, both reactionary and radical strategies had in common the articulation of a neoindividualism, and the call for an individualist space protected from the demands/of the 'other'. (2003: 7–8)

Martinez argues that the Beats' ersatz resistance was based on misogyny and the appropriation of Mexican and African American identities. Ann Charters acknowledges that 'Kerouac's book [. . .] reflects the prevailing social attitudes about women and racial minorities', but suggests that 'the chance to go on the road with Sal Paradise and Dean Moriarty, two great American "courage-teachers"' outweighs such inescapable attitudes (1991: xxix).[9] In his psychoanalytically-oriented analysis of the Beats in *Taking It Like a Man*, David Savran argues that their work is imbued with the melancholy of loss – a loss of joy and belonging symptomatic of 'the suburbanized, bureaucratized, commodity culture of postwar America' (1998: 62–3).

On the Road is therefore a complex text and open to different interpretations. The following discussion concentrates on the notion of the 'road' as a space in which masculinity may be performed differently from the spaces of the Organization and the suburbs. The masculinity represented in *On the Road* depends on a macho individualism and an 'othering' of women, ethnic groups and homosexual men.

The masculine individualism articulated in *On the Road* derives primarily from the persona of Dean Moriarty, who is seen as a cowboy: 'My first impression of Dean was of a young Gene Autry – trim, thin-hipped, blue-eyed, with a real Oklahoma accent – a sideburned hero of the snowy West' (Kerouac [1957] 2000: 4). This description is juxtaposed with Sal Paradise's impression of Moriarty's wife, Marylou, who is a 'pretty blonde', but 'awfully dumb and capable of doing horrible things' (4). The next morning Dean gets her to prepare breakfast and sweep the floor (4). Within a week, Marylou has gone back to Denver and is described as a 'whore' (5). These two complementary descriptions epitomise the way in which a set of masculine values is first idealised and then shored up through the attribution of other contrasting characteristics to women and the feminine. (Sal's assessment of Dean also involves a scopophilic scrutiny full of homoerotic desire – an aspect that is considered below.)

Manuel Martinez points out the rhetorical power of the cowboy in this period. By 1959 there were thirty-five westerns broadcast weekly on national television, and eight of the ten top shows were westerns (Martinez 2003: 74). If the cowboy personified and embodied the essence of a macho masculinity, then he also signified the 'West', the frontier on which expansion, movement and change defined 'America'. Dean Moriarty represents a macho notion of the frontier in his cowboy persona, his inexhaustible movement on the road and his oppositional location on the edge of American society.

To be 'on the road' is to avoid the stasis of domesticity and thereby repudiate the 'domestic ideology' of the period. As Dean tells Sal: 'no matter where I live, my trunk's always sticking out from under the bed, I'm ready to leave or get thrown out' (Kerouac [1957] 2000: 229). To '*move*' is to leave 'confusion and nonsense behind' and to perform the 'one true and noble function of the time' (121). To be on the road is also to live an individual life – 'you cut along and make it your own way', according to Dean (229). And he adds that this is a test of masculinity: 'He ain't a man 'less he's a jumpin' man' (229).

Dean's constant movement on the road is expressed in driving at excessive speed, taking risks and demonstrating great skill. This is perhaps epitomised in the journey to Chicago in the Cadillac limousine (204–20), which, in a repudiation of consumer values, ends with the car wrecked (220). Not only is it notable that none of the female characters ever drives, the macho element of Dean's driving is made apparent in the episode of the 'fag Plymouth' (187–91). Sal and Dean have arranged a lift through a travel bureau and they have a ride with 'a tall, thin fag who [. . .] drove with extreme care'. Moreover, his 'fag' car was 'effeminate' and had 'no pick up and no real power' (187). The journey is broken in Sacramento and there is there an ambiguous exchange in the hotel room where the driver admits to his homosexuality.[10] There is some negotiation with Dean, who has been 'a hustler in his youth', while Sal hovers in the bathroom (190). The only clear outcome of this is that the driver agrees to Dean taking over the driving, with Dean's driving terrifying the other passengers. A cautious, effeminate homosexuality is driven out in this display of virile masculinity.

The novel's assertion of a particular masculine identity is further achieved through a constant misogyny in the representation of the female characters. The contrasting perspectives on Dean and Marylou have already been noted, as has Dean's view of women (and his children) as disposable in his constant readiness to move on. The novel also articulates very clearly the conventional dichotomy between women as sexual objects and as mothers. The women in the novel are constantly represented as subject to the sexual needs of the male characters. For example, when Sal first visits Denver, he discovers that Dean is running a complex schedule involving two women – Marylou and his 'new woman', Camille – and Carlo (38–9).[11] Moreover, Dean's sexual power extends to the provision of girls to others as he promises to 'fix [Sal] up' (39). What really counts is the depth of male bonding, while sexual needs with women may be fulfilled in superficial encounters. Later, the relationship between Dean, Sal and Marylou blends into the sort of homoerotic triangle discussed by Eve Sedgwick in *Between Men*. Dean first claims Sal as his buddy and then it becomes apparent that he wants Sal 'to work Marylou' (118). Marylou apparently agrees, but Sal is uncomfortable being watched by Dean, and significantly the bed in which he fails to perform is described as the 'deathbed of a big man and sagged in the middle' (119). In this exchange there are two significant points: first, that Marylou is given no significant agency – later, Sal realises that 'Marylou had no real interest in me;

she was trying to reach Dean through me, his buddy' (155) – and secondly, that the exchange masks the real homoerotic desire that Sal has for Dean.

The homosocial/homoerotic continuum is similarly invoked late in the novel in the final road trip when Sal and Dean, with Stan Shephard, drive to Mexico. This is the trip that Sal describes as 'the most fabulous of all', to the 'magic *south*' (241), 'us flying down the curve of the world into other tropics and other worlds' (242). This excitement over the exotic potential of the south is echoed in the visit of the three men to a Mexican whorehouse in Gregoria, after smoking marijuana. The visit is represented as a collective endeavour as they dance together and 'switched the girls' (262, 264). Moreover, as they cavort, 'a good twenty men leaned in [the] window, watching' (262). These aspects of the visit establish it as a demonstration of masculine sexuality, where the men perform for each other as well as for themselves, where that sexuality is performed on female bodies in an economic transaction, which is expected to make as much money as possible from these 'rich' Americans. Here also, white masculinity is reinvigorated in relation to an exotic Other as Sal describes the experience as 'a long spectral Arabian dream in the afternoon in another life – Ali Baba and the alleys and the courtesans' (264).

These women are exoticised and sexualised, and consequently rendered subject to the whims of the men, but are then endorsed as 'great girls'. On the other hand, as mothers or partners, women are relegated to the domestic space of the 'sewing circle' (176). The domestic space is feminine and Dean, with his ever-ready trunk, constantly escapes from it into the masculine space of the road. As has been noted, women in American culture have been seen as the guardians of conscience and it is this role that the 'sewing circle' is shown to adopt. When Sal stays in San Francisco with Dean, his wife, Camille, throws them out. The next day they are at a gathering with friends where Dean is accused by Galatea:

> You have absolutely no regard for anybody but yourself and your damned kicks. All you think about is what's hanging between your legs and how much money or fun you can get out of people and then you just throw them aside. [. . .] It never occurs to you that life is serious [. . .] (176)

Dean leaves the room and stands outside on the pavement. Sal perceives that: 'Bitterness, recriminations, advice, morality, sadness – everything was behind him, and ahead of him was the ragged and ecstatic joy of pure being' (178). The attitude of Camille, Galatea and the other women is compared unfavourably with the nameless wife of Walter, an African American whom Dean and Sal have met that evening as they tour the jazz clubs. Walter takes them home for a beer (185). They disturb his wife's sleep in the small apartment, but she just 'smiled and smiled. She never asked Walter where he'd been, what time it was, nothing'. Dean comments on this as they leave: '[T]here's a *real* woman for you. Never a harsh word, never a complaint, or modified; [. . .] This is a man, and that's his castle' (185). The narrative thus constantly constructs masculinity in relation to the female Other, repudiating the feminine space of the domestic and the policing of morality.

This macho masculinity also intrinsically challenges the compromised masculinity of feminised modern American culture – contained in the spaces of the corporation and suburbia. As has been discussed in relation to *The Man in the Gray Flannel Suit*, the feminisation of American culture, together with contemporary anxieties about homosexuality, particularly required men to reject any hint of homosexual identity. The novel both asserts an aggressive heterosexuality and evinces homophobia, as has been seen in the episode of the 'fag Plymouth'. Homophobic attitudes are recurrent through the novel, for instance in the jazz club in San Francisco when they see 'a horrible sight in the bar: a white hipster fairy had come in wearing a Hawaiian shirt and was asking the big drummer if he could sit in' (182). Yet the text also constantly brings the homoerotic into the narrative. The ambiguities in this echo the ambiguities in Kerouac's personal life. In her Introduction, Charters notes that Kerouac's revisions to the novel included the excision of references to the homosexual relationship between Carlo (Ginsberg) and Dean (Cassady) (1991: xxiv). There may have been revision of this sort because Viking were very concerned about libel when they first published the book (see Dittman's biography of Kerouac [2004]). However, Gore Vidal records a conversation with Allen Ginsberg in which Ginsberg says that Kerouac would not admit his homosexual acts because of his mother, who was 'a monster. She hated me because I was a fag. Worse, I was a Jew too' (Vidal 1995: 233). In his biography of Kerouac, Michael Dittman refers to his 'divided nature: although he would rant endlessly about the evils and moral turpitude of homosexuality, he also flirted and experimented with Ginsburg and Cassady' (2004: 57).[12] Certainly in the atmosphere of post-war America, to admit publicly to homosexual activity was brave and risky.[13] It was inevitable therefore that the novel's assertion of a macho masculine identity correspondingly involved the repudiation of homosexuality. And yet, as has been noted, Sal considers Dean with desire, and their relationship is suffused with homoeroticism even as they display an exaggerated heterosexuality. The construction of masculinity in the novel may be seen to work on a set of exclusions that emphasise a particularly macho set of characteristics, but with the homophobia/homoerotic connection, there is an underlying ambiguity.

Masculine identity is also established through the association of Dean and Sal with marginal characters in American society – hobos, farm workers, railway workers, jazz musicians and African Americans, and immigrant Mexican workers. In a notorious passage, Sal expresses this very clearly when he is walking in Denver, wishing

> I were a Negro, feeling that the best the white world had offered me was not enough ecstasy for me, not enough life, joy, kicks, darkness, music, not enough night. [. . .] I wished I were a Denver Mexican, or even a poor overworked Jap, anything but what I was so drearily, a 'white man' disillusioned. (163–4)

Norman Mailer's essay 'The white Negro' considers the sort of aspiration expressed by Sal, but in 'The black boy looks at the white boy', a response to Mailer's essay, James Baldwin discusses this passage, describing it as 'offensive nonsense', and while he notes that it articulated a 'thin pain', he regards this pain as about a dream, not reality ([1961] 1964: 188). Kerouac's attitude is illustrative of how American writers in the post-war period 'mythologize movement' (Martinez 2003: 12). In novels like *On the Road* the characters move into the periphery of American society, associating with marginalised subjects, but they can always move back to the centre. For Martinez, this movement means that the Beats appropriate the figure of the Mexican and the African American in what 'is a nostalgic and romantic search for a cultural/social space as yet unterritorialized and regulated by external forces' (2003: 28). It can be argued that part of this nostalgia is to recuperate older forms of masculinity.

In 'Jazz America', an essay that complements Martinez's analysis, Douglas Malcolm argues that Kerouac's claim that his writing is analogous to jazz improvisation amounts to a form of appropriation of this element of African American culture. Malcolm maintains that Kerouac's representation of jazz rests on a Romantic and primitivist ideology of spontaneous expression that is far from the technical accomplishment required to improvise effectively in jazz (1999: 106). He concludes that in fact the form of Kerouac's prose owes more to modernist writers than to jazz improvisation (107). In terms of the description of jazz and jazz musicians, there is a claim to masculinity by association and also to a 'madness' that emphasises the way in which the experience of the music is beyond normal American mainstream culture. This is perhaps most apparent in Sal's brief history of American jazz, in which there are, first, the 'mad musicians' in New Orleans; followed by Louis Armstrong, who 'blows his top'; 'vigorous and virile' Roy Eldridge; 'mad Thelonious Monk and madder Gillespie'; and a 'flipped' Charlie Parker (Kerouac [1957] 2000: 218). Kerouac's particular representation of the spontaneity and 'madness' of jazz is harnessed to a discourse claiming an equivalent style of writing and of self-expression. This is articulated with the ideology of Romantic alienation to construct a masculine identity resistant to the conformity and feminisation of modern American culture.

Perhaps Malcolm's most telling example of Kerouac's refusal of the realities of African American experience comes in an episode where, on a rare occasion, Sal does some work. He has taken up with Terry, a young Mexican woman, in California, and they are broke. They end up in a tented encampment picking cotton with some Okies, African Americans and Mexicans (86ff). Sal admits to being incompetent, but enjoys resting when he wants to, with his 'face on the pillow of brown moist earth' (87). Around this is a patronising and sentimental attitude to back-breaking labour – the Okies 'loved to work' and had advanced to 'a kind of smiling respectability in better tents' (86, 87). The 'Negro couple [. . .] picked cotton with the same God-blessed patience their grandfathers had practised in antebellum Alabama' (87). When Sal realises that his situation is far from ideal he prays to God that he might be able to do something for the 'little people I loved' (87).[14] Malcolm refers to Kerouac as celebrating 'manual labor while seemingly utterly unaware of slavery' (98). Sal lasts a few days in this situation and then sends a postcard to his aunt asking for another $50 (89). He then sends Terry back to her family and returns home to New Jersey. Sal thus always has available an exit from poverty and life in the margins of America that simply was not available to the elderly Negroes, Mexicans like Terry, and the Okies. In Martinez's terms this is a kind of tourism that allows Sal to claim the trappings of a marginal identity, which authenticates his masculinity.

So far, this reading of *On the Road* has traced the construction of an assertive masculinity that distinguishes itself from the conformity of American culture through its mobility and association with marginal or oppositional elements of society; this masculinity is further defined against the 'Other' of women and homosexuals. However, I want now to consider aspects of the narrative that suggest some brittleness in this masculine persona.[15] This emerges in considering more closely Sal's relationship with Dean – the axis of the novel around which all the action and movement occurs. Sal is the narrator and, as readers, we are borne along on his description of the events of the novel. Dean's appearance in Sal's life is the mainspring of the novel's action, as is clear from the very first sentence; moreover, Sal is infatuated with Dean. Dean becomes Sal's mentor and guide, not only because he will be the source of new experiences for this ambitious writer, but because he also seemed like 'a long-lost brother' (9). However, the novel is also, of course, written as an account of past events, and from the beginning, Sal notes that 'With the coming of Dean Moriarty began the part of my life you could call my life on the road' (3). Part 5 of the novel marks the end of that phase of his life. The change here involves Sal's marriage to Laura, 'the girl with the pure and innocent dear eyes that I had always searched for and for so long' (278). As this suggests, Sal had always in mind the prospect of retiring from the 'road' and settling down in marriage: 'All these years I was looking for a girl I wanted to marry' (105). There is a way then in which Sal is himself always 'homeward bound' (to borrow the title of Elaine Tyler May's book). After Sal has abandoned Terry and the cotton pickers he returns to his aunt's home and consumes everything in the icebox. With the money that Sal has sent back they decide to buy a refrigerator, 'the first one in the family' (96), thus participating in the consumerism that marked the post-war years.[16]

Sal also enjoys the 'great rag rug woven of all the clothes in my family for years, which was now finished [by his aunt] and spread on my bedroom floor, as complex and rich as the passage of time itself' (96). Sal's attachment to home and family reminds the reader that he is essentially a follower of Dean, and although he is a willing participant in the excesses of life on the road, he is also a writer and observer, who has some distance from Dean. This introduces ambiguity into the whole ethos of the road. It is perhaps most clearly expressed when Sal, who is in Denver, learns that Dean is on his way there to drive them to Mexico. Sal has a vision of Dean,

> a burning shuddering frightful Angel, palpitating toward me across the road, approaching like a cloud, with enormous speed, pursuing me like the Shrouded Traveler on the plain, bearing down on me. [. . .] I saw his old jalopy chariot with thousands of sparking flames

shooting out from it; I saw the path it burned over the road; it even made its own road and went over the corn, through cities, destroying bridges, drying rivers. It came like Wrath to the west. (236)

The 'Shrouded Traveler' was part of an earlier vision of Sal's and was agreed with Dean to be a figure of Death. So Dean is here imagined as a destructive angel wreaking havoc. He has 'gone mad again', and this repetitious madness no longer seems to be the simple attraction that it once was. The trip to Mexico indeed ends in Mexico City with the 'rat' Dean abandoning Sal, who is suffering from a delirious fever (275–6).

There are then ambiguities in the novel, about masculinity and sexuality, about the contrasting attractions of home and the road, and these are embodied in the character of Sal. Moreover, in its representation of jazz and the marginal, the novel is not simply exploitative. However much it is true that Sal is an observer who can retreat from the margins at will, the novel is a protest against the dominant narrative of white middle-class America and its ideologies of work and domesticity, and at the least represents aspects of the lives of others who do not fit easily into that mould. Kerouac himself was brought up in a Catholic French-Canadian household, while Sal is from an Italian background. As Elaine Tyler May records, such ethnic groups had been marginalised before the Second World War, but became incorporated into the dominant 'white' narrative after the war (1999: xx). Kerouac of course grew up before the war (he was born in 1922), speaking a local French dialect, *joual*, before he spoke English. It is possible to argue therefore that in *On the Road*, Kerouac, while identifying with the marginalised, seeks to distance himself from them as he constructs an *American* male identity through his writing. In particular he identifies with Dean, the 'cowboy', as embodying an incontrovertible American masculinity, drawing on this example as a way of negotiating a sense of belonging in a society that gave few favours to the marginalised.

J. D. Salinger, *The Catcher in the Rye*

In its representation of Holden Caulfield's adolescent perspective, *The Catcher in the Rye* (1951) echoes *The Man in the Gray Flannel Suit* in representing the complexities and contradictions of masculine identity in the period. In particular, I argue that the novel emphasises the constructed nature of a gendered identity while undermining essentialist notions of gender through the association of Holden Caulfield with the feminine.

Responses to *The Catcher in the Rye* have been diverse and fluctuated with the shifting context in which writers have considered its themes. For example, in a 1951 review published in the *Saturday Review of Literature*, Harrison Smith writes about the novels of 'despair and frustration' that many younger writers have been producing:

> The sour note of bitterness and the recurring theme of sadism have become almost a convention, never thoroughly explained by the author's dependence on a psychoanalytical interpretation of a major character. The boys who are spoiled or turned into budding homosexuals by their mothers and a loveless home life are as familiar to us today as stalwart and dependable young heroes were to an earlier generation. We have accepted this interpretation of the restlessness and bewilderment of our young men and boys because no one had anything better to offer. (Smith 1951)

Smith argues that the novel does not 'attempt to explain why all boys who dismay their elders have failed to pass successfully the barrier between childhood and young manhood', although he quotes the advice given to Holden Caulfield by his ex-teacher, Mr Antolini: 'The mark of the immature man is that he wants to die nobly for a cause, while the mark of a mature man is that he wants to live humbly for one' (Salinger [1951] 1994: 169). Smith's approach reflects two contemporary obsessions – with the explanatory potential of psychoanalytic approaches, and with mothers' undermining of young men's manliness. Broadly, Smith echoes some of the concerns about a feminising shift in American culture, with the consequence that a clearly defined masculine identity (embodied in 'stalwart and dependable young heroes') has been swept away, leaving young men bewildered.

In her essay, 'Masculine protest in *The Catcher in the Rye*', Sally Robinson has read the novel in relation to such texts as *The Lonely Crowd* and *The Organization Man* as resisting the pressures on traditional masculinity of a conformist and feminised culture. She concludes:

> Holden's lament is [. . .] part of a larger tradition of masculine protest: protest against threats to masculinity and protest as an expression, however compromised, of masculine power and authority. [. . .] That protest has the effect, not of creating *new* forms of masculinity, but of creating a nostalgic desire for the old forms, even as those forms become increasingly impossible to maintain. (2007: 76)

I agree that *The Catcher in the Rye* does not create or represent new forms of masculinity, but I argue that its engagement with masculinity is more complicated than a nostalgic desire for old forms of masculinity; nor does it simply express masculine power and authority.

The ambivalence of Holden Caulfield towards the expectations of the adult male and his attraction to the feminine are embedded in the narrative structure of the novel and metaphorically represented in his enthusiasm for 'digression', which he explains to his ex-English teacher, Mr Antolini. He recounts that his Oral Expression teacher at Pencey, Mr Vinson, demanded that speakers '*un*ify and *sim*plify all the time' (Salinger [1951] 1994: 166). If a speaker failed to keep to the point, the rest of the class yelled 'Digression!' (165). However, Caulfield likes digression, which he believes is 'more *in*teresting' (165). Vinson's view of the ideal trajectory of narrative can be characterised as conventionally rationalistic – direct, logical, purposive – traits commonly associated with masculinity. 'Digression', which is not linear, fits, on the other hand, with certain notions of the 'feminine'.[17] Caulfield's preference for digression can therefore be seen as a rejection of the rational, structured speech of male authority in preference for a more feminine mode of narration. Digression is characteristic of Caulfield's narrative voice, so the form of the novel itself works to disrupt a simple masculine point of view. Caulfield's association with the digressive and the feminine also makes a significant contribution to the novel's critical relationship to male coming-of-age narratives. Caulfield tells his readers in the first sentence that he will not be going into 'all that David Copperfield kind of crap' (1). Unlike other male narrators of fictional biography, who look back on their adolescence from maturity, Caulfield remains ambiguously located at the end of the novel, associated with the feminine, and with his development into conventional adult masculinity open to doubt (192).

Holden Caulfield's frustration and alienation as he attempts to move from adolescence into an adult masculine identity are revealing of the constructed and artificial nature of gender identities. This can be seen in his attempts to occupy an adult male identity in the public spaces of New York. The theme of 'phoniness' in the novel is crucial to Caulfield's perception of identity and is related to the notion of performance. Caulfield's journey through the novel may be read as a search for an authentic male identity, and his abhorrence of 'phoniness' may be considered as a repudiation of aspects of contemporary consumer and mass culture that are part of the feminisation of American society. This is an element of Caulfield's critique, but it also involves a recognition that identity is always a performance. This is noticeable when he goes with his girlfriend, Sally, to see a play starring the Lunts, who were contemporary celebrity actors. While he admires their performance, he says that they were 'too good' (113): 'If you do something *too* good, then, after a while, if you don't watch it, you start showing off' (113–14). So the Lunts' skill becomes diverted from a representation of characters to a display that emphasises the artificiality of the theatrical performance itself. Significantly, what happens on the stage is echoed in Caulfield's observations of the audience in the interval: 'You never saw so many phonies in all your life, everybody smoking their ears off and talking about the play so that everybody could hear and know how sharp they were' (114). The critical stance of the narrative questions the availability of an authentic subjectivity.

The performance of identity, however, bears most strongly on sixteen-year-old Caulfield himself. He is in the liminal state of adolescence – a set of social, psychological and physiological processes through which subjectivity is transformed. Transformation of a particular kind is offered by Caulfield's expensive boarding school in Pennsylvania – Pencey Prep. The school claims that 'Since 1888 we have been molding boys into splendid, clear-thinking young men' (2). The school's claim is significant in its articulation of an understanding that 'men' are socially shaped during adolescence. The claim to 'mold' boys may also be seen as a kind of physical production line and there is an emphasis on embodiment through the novel. Early on, Holden Caulfield describes himself: 'I act quite young for my age sometimes. I was sixteen then, and I'm seventeen now, and sometimes I act like I'm about thirteen. It's really ironical, because I'm six foot two and a half [. . .]' (8). The relationship between embodiment and subjectivity is therefore complex: while Caulfield has an adult body, he does not behave as an adult male. This contradiction works through the novel as Caulfield's experiences set up an ironic distance between his physical maturity and his inability to operate as an adult male in the cultural spaces of Manhattan.

In order to explore this further, it is necessary to consider Caulfield's embodiment in the context of different material spaces. Most of the narrative of the novel is focused on his experiences in Manhattan after he has run away from Pencey Prep. It is apparent from Caulfield's account of his trip that as the son of well-to-do New York parents, he is familiar with the cultural geography of the city and able to negotiate his way through its spaces. For example, when he first arrives in New York he is able confidently to direct the taxi driver to an appropriate hotel. Salinger himself was brought up in Manhattan and the novel is rooted in the actualities of pre-war, metropolitan, middle-class social life. Indeed, from the *New York City Guide* of 1939, with its detailed maps and listings of hotels and night spots, it is possible to identify most of the places Caulfield visits and to trace his journey right through to the carousel marked on the map of Central Park (*New York City Guide* 1939: 277). It is, therefore, a sophisticated, white, heterosexual metropolitan masculinity that Caulfield seeks to occupy as he sets out in Manhattan after he has left Pencey. However, as Caulfield recounts his experiences in the public spaces of adulthood, it becomes clear that although he has moved beyond childhood, he cannot effectively embody Manhattan masculinity. While he can direct the taxi driver to a hotel, his conversation with the driver is notably inappropriate, ending with asking the driver to have a drink with him. Such an invitation can be seen as a misguided attempt to employ the codes of masculine social interaction and signifies both Caulfield's aspiration to manhood and his unconscious distance from it. Moreover, Caulfield's inability to act appropriately reinforces the suggestion that the masculinity to which he aspires is ultimately a performance. The contradictions in Caulfield's perception of phoniness and his own desire for authentic manhood point up for the reader the constructedness of a social identity.

The suggestion that masculine identity is a performance continues as Caulfield tries and fails to be the 'man about town' in touring the bars and nightclubs of New York. For example, he goes to the Lavender Room of the Edmont Hotel, where he is staying, but he is given a 'lousy table' and then, because he is underage, is refused the Scotch and soda he tries to order (62). In this episode the narrative exposes Caulfield as a problematical narrator and engages the reader's sympathy with the female characters. Sitting at the table next to him in the Lavender Room are three 'girls around thirty or so. The whole three of them were pretty ugly, and they all had on the kind of hats that you knew they didn't really live in New York, but one of them, the blonde one [Bernice], wasn't too bad' (62). Here Caulfield makes a number of judgements about the young women: about their physical appearance, their age and their provincialism. He names them as 'girls', thus positioning them within his imagined sexual orbit, and his behaviour from then on corresponds with this assumption. The reader may be drawn into Caulfield's value judgements, yet, as the episode moves on, the narrative serves to question and complicate the interchange. Caulfield is acting as if he is a grown-up, but he is refused an alcoholic drink because he is underage: despite his claims about his appearance, he is obviously not an adult. It is in this light that his 'giving the three witches at the next table the eye' must be seen (63). Caulfield claims that their response was to start 'giggling like morons', but the reader might in fact begin to appreciate the young women's point of view: Caulfield probably does cut a rather absurd figure. This opens to question his assumption that he is entitled to make these sexual and class judgements about them. This is reinforced after he has been dancing with Bernice and he sits down with the women, even though, he says, they 'didn't invite me to sit down at their table – mostly because they were too ignorant' (65). Caulfield here draws on the codes of conventional male behaviour in imposing himself uninvited on the space occupied by the women, but it is clear that it is his behaviour rather than theirs that is 'ignorant'. Moreover, as the scene in the Lavender Room unfolds, Caulfield's attempt to perform the conventional male role is undercut by his identification with the young women. Like the women, he is vulnerable and marginalised in New York, and, as the narrative unfolds, his helplessness and frailty are increasingly exposed. By associating Caulfield with female characters, and expressing his ambivalence to the male world of work and responsibility, the novel questions conventional notions of masculinity.

Indeed, the representation of the female characters through the novel contributes to the complexity of the representation of gender.[18] The novel's women have received little critical attention and this may be a result of Salinger's decision to narrate the novel in Caulfield's voice, thus limiting the narrative to a single male perspective that renders the female characters marginal. In one sense, Caulfield's view of women is unremarkable for an adolescent male in 1950s America; he frequently echoes conventional attitudes that reflect women's subordinate social status at this time. Here, for example, is Caulfield sitting in the lobby of the Biltmore Hotel, waiting to meet Sally:

> [. . .] there were about a million girls sitting and standing around waiting for their dates to show up. Girls with their legs crossed, girls with their legs not crossed, girls with terrific legs, girls with lousy legs, girls that looked like swell girls, girls that looked like they'd be bitches if you knew them. It was really nice, sightseeing [. . .] (111)

Caulfield's 'sightseeing' could thus be regarded as typical of an objectifying and sexualising male gaze. Furthermore, he assumes that the inevitable destination of the young women at the Biltmore is marriage (111). It may be argued, however, that the novel offers a more complex representation of Caulfield's interactions with the female characters than might initially appear. For example, at the Biltmore, Caulfield positions himself as a sophisticated heterosexual man about town, and yet, while he watches and judges the young women, he is in fact identified with them: he too is sitting and waiting for his date, just as they are. The novel suggests, therefore, that Caulfield's image of himself as a conventional adult male is a delusion. Indeed, because he is an unreliable narrator, his perception of what is happening around him and his account of other characters cannot be taken at face value. Particularly in relation to the female characters, the text's continual revelation of Caulfield's misperceptions, inconsistencies and uncertainties creates doubt about how to interpret his attitudes to women and his descriptions of their behaviour. By focusing on two aspects of Caulfield's relationships with female characters – in terms of sexuality and mothering – it becomes evident that Caulfield is strongly identified with the feminine and the maternal. Thus, while Caulfield may appear to uphold conventional attitudes to women, his identification with the feminine expresses a complex relationship with the dominant model of masculinity.

Sally Hayes is one of the most prominent female characters in the novel. Caulfield feels both attracted to and repelled by Sally: 'She gave me a pain in the ass, but she was very good-looking' (96). He responds to her in conventional ways, willing to engage in sexual fantasies about her, 'horse around' with her in the taxi (112) and admire her in her 'little blue butt-twitcher of a dress' when they go skating (116). Given the expectation of marriage as a natural trajectory for young women like Sally, she might be regarded as a potential partner for Caulfield. He enunciates this possibility when he sees her arrive at the Biltmore, proclaiming: 'I felt like marrying her the minute I saw her' (112). Caulfield's sexual interaction with Sally is not entirely successful, however: although he believes he is 'seductive as hell' in the taxi, he almost falls off his seat twice (113). The implication is that Caulfield cannot play the role of adult partner successfully and, when he suggests running away with Sally to New England – which is partly a sexual fantasy and partly an attempt to escape the phoniness that Caulfield sees everywhere – she refuses. At this point, Caulfield's perception of her as desirable shifts and he repositions her as a judgemental mother. As has been noted, Geoffrey Gorer argued that the American conscience was 'predominantly feminine', and maintained that this was problematic for the American male, who carried around inside him 'an ethical, admonitory, censorious mother' (1948: 54). In what Caulfield perceives as her moralistic and restrictive reaction to his plan, Sally may be deemed to be speaking as the 'censorious mother' identified by Gorer, and Caulfield responds with a final insult that rejects Sally and her values: 'You give me a royal pain in the ass' (120).

However, while the text is sensitive to Caulfield's struggle to negotiate a place in the world, it simultaneously suggests that his judgement of Sally is open to question and that his representation of her should be read as both flawed and limited. Through the scenes with Sally, Caulfield presents her in an unflattering light: she is 'the queen of the phonies' (105), the embodiment of the inauthenticity that he is so anxious to avoid. Yet Caulfield's ambivalence also involves some hypocrisy: a phoniness of his own. While he thinks Sally is a 'pain in the ass', he also tells her that he loves her, while admitting that this is a lie (113). Moreover, Caulfield's inconsistent attitude and extreme behaviour, such as lighting matches (116) and shouting (117), inverts the idea that it is Sally who is the 'royal pain in the ass'. In these ways, the text calls into question Caulfield's assertions about what is or is not authentic. What emerges, in fact, is an identification of Caulfield with Sally in terms of their social class and cultural interests. Caulfield's hostility towards Sally may then be read as a projection of anxiety about the authenticity of the male role to which he aspires. While this reassessment of the narrative does not claim any autonomy or genuine agency for Sally, it opens up the possibility of a more sympathetic reading of her and raises important doubts for the reader about Caulfield.

While Caulfield's relationship with Sally might be seen through the prism of conventional teen dating, further episodes engage more directly with the sexual mores of the period. Critics have often interpreted Caulfield's resistance to sexual contact as his clinging to innocence, but it could alternatively be seen as evidence of his resistance to heteronormative conventions. According to 1950s middle-class moral codes, sex should be constrained, particularly because pregnancy outside marriage provoked severe disapproval. Abortion and birth control were not accessible, so the answer was 'petting', which required complete control of the boundaries of sexual contact to avoid pregnancy. As Mead wrote in *Male and Female*, this control was the responsibility of the girl: 'the boy is expected to ask for as much as possible, the girl to yield as little as possible' (1949: 290). As Caulfield puts it, a girl who isn't a prostitute 'keeps telling you to stop' (83). The allocation of control to the 'girl' implies that the female has no desire of her own, other than to control her partner, thus denying the possibility of active female sexuality. These circumstances are exemplified in the example of Caulfield's roommate at Pencey, Stradlater, who is sexually aggressive and unscrupulous:

> What a technique that guy had. What he'd do was, he'd start snowing his date in this very quiet, *sincere* voice – like as if he wasn't only a very handsome guy, but a nice *sincere* guy, too. [. . .] His date kept saying, 'No – *please*. Please, don't. *Please*.' But old Stradlater kept snowing her in this Abraham Lincoln, sincere voice, and finally there'd be this terrific silence in the back of the car. (43–4)

In this anecdote, Stradlater's approach to sex is described as genitally focused and emotionally disengaged, typifying dominant notions of masculine sexuality: lust that must be satisfied, unconnected with affection. Caulfield understands that most guys are like Stradlater and don't stop when asked to, although Caulfield does so (83). Moreover, somewhat apologetically, he admits that he 'can never get really sexy – I mean *really* sexy – with a girl I don't like a lot' (133).

Caulfield's perception of Stradlater's technique turns to anxiety when he learns that Stradlater has a date with Jane Gallagher. In their markedly different responses to Jane, the narrative contrasts Caulfield and Stradlater. Unlike Stradlater's phallic obsession, Caulfield's summer relationship with Jane, characterised by companionship, hand-holding and Jane's stroking of Caulfield's neck, is represented as touching and sensuous, polymorphous in its engagement of multiple areas of the body. This difference may again be considered in terms of digression. The trajectory of Stradlater's sexuality is unified and simplified in its objective: it is a sexuality that exploits discrepancies of power in contemporary gender relations. In contrast, Caulfield is hesitant. Not only does he not go to see Jane when she is at Pencey, throughout his time in New York, the reader is teased with the prospect of Caulfield speaking to her on the phone; but he either defers the call or fails to make contact. In the sharp distinction between Stradlater's approach and Caulfield's empathy with Jane, he is identified with the feminine. Such identification is suffused with an ambiguity about sexuality and its relationship with gender that is disruptive of conventional expectations. It is not that Caulfield simply identifies with a conventional notion of female sexuality, but rather that his distance from a crude masculine phallic sexuality throws open to question the stereotypes associated with femininity and masculinity.

The social and moral codes involved in middle-class sexual exchanges do not apply in Caulfield's episode with Sunny, who is a prostitute. Caulfield's avoidance of sex with her may be read as consistent with his need for an emotional connection in sexual contact. The key moment occurs when Sunny unexpectedly removes her dress. This sudden transformation reveals the true nature of the circumstances: those in which her body becomes an object in a financial transaction. His despair at the lack of emotional contact is reinforced by his identification with her: 'She was around my age' (85). He begins to empathise with her and this identification means that he must refuse the emotionless sexual contact that prostitution offers.

Caulfield's distance from conventional male sexuality is connected with other key signifiers of masculinity – courage and violence – in an episode that further emphasises the constructed nature of masculinity. In imagining violence, the novel articulates a tension between the idealised sophistication of Manhattan and the realities of Salinger's war experience.[19] Caulfield's sexual opportunity with Sunny is offered to him by the elevator operator, Maurice, when he returns to his hotel in New York. After Caulfield decides not to go through with sex, there is a dispute about her payment, which brings Maurice to Caulfield's room. Caulfield's failure to step towards male adulthood by gaining an initial sexual experience is reflected in his physical vulnerability in relation to Maurice. First, under pressure, he begins to cry (92) – his body fails him, expressing childish (or perhaps 'feminine') emotional weakness. Then Maurice 'snapped his finger very hard on my pyjamas . . . it hurt like hell' (93). This humiliating assault on his genitals is followed by a punch in the stomach. Maurice and Sunny leave, with Caulfield lying on the floor in agony. Eventually, he gets up:

> About halfway to the bathroom, I sort of started pretending I had a bullet in my guts. Old Maurice had plugged me. Now I was on my way to the bathroom to get a good shot of bourbon or something to steady my nerves and help me *really* go into action. (93)

Caulfield imagines himself getting his gun and ringing for the elevator. As soon as the doors open, Maurice screams for mercy,

> But I'd plug him anyway. Six shots right through his fat, hairy belly. [. . .] Then I'd [. . .] call up Jane and have her come over and bandage up my guts. I pictured her holding a cigarette for me to smoke while I was bleeding and all.

There is a juxtaposition here of sexuality and violence. First, his shooting of Maurice in his 'fat, hairy belly' implies a castrating act of revenge for Caulfield's humiliation; then the consoling appearance of Jane is represented as the reward for 'the man of action'.

The narrative immediately continues:

> The goddam movies. They can ruin you. I'm not kidding.
> [. . .] Then I got back into bed. It took me quite a while to get to sleep – I wasn't even tired – but finally I did. What I really felt like, though, was committing suicide. I felt like jumping out the window. (94)

The novel here shows the disparity between the artificiality of the cultural constructions that bear down on Caulfield and his authentic feelings – 'what I really felt like'. The fantasies of masculinity derived from the movies offer a consolation. However, Caulfield is aware of being contained within the artificial cinematic tropes of tough masculinity – guns, girls and cigarette smoke. This perception and his vulnerability generate what he represents as an authenticity of feeling, but in fact it summons up feelings of violent anger that he directs against himself. Yet while the novel criticises this performance of a certain style of contemporary masculinity, it doesn't offer Caulfield a viable alternative masculine subjectivity. So his failure to act according to dominant ideals of masculine strength and self-assertion leave him loathing himself.

The Catcher in the Rye is also disruptive of gender roles in its representation of the maternal. Caulfield's connection with mothering is twofold: he both seeks out maternal women and manifests maternal impulses himself. Reading the novel in the light of D. W. Winnicott's psychoanalytic notion of 'holding' and maternal care allows the central metaphors of the novel – falling and catching – to be read in relation to mothering.[20] Winnicott was a British psychoanalyst whose post-war writings on infant development reflected the focus on the child–mother relationship central to psychoanalytic work of the period.[21] Winnicott argued that the period of infant care before the infant developed a sense of himself or herself was critical to psychic development. In this stage the child was dependent on the mother, and in 'The theory of the parent-infant relationship' Winnicott names this as the 'holding' stage. For Winnicott, '[h]olding includes especially the physical holding of the infant which is a form of loving' ([1960] 1979: 49). *The Catcher in the Rye* presents a series of images and events connected to falling and catching: Allie's death and his baseball catcher's mitt; the little boy risking the traffic as he walks along singing Burns's song; the suicidal fall of

James Castle; Caulfield's own sense of falling and disappearing. Winnicott's emphasis on holding in relation to maternal care is useful in that it reveals that Caulfield's desire to 'catch' (hold) others and be saved from falling himself can be understood in terms of his desire to mother and be mothered.

Indeed, from its opening dedication to Salinger's own mother, the novel continually returns to the archetype of the mother in its representation of female characters. This is perhaps not surprising given an obsession with the 'mother' in other contemporary discourses, much of it markedly controlling and misogynistic. Perhaps none was more remarkable than Philip Wylie's *Generation of Vipers* (1942), which became notorious for its introduction of the concept of 'momism'. Wylie's notion of momism suggested that American women had persuaded men of the extraordinary value of mothers, turning this validation into a form of ideology. He asserts that:

> [. . .] megaloid mom worship has got completely out of hand. Our land, subjectively mapped, would have more silver cords and apron strings crisscrossing it than railroads and telephone wires. Mom is everywhere and everything and damned near everybody [. . .] (Wylie 1942: 185)

As a consequence, for Wylie, America was a 'matriarchy in fact if not in declaration' (50). In *Their Mothers' Sons*, Edward A. Strecker argues that when young men 'failed' the test of maturity when faced with combat, 'In the vast majority of case histories, a "mom" is at fault' (1946: 23–4). Wylie's and Strecker's views foreground an element of hostility towards women in 1950s America.

Such hostility to women is also evident in popular attitudes to female sexuality derived from psychoanalytic theory. For example, in Ferdinand Lundberg and Marynia Farnham's *Modern Woman: The Lost Sex* (1947), it is claimed that

> for the sexual act to be fully satisfactory to a woman she must, in the depths of her mind, desire, deeply and utterly, to be a mother. If she does not so desire, if she regards the sex act as ending with orgasm, it will be sensually unsatisfactory in various ways, and will often fail to end in orgasm. (1947: 265)[22]

Such claims demonstrate the ways in which Freudian psychoanalytic theory, with its emphasis on vaginal intercourse, was co-opted into conservative discourses about women's natural role as mothers.

Active female sexuality was therefore expected to be confined to the heterosexual marital bed, and Alfred C. Kinsey's *Sexual Behavior in the Human Female* (1953), with its account of women's sexual behaviour that went far beyond what was considered appropriate, caused outrage.

This conventional connection between female sexuality and mothering colour Caulfield's attitudes to women. When he meets Mrs Morrow on the train his behaviour reflects his attempt to be a sophisticated adult. He assesses her as a woman who was 'very good-looking' with 'quite a lot of sex appeal' (48 and 49) and, initially, he tries to relate to her as an adult, rather flirtatiously offering her a cigarette and trying to buy her a drink. Having failed to establish an erotic connection with her, Caulfield slips into a more comfortable exchange, regarding Mrs Morrow as maternal rather than sexual. He is prepared to tell substantial lies to hold her attention, not least his invented illness, which demands from Mrs Morrow exactly the sympathy that will be lacking when his own mother discovers the truth. Thus, Caulfield's projection onto Mrs Morrow of an idealised mother–son relationship articulates his craving to be mothered.

Caulfield's desire to be mothered is complicated by his identification with his mother. He only describes her briefly, usually referring to her anxious disposition and on one occasion describing her as 'very hysterical' (45–6). Although 'hysteria' is a condition traditionally associated with women, Caulfield also manifests 'hysterical' symptoms in relation to Allie's death: breaking all the windows in the garage (34). Such similarities align Caulfield with the maternal. Caulfield's family name also connects him to the maternal. Critics have pointed out that while Caulfield begins his story by disassociating himself from 'biographical' fiction such as *David Copperfield* (1849–50), his name and other aspects of *The Catcher in the Rye* in fact connect him to Charles Dickens's novel – firstly, in the 'field' that Caul*field* and Copper*field* share, but also in the 'caul', which is a membrane from the womb which may cover a baby's head at birth (see Fleissner 2001). David Copperfield tells us that he was born with a caul, which is considered to be a sign of good luck (Dickens 1850: 7). I suggest, however, that Caulfield's 'caul' signifies his connection to the maternal.

Caulfield's need to be mothered, together with his failure to master the codes of masculinity, and his association with the feminine, emphasises his vulnerability as an adolescent. This is the corollary to the creative making of a self in the processes of adolescence – being 'in between' may result in an instability of identity – a state where a sense of self may evaporate, where the pressures to adopt a normative gender identity within dominant cultural expectations crack the subject.

Caulfield's bodily vulnerability is shown in a number of ways in the text but perhaps the most dramatic is the trope of 'falling', which might be seen as a psychological symptom but which he experiences as an overwhelming physiological sensation. These attacks occur in the liminal space between the road and the pavement. His first recounted experience is associated with the cold and his visit to Spencer at Pencey College:

> Anyway, as soon as I got my breath back I ran across Route 204. It was icy as hell and I damn near fell down. [. . .] After I got across the road, I felt like I was sort of disappearing. It was that kind of crazy afternoon, terrifically cold, and no sun out or anything, and you felt like you were disappearing every time you crossed a road. (4)

This experience becomes a terrifying symptom of his collapse at the end of the novel. He is walking up Fifth Avenue:

> Then all of a sudden, something very spooky started happening. Every time I came to the end of a block and stepped off the goddam curb, I had this feeling that I'd never get to the other side of the street. I thought I'd just go down, down, down, and nobody'd ever see me again. Boy, did it scare me. (178)

This experience is connected with the prediction of his former teacher, Antolini, that he is heading for a 'terrible fall'. Antolini tries to explain to Caulfield that there might be other ways of growing into manhood than what seems obviously available. He describes the 'horrible' kind of fall experienced by 'men who, at some time or other in their lives, were looking for something their own environment couldn't supply them with. [. . .] So they gave up looking' (169). Antolini's anticipation of Caulfield's experience suggests that his crisis is indeed a problem of masculinity.

Yet Caulfield also observes a young boy confidently occupying that border zone between the road and the pavement. The boy is seen as potentially in danger – 'cars zoomed by, brakes screeched all over the place' (104). Yet 'The kid was swell. [. . .] He was walking in the street, instead of on the sidewalk, but right next to the curb' (104). In a 'pretty little voice' he is singing: 'If a body catch a body coming through the rye'.

It is this that Caulfield recalls when he is trying to answer his sister Phoebe's question about what he would 'like to *be*' (155). He pictures thousands of small children in a field and he would be 'the catcher in the rye' stopping these children from going over a cliff (156). This response, and his feelings of contentment as he sits watching Phoebe sleep (144), reveal Caulfield's own maternal drive. In his adaptation of Burns's song, changing the word 'meet' to 'catch', Salinger replaces the sexual overtones of the original with an image of maternal care and protection. In imagining himself catching the children and preventing them from falling, Caulfield is identified with a maternal role that closely parallels Winnicott's notion of holding: an identification that is echoed in his first name. In actively connecting Caulfield with maternal care, the novel subversively disconnects the pervasive equation of the female with the maternal in a manner that destabilises the novel's otherwise predictable understanding of women as the only permissible source of comfort and compassion.

In conclusion, there is a persistent association of Caulfield with the feminine and the maternal that runs counter to his sometimes conventional responses to the female characters. The novel's subtle alignment of Caulfield with the feminine is a significant element in its critical relationship to the tradition of masculine coming-of-age narratives because it questions the protagonist's desire to mature into the conventional male role. Caulfield's 'digressions' challenge the phallically oriented model of male sexuality that dominated post-war America. His identification with the feminine and maternal thus offers a critique of contemporary discourses about gender and sexuality. Moreover, Caulfield's failed attempt at adult male embodiment in the spaces of Manhattan, together with his refusal to conform to the conventions of male identity, are a measure of the novel's opening up to critical scrutiny the cultural expectations of men and the ways in which behavioural codes were rehearsed in the mass media, such as the movies.

Edna Ferber, *Giant*

In 1952 Edna Ferber was a widely read and well respected writer who had won the Pulitzer Prize in 1925 for *So Big*, while her 1926 novel *Show Boat* had been turned into a successful musical. She had developed a close working relationship with Hollywood, and between 1918 and 1960 no fewer than twenty-five films were made from her work, including *Giant* (1956), which starred Elizabeth Taylor, Rock Hudson and James Dean in his final movie.[23]

Ferber's interest was in historical and social themes and these are evident in *Giant*, which is set in Texas and concerned with the interconnections between gender, race and modernity in American identity. The frame for this view of Texas is a family history from the 1920s to the late 1940s. The plot is organised around the marriage of Leslie Lynnton, the daughter of an eminent Virginian doctor, to Jordan Benedict, a Texan with a cattle ranch of millions of acres. Leslie has been well educated and raised by her father to take an independent, liberal view of the world, and it is this perspective that she brings to bear on Texan masculinity, wealth and racism when she moves to the ranch.

While their wealth and the physical location of the Benedicts' marriage is far from the middle-class suburban norm described earlier in the chapter, the novel broadly conforms to post-war attitudes to femininity, marriage and the home. However, in its exploration of the relationship between masculinity and race in the vast physical environment of Texas, the novel opens up significant new themes relevant to the post-war period in America.[24] The white cattlemen of Texas dominate the spaces of Texas on horseback, in their automobiles and, after the Second World War, in the air. Unlike the characterisation of Dean Moriarty, here the cowboy is open to critique rather than standing as a mythological persona. American national identity remained inseparable from the white male citizen, and the novel shows how a hegemonic white masculinity creates and sustains a dominant position through the marginalisation of women and other racial groups.

The novel opens in the late 1940s before turning back to the 1920s and the marriage of Jordan Benedict and Leslie Lynnton. The first few chapters focus on preparations for an event celebrating the opening of a new airport built by Jett Rink, who is a rich oilman. Wealthy Texan society – together with celebrities, foreign dignitaries and politicians – has been invited to the celebration, which will take place in Rink's hotel by the airport. Leslie and Jordan Benedict with their daughter, Luz, their son, Jordy, and his wife, Juana, are staying at the hotel. Mexicans are only allowed into the hotel as workers and, according to hotel policy, Jordy's wife Juana is therefore excluded from the hotel's beauty parlour. Jordy confronts Rink, who responds by assaulting him. Benedict is ready to attack Rink, but Leslie restrains her husband and says, 'You see. It's caught up with you, it's caught up with us' (51). 'It' may mean racism in the context of the Benedicts' ranch, or be a reference to the complex legacies of wider Texan history, which Leslie sees as involving violence, exploitation and racism. In the confrontation between Rink and Jordy these legacies are expressed through the tropes of masculinity. Jordy intervenes because his honour has been impugned in the insult to his wife, and violence is his means of resolution. It is these issues that the novel then proceeds to explore through Leslie's experience of Texas. In discussing the novel, I begin by focusing on gender, examining how far Ferber deconstructs conventional assumptions about the differences between white men and women held at the time. I then consider how Ferber relates the issue of Texan masculinity to that of race.

Ferber's novel has an omniscient narrator, but is focalised through Leslie Lynnton/Benedict, and it is through her fresh, Eastern perspective that the reader is to understand Texas, its wealth, its ranches, its cowboys and its Mexicans.[25] Cattle ranching is shown to be essentially a male preserve. Benedict tells Leslie that in Texas 'the cattle come first, then the men, then the horses, then the women' (43), and Leslie notes that there are no arrangements 'for the comfort of women in this man's world of Texas' (113–14). The wealth of these white Texan ranchers is based on a power that rests on the threat of violence, shown by the well-stocked gun case at the entrance to the Reata ranch. Texan power is exercised by white men; Benedict himself claims to Leslie: 'I run everything and everyone that has the Reata brand on it.' In response, Leslie asks whether that includes her, and recollects Lord Acton's remark about the corruption wrought by the exercise of absolute power (284). The Texan men are constantly represented as hypermasculine: they had somehow taken on 'physical dimensions in proportion to the vast empire they had conquered [. . .], as male as bulls, massive of shoulder [. . .]' (45). Jordan Benedict is the 'mighty male' (68), a 'figure of steel and iron and muscle' (177). Masculinity is asserted in relation to women through this male animal presence and through the exclusion of the women at social gatherings. Early on, at a barbecue, Leslie notices how the men separate themselves from the women and that when they do speak to them, they change their tone, 'as adults change when they speak to little children, coming down to their mental level' (153). Similarly, later in the novel, Leslie is cold-shouldered by Benedict and their male friends when she tries to join their conversation because it is, as Benedict says, about 'ranch stuff', 'business', and she is told by the lawyer Lew Morey, 'Now now you don't want to fret your head about such talk' (277). Another male friend, Pinky Snyth, explains that they are fixing things 'so that you girls can have all those doo-dads you're always buying', and the misogyny is openly expressed by Benedict in his view that Leslie's fine mind 'is pretty damn repulsive. In a woman, that is.' Leslie responds that they 'ought to be wearing leopard skins and carrying clubs and living in caves' (241).

Texan masculinity relies then on a denigration and domination of women, but the novel also suggests that this masculinity may not be as monolithic as it pretends. Leslie finds an ally in Uncle Bawley, the family's elder statesman. His characterisation hints at a breach in the universal heterosexuality of Texan culture. His nickname – Bawley – has been given to him because he has an allergy to cattle that causes his eyes to stream continuously and he had to 'fist-fight [his] way through school and college' to avoid being called a 'sissy' (220). Moreover, he is something of a dandy, with a 'gentle voice [. . .], fine linen [. . .], glove-fitting boots' (219), and it turns out that his ambition was to be a pianist rather than a rancher. Uncle Bawley has had no relationship with women and no woman has ever set foot in his house – a retreat where he 'nursed his loneliness and unfulfillment' (275). Uncle Bawley does not therefore conform to conventional expectations of gender identity. Nor indeed does Leslie and Jordan Benedict's son, Jordy, who eschews his expected path as Benedict's successor on the ranch and instead pursues a career as a doctor. Moreover, he is closely attached to the local Mexican doctor and marries a Mexican woman, Juana. There are also female members of the family who threaten the boundaries. Benedict's older sister, Luz, ran the household before his marriage, and 'she can also do anything a cowboy can' (88). Unlike the other Texan women, who 'dress like mad' because they have nothing else to do, Luz doesn't worry about 'chiffon and paillettes and fancy riding pants' (146), and she is described as preferring to 'work cattle than make love' (147). Leslie and Benedict's daughter is also Luz and, like her namesake, takes to horses 'as other little girls demand dolls and lollipops'. Rather than dress in pink like other girls as she grows up, she is found down in the corral in 'pants and shirt' or 'sprawled, grease-grimed, over a balky Ford' (339).

However, none of these disruptive characters is ultimately able to break through the bounds of conventional gender roles. Leslie herself is unconventional in being opinionated and challenging, but in many respects she conforms to normative expectations of women in her marriage and mothering, and wants to run the Benedict household: 'a wife wants to manage her own household and plan things and decide things and be alone with her husband' (99). In this her attitude reflects Elaine Tyler May's argument that women in the postwar period 'embraced the homemaker role as significant, important and fulfilling' (1999: 45).

In relation to women and any form of deviant male identity, Texan masculinity is dominant, but the novel also offers a serious critique of the way white masculinity asserts its superiority in relation to a racial other, defined as Mexican. The first layer of the critique lies in Leslie's reading and recounting of the history of Texas, which challenges the ideology of white Texan culture. When she first meets Benedict in Virginia, she spends the night reading about Texas and the next morning confronts him with the accusation: 'We really stole Texas [. . . a]way from Mexico' (74). By 'we' she means the United States, but as the novel unfolds, her understanding shifts to see that the white Texans effectively stole ownership of the land from the Mexicans through the Spanish Land Grants. She sees its violent past written into Texas, from the Spanish conquistadores to the white northern men who conquered the land and its people, and who now see themselves as the 'white Americans', the 'big men' (200–1). At the Alamo, she notes the racial element in the paintings of its defence, showing 'brave white Americans rising superior over the dark-skinned Mexicans' (262). In a further series of events, Leslie is brought face to face with discrimination in Texas – the poor pay and poverty of the Latino population, the exploitation of migrant workers, the lack of medical care and education, the undermining of political rights, and crude segregation. A visiting exiled European king remarks on the Reata ranch's 'serfs' and although he is corrected and told that they are all 'free Americans', the novel endorses his perspective. The masculine hierarchy on the ranch is shown in the way young vaquero[26] boys have slept on the floor outside the senior Benedict males' bedrooms – a practice that Leslie calls 'feudal' (179).

In fact the origins of the white Texan male culture of the cowboy lie in Spanish and Mexican culture. When Benedict and Leslie arrive together at Reata for the first time they are met by fifty men on horseback. They are wearing 'the uniform that the Mexican charro had worn three hundred years before and that every American cowboy [. . .] had copied' (102). It is not just a matter of appearance, as the management of the cattle depends on the outstanding horse-riding skills that have also been learned from the Mexicans. Indeed, white Texan culture is shown in the novel to be heterogeneous and bilingual, contradictory in the pride in its history – in the tradition of the fiesta, for example – while hostile to the racial other. An ambassador from South America, who is himself temporarily excluded from Rink's hotel party because he looks like a 'cholo',[27] comments that 'It is curious that the citizens of Texas have adopted so many of the ways and customs of the people they despise' (44, 46). The marginalisation of the Spanish-speaking,

Latino part of the population is of course a matter of economic and political control. Justification for the exploitative and paternalistic relationship of the ranch with its Latino workers lies in the view that they are lazy and have to be made to work, and that their culture is supposedly of no value. As Benedict says, 'They're full of superstitions and legends. They believe in the evil eye and witchcraft and every damn thing' (187).

The white male character who displays most overt hostility to the Mexicans is Jett Rink. Rink starts as a general ranch worker with particular skills in fixing machinery. He is economically deprived, like the Mexicans on the ranch, and behaves aggressively to the Benedicts. He is one source for Leslie's understanding of the realities of the white acquisition of land in Texas (194) and is also responsible for introducing Leslie to the realities of Mexican life. However, he is dismissive of the Mexicans, saying that they 'sure ain't white' and excluding them from being Americans (194). He is very ambitious and becomes extremely wealthy after oil is found on the small parcel of land that was originally given to him by the Benedicts. Once he has acquired his wealth Rink behaves more outrageously, often drunk and aggressive, and displaying his wealth ostentatiously, becoming a 'living legend' (352). He is also seen by the younger Luz as 'a kind of modern version of the old buccaneer type' (360). The narrative projects Rink as a vulgar materialist symptomatic of the worst traits of oil-rich Texas. Rink in fact signifies in a complex way in relation to class, gender and race in the novel. In terms of gender and race, as a white man he occupies a dominant identity, but early on, as an impoverished white man, he hovers on a borderline where he risks compromising what status he has as a white.[28] Rink is therefore determined to uphold the social and racial boundaries that relegate the Mexicans, given his lack of economic status. Once he is rich he is able to behave however he wants without damaging his white male identity, rather in fact enhancing his masculinity in becoming a 'buccaneer'. As far as race is concerned, he uses his new position to police the boundaries strictly, for example in his hotel, which is where Juana is excluded from the beauty parlour and the ambassador is identified as a 'cholo'.

In Rink, therefore, white Texan masculinity asserts itself in a cruder and more brazen form than it does with Benedict, the wealthy rancher. Yet both Benedict and Rink are central to the novel's attempt to deconstruct Texan masculinity and racism. The events at Rink's hotel, described above, will be anticipated at the end of the novel when Leslie, with her daughter Luz, her daughter-in-law Juana and her grandson, Polo, call in at a roadside diner. Leslie, who has dark hair, sits down with Juana and Polo, only to be told by the male owner to leave: 'We don't serve Mexicans here' (394). Luz, with her blond hair and blue eyes, arrives after parking the car, and a brief confrontation follows, but the Benedict family is forced to leave.[29] This episode has been immediately preceded by Leslie reflecting on changes to the town of Benedict, marked particularly by the post-war modernity of plate-glass windows reflecting 'the dazzling aluminum and white enamel objects within' – refrigerators, washing machines and vacuum cleaners (389). The younger generation of the Benedict family embodies this modernity in their refusal of the family traditions and in their multi-racialism. The diner owner's comment on Leslie – 'the old one was [Mexican], black hair and sallow, you can't fool me' – in its misidentification makes a fool of him and deconstructs racism (395). Yet Benedict himself holds similar views, referring to his grandson as a 'cholo' and describing his doctor son as 'no real Benedict', working down in 'Spigtown with the greasers in Viencito' (401). But, as with Rink struggling violently to maintain the colour bar in his hotel, Benedict too is shown to be a man out of time: 'Things are getting away from me. Kind of slipping from under me, like a loose saddle. I swear to God I sometime feel like a failure' (401). In this the novel traces the tensions between traditional white masculinity and American modernity after the Second World War. Leslie, in contrast, is full of hope for a future in which Jordy and Luz can be seen as 'a real success'.

The novels considered in this chapter have brought light to bear on some contradictions in the conventions of masculinity in post-war America. On the one hand, men are expected to fit into American social structures and perform as husbands and fathers in the spaces of the workspace and the suburb, while on the other they must express a virile individualism in resistance to the supposed homogenisation and feminisation of that culture. Wilson's novel problematises this dilemma and attempts to stabilise Rath's masculine identity through heterosexuality, paternity and authenticity. *On the Road* responds with a strong macho assertion of supposedly masculine traits. However, if one views Kerouac himself as negotiating the shifts in identity accompanying the assimilation of 'white' ethnic minority groups into middle-class American culture, the macho response of *On the Road* might be indicative of anxieties experienced by such men. *The Catcher in the Rye* and *Giant* offer a more provocative challenge to contemporary notions of masculinity. I have argued that Holden Caulfield rejects the possible models of masculinity available but comes to an impasse reflected in the circularity of the story. *Giant* offers a critique of what might be regarded as a traditional manifestation of masculinity – broadly identified as inner-directed by Riesman – showing how it depends on the assertion of racial and gender difference that is inappropriate in modern post-war America. What is apparent is yearning for an uncomplicated form of male identity, but evidence of instability in expectations of men in a period of cultural change.

Notes

1. Mills here reflects the Frankfurt School view that mass culture was the product of capitalism and intended to manipulate consumers.
2. See the discussion of momism below, and in Chapter 2.
3. The role of men in domestic spaces is discussed by John Tosh in *In a Man's Place*. He emphasises the importance of the domestic sphere to masculinity: 'To establish a home, to protect it, to provide for it, to control it, and to train its young aspirants to manhood, have usually been essential to a man's good standing with his peers' (1999: 4).
4. In *Homeward Bound*, May argues that generally middle-class suburban women were more dissatisfied with home and marriage than men, whose principal sources of anxiety and concern were to do with the workplace (see May 1999: ch. 8).
5. The term 'queer' as a reference to homosexuality was in common usage at least from the 1920s, and that meaning recurs in a number of the novels discussed.
6. Gorer was an English social anthropologist who had trained with Mead, so his views may have been influenced by hers.
7. The actual publication date of *On the Road* is later than the chronological focus of this book. However, Kerouac completed a full draft of the novel in April 1951; this was the notorious paper roll manuscript, which had taken him just a few weeks to write. It is also the case that the novel is primarily based on Kerouac's experiences with Neal Cassady in 1947–50, so despite the fact that Kerouac revised the original manuscript as it went through its tortuous route to publication, it is legitimate to regard the novel as a representing the late Forties and early Fifties. (See Ann Charter's 1991 'Introduction' to the 2000 Penguin edition of *On the Road* and Adam Gussow's article 'Bohemia revisited' for various perspectives on Kerouac's development of the novel.)
8. Reactions to *On the Road* on its publication primarily saw it as a protest against contemporary American culture. *Life* described the Beats as 'against virtually every aspect of American society' (quoted in Erhenreich 53). Ann Charters quotes the *Village Voice* review, which called it 'a rallying cry for the elusive spirit of rebellion of these times' (viii).

9. Charters is here referencing Ginsberg's poem 'A supermarket in California', which describes Walt Whitman as 'dear father, graybeard, lonely old courage-teacher' (Ginsberg 1956: 30).
10. There is no ambiguity in the original scroll, in which Dean gives 'him a monstrous huge banging', but is still unable to extract any cash from the man (Kerouac 2007: 307).
11. Carlo is a representation of Allen Ginsberg, who had an intermittent sexual relationship with Neal Cassady.
12. Vidal describes a sexual encounter with Kerouac at the Chelsea Hotel, claiming to have fucked him (1995: 218 and 229–34). He quotes Allen Ginsberg as saying that he used to 'blow' Kerouac every now and then, but also says that while Kerouac liked company in bed, 'he wasn't all that keen on the sex part – with men' (218).
13. See the Introduction and Chapter 3 below. Ginsberg's profession of his own homosexuality on the publication of *Howl* in 1956 caused great controversy.
14. There is some irony here, as Kerouac notes that no one was paying any attention to his prayer (88).
15. In considering Leslie Fiedler's attack on the Beats in 1965, Savran argues that the 'Beat is masculinized by virtue of his resuscitation of the entrepreneurial and maverick self, yet simultaneously feminized both by his sexual dissidence and by the practice of writing itself, that is, by his association with the cultural and artistic sphere' (1998: 65–7).
16. There is an interesting comparison here with Arthur Miller's *Death of a Salesman*, where for Willy Loman the repayments on unreliable refrigerators and cars symbolise his ambiguous, frustrating and destructive relationship with 'success' in the same period: 'Whoever heard of a Hastings refrigerator? Once in my life I would like to own something outright before it's broken!' (Miller 1940: Act 2, 56–7).
17. Julia Kristeva analyses changing feminist approaches to time in 'Women's time' ([1979] 1986).
18. A fuller version of this analysis may be found in my essay '"Digressing from the point": Holden Caulfield's women' (C. Baldwin 2007).
19. See Hamilton 1988: 85–95.
20. I am indebted to Dr Edith Frampton for introducing me to Winnicott's notion of 'holding'.
21. For a discussion of developments in psychoanalytic theory in relation to infant development, see Zaretsky (2004): ch. 10.
22. Contemporary attitudes to sexual behaviour are discussed more fully in Chapter 3.
23. See J. E. Smyth, *Edna Ferber's Hollywood* (2010), for a discussion of Ferber's relationship with Hollywood and a useful summary of her career as a writer and the themes of interest to her.
24. Here the focus is on the cultural and economic legacy of Spanish colonialism, and Mexican occupation of the south-west of North America,

whereas Chapters 4 and 5 respectively consider Jewish American and African American writers. A significant difference in this chapter is that the account is written by a white woman, albeit one from a Jewish background, rather than a Latino American author.
25. The novel uses the term 'Mexican' throughout and I have mostly followed that usage for simplicity in discussing the novel. Where I am referring to a more modern perspective I have used the term Latino, although, because of the complexities of history, there is as yet no universally agreed term of identification. 'Mexican' might imply a migrant from 'Mexico', but of course until the annexation of Texas into the United States in 1845 and the Mexican Cession of 1848, the population of the south-west of the modern United States were of Mexican nationality. Such Mexicans were of mestizo heritage, that is, of mixed Indian/Spanish/African origins. See Laura E. Gómez (2007) for a discussion of the history and her argument that Mexicans constitute a racial group in the United States.
26. Mexican cowboy.
27. An insulting term for a Mexican.
28. His assertion that the Mexicans are not 'white' is legally incorrect. As Gómez puts it in *Manifest Destinies*, Mexican Americans were legally constructed racially as white, but socially constructed as non-white and racially inferior (2007: 4).
29. The film of *Giant* culminates with this scene and has Jordan Benedict – Rock Hudson – present. He has a brutal fight with the diner owner and, although losing, thus redeems white Texan masculinity from the accusation of racism. The film was popular in Texas, in marked contrast with Ferber's novel (see Smyth 2010: 199 and 213–15).

Chapter 2

'Everything in him had come undone':[1] Violent Aggression, Courage and Masculine Identity

This chapter examines the relationship between aggressive and violent behaviour and male identity. Male violence is a significant element in many of the novels discussed in this book.[2] For example, as we have seen in Chapter 1, *Giant* represents both interpersonal aggression in the clash between Jett Rink and Jordan Benedict, and the history of violence and oppression in Texas. Novels discussed later in the book make connections between sexuality and violence, while others represent violence as a reaction to cultural oppression. In considering such novels and other contemporary discourses that analysed the relationships between masculinity, aggression and courage, what becomes apparent is contestation at the heart of these issues. Differences emerge over whether or not men are naturally aggressive and violent. Writers who expect men to be aggressive maintain that a lack of aggression is explained by constraining cultural influences.

Not surprisingly, much of the focus on male violence and aggression in the period following 1945 was on the performance of American men in the Second World War. Accordingly, the primary focus in this chapter is on two major war novels – Norman Mailer's *The Naked and the Dead* (1948) and James Jones's *From Here to Eternity* (1951) – which are discussed in relation to post-war debates in America about the performance of American servicemen and the implications for American national identity. However, the chapter begins with a discussion of Jim Thompson's *The Killer Inside Me* (1952), whose main character is a murderous psychopath. In an extreme form, Thompson's novel manifests the anxieties about the feminisation of American culture and the related hostility to women that are a recurrent characteristic of the period. The significance of psychiatric explanations of behaviour in the novel connects it with the contemporary discourses about aggression, violent behaviour and courage that are permeated with psychological theory. Furthermore, in its representation of male sexuality, the novel anticipates Chapter 3.

Jim Thompson, *The Killer Inside Me*

Thompson's *The Killer Inside Me* (1952) introduces significant connections between sexuality, masculinity and violence. In particular, Lou Ford, the narrator and main character, is a psychopath with a 'sickness' that he attempts to repress (J. Thompson [1952] 2006: 6). This characterisation suggests that his murderous impulses are the mark of a dysfunctional masculinity.[3]

Ford is a deputy sheriff in Central City, in the Texas oil belt, and has adopted a public persona that is dumb, laid-back and given to spouting clichés and banalities, but he claims to the reader that he is intelligent and well read, with a father who was a doctor. In his self-description he both lays claim to a masculinity linked to the Texan cowboy, and reveals a narcissism:

> I was still wearing my Stetson, shoved a little to the back of my head. I had on a kind of pinkish shirt and black bow tie, and the pants of my blue serge suit were hitched up so as to catch up on the tops of my Justin boots. Lean and wiry; a mouth that looked all set to drawl. A typical Western-country peace officer, that was me. (23)

Ford's story describes his 'sickness', which is what he claims has warped his character and sexuality. In this representation of mental illness, Ford's self-diagnosis reflects the attention to psychiatric theory in the period. Ford's insight into his condition draws on his father's 'endless files of psychiatric literature' (22). He quotes from Emil Kraepelin, one of the pioneers of investigation into schizophrenia (see Payne 2002), identifying himself as manifesting the symptoms of dementia praecox. Kraepelin regards the onset of the illness as usually beginning around puberty, and that it is 'often precipitated by a severe shock' (197). The shock for Ford is his sexual initiation at around fifteen by Helene, his father's housekeeper (his mother had died when he was an infant). He is traumatised primarily by the reaction of his father, who, on discovering what has happened, banishes Helene and thrashes Ford (94–5). He claims that he then carried a 'burden of fear and shame [. . .] that I could never get shed of' (195). As a result he is socially aggressive, 'striking at people' through clichés and platitudes (3). However, for Ford the 'real way' to express his aggression is violence against women: because he cannot kill Helene, he wants to 'strike back at any of them, any female [. . .], and it would be the same as striking her' (195).

Thompson's novel is written within the broad conventions of noir crime fiction, for example in its muscular, demotic prose and male world view. Yet it also has complex formal elements – for example, a first-person narrator who records his own last words as he is shot. Ford is also clearly an unreliable and self-serving narrator, and the effect of this is to deconstruct the conventional element of crime fiction in which the male lead – often a private detective – is the personification of a quest for truth, which succeeds in setting the world back in balance, at least for the time being. In contrast, in Thompson's novel the perpetrator of violence and mayhem is a law officer. In its disenchanted representation of an everyday life infused with banality and undercurrents of seaminess and corruption, the novel has been seen as a critique of post-war America. Yet I want to argue that this critique also rests on assumptions about gender, sexuality and masculinity, and that through its representation of women, the novel reinscribes structures of gender and power.

Ford's narrative recounts the story of how he attempted the double murder of a prostitute, Joyce Lakeland, with whom he has been having a sadomasochistic affair, and Elmer, the son of Chester Conway, the local 'big man' (33) and owner of a large construction company. His motive for killing Elmer Conway is in revenge for the murder of his adopted brother Mike Dean, who was a building inspector and a thorn in Chester Conway's side on a particular project. Ford then commits two further murders designed to protect himself. The first of these is Johnnie, a teenage tearaway whom Ford throttles in a police cell, making it look like suicide. This apparent suicide seems to quell local suspicion of Ford, but he decides he needs to move away. His fiancée, Amy Stanton, has doubts about him that may develop and make him a suspect, so he murders her instead of eloping with her. At the end of the novel, it is confirmed that Joyce Lakeland has survived his assault and is brought to confront him at his home. The confrontation is a violent one, as planned by Ford. As his house catches fire, he stabs Lakeland and dies in a flurry of police shooting.

The two women who are attacked, Joyce Lakeland and Amy Stanton, are subject to conventional attitudes to female sexuality. Joyce Lakeland is a prostitute who has moved into the area and initially Lou Ford is asked by the sheriff to check her out and decide whether she should be moved on or not. Ford's initial reaction is 'The good Lord had known just where to put that flesh where it would *really* do some good' (6). Amy Stanton on her first appearance is described as 'a mighty pretty girl' and with 'probably the second prettiest rear end in West Texas' (24). Both women are therefore sexualised and objectified through bodily description. Lakeland embodies a dangerous and illicit sexuality, while at the respectable end of female identity, Stanton is a potential wife and mother. Amy expects to marry Ford, but he has been showing reluctance since Lakeland has turned up and he won't marry someone who is a 'bossy little gal with a tongue like barbed wire and a mind about as narrow' (33). Amy therefore stands for the conventional trajectory in post-war American sexual relations, towards marriage and family, with Ford seeing his independence supposedly shackled to a constrictive feminine morality. Conventional views about the sexually active woman are clearly indicated. When after the deaths of Joyce Lakeland and Elmer Conway, Ford is questioned about who he was with, Amy's name cannot be brought up as she is a 'nice' girl (57). Lakeland on the other hand is a prostitute, and the assault on her arouses no social sympathy.

In the novel male sexuality is accompanied by sadistic violence. Lou Ford claims a virile sexuality in sustaining relationships simultaneously with Joyce Lakeland and Amy Stanton. He claims that both Lakeland and Stanton enjoy the sadistic element of their sexual relationship. At one point he claims, 'Let Lou Titillate Your Tail' (112). He falters at one point with Amy, but he injects himself with Vitamin B and a male hormone so that she wouldn't be 'disappointed again. [. . .] Whether my trouble had been psychosomatic or real, the result of too much tension or too much Joyce, I wouldn't have it tonight. Little Amy would be tamed down for a week' (82). Lou Ford wishes to establish his virility, while exerting sexual control of these women through violence.

However, Ford's violent impulses are not restricted to sadistic sex, and Joyce Lakeland and Amy Stanton are reduced to shattered flesh and bone in the graphic descriptions of the violence inflicted on them. This is Ford's description of the murder of his fiancée.

> I killed Amy Stanton on Saturday night on the fifth of April, 1952, at a few minutes before nine o'clock. [. . .]
> She smiled and came towards me with her arms held out. 'I won't darling. I won't ever say anything like that again. But I want to tell you how much –'

> 'Sure,' I said. 'You want to pour your heart out to me.'
> And I hit her in the guts as hard as I could.
> My fist went back against her spine, and the flesh closed around it to the wrist. I jerked back on it, I had to jerk, and she flopped forward from the waist, like she was hinged. (152, 164–5)

Here Ford's brutal description incorporates sexualised imagery of penetration, and the projection of emotion onto the feminine.

Anne Campbell's survey of gender and aggression, *Men, Women, and Aggression* (1993), which deconstructs generalisations about aggression, is a useful frame within which to consider Thompson's novel and the representation of violence and aggression in mid-century America. Although her analysis is culturally bound to American attitudes at the time of her research, it does confirm the continuing currency of expectations both of and by men. Culturally, aggression is seen as intimately connected with masculinity: 'For some men the reward for behaving aggressively is a boost to their shaky sense of self-worth, since it is a public demonstration of their manliness, about which they have profound doubts' (A. Campbell 1993: 11). Furthermore, she argues that male aggression imposes control, thereby creating winners and losers and affirming the masculine hierarchy (55–6). Campbell's methodology favours social representation – how individuals represent their behaviour in a social context. While such an approach helps an understanding of how men and women see their behaviour, it tends to be less revealing of broader cultural determinants. Male aggression imposes control, but such aggression derives from a cultural context in which male control is an expectation and violence a legitimate means of achieving it. In Campbell's terms, then, aggression is less a natural concomitant of masculinity and more a culturally produced instrument of power and control.

Ford's violent aggression – including the conflagration through which he engineers both his own death and that of Joyce Lakeland – may therefore be seen as a means of exercising control. Connell argues that there is a connection between hegemony and violence – the unequal relations of power between men and women may be enforced with violence, especially if male dominance is challenged (1995: 83). In the novel threats to Ford from men or women are met with violence as he seeks to control circumstances. However, the most extreme descriptions of violence in the novel relate to Joyce Lakeland and Amy Stanton, and mark his pathological hostility to women. In identifying a woman as the agent of his sickness, the novel resonates with topical cultural anxieties about gender and sexuality. Moreover, while Ford asserts his heterosexual virility in terms of the sexual response of Joyce Lakeland and Amy Stanton, it is also possible to see their active female sexuality as a source of anxiety. Ford's self-administration of drugs to ensure his potency can be seen as a means of controlling female sexuality.[4] So, although Ford's psychic development is represented as disrupted and this is supposed to explain his violent sexuality and psychopathology, his behaviour is reflective of contemporary hostility towards women, and can be seen as a response to the purported threat to masculinity in post-war America.

'Warrior values' and Male Identity

In turning from Ford's individual violence to the position of American servicemen in the Second World War, it is useful to consider further theoretical analysis. Such analysis helps provide a framework for a retrospective consideration of the discourses linking masculinity and violence in mid-twentieth-century America. A central element of the ideology of masculinity is the notion of the 'warrior'. In a brief survey, 'Warrior values', Barry McCarthy traces the changing manifestations of the warrior ethic in a variety of historical and cultural circumstances. He identifies a set of categories which are common across cultures, but which he describes as heuristic rather than conclusive: physical courage; endurance; strength and skill; honour. He considers there is an 'almost universal, intimate bond between warrior values and conventional notions of masculinity' (B. McCarthy 1994: 105). McCarthy argues that 'masculine role prescriptions' in contemporary Western culture 'continue to emphasise qualities which are often little more than slightly diluted versions of warrior values' (118). McCarthy further emphasises that theories of aggressive drives or instincts have proved inadequate explanations of why young men adopt the warrior role, and that the representation of the experience of war is consistently negative (106–7). Few men are able to sustain exposure to combat without psychological deterioration and breakdown, and the pleasures and satisfactions reported by twentieth-century soldiers are 'overwhelmingly those associated with comradeship, and the sensual and aesthetic experiences of survival' (106–7). Some significant points may be noted from McCarthy's analysis. First, the pervasiveness of the ethos of the warrior in relation to masculinity in industrialised Western culture in peacetime, and not just in war. Secondly, that the primary site for the expression of these values is the male body, which must not only display strength and skill, but which is also the medium through which the values of courage and honour are expressed. Conversely, the male body is vulnerable to injury and death in violent conflict.

Such issues can be further illuminated through Connell's theory of 'hegemonic' masculinity (see pages 19–20 above). The notion of hegemonic masculinity is particularly appropriate in considering how novels represent the institutional workings of the military, and the effects of the inculcation of certain 'masculine' aptitudes and attitudes on characters in the novels. Central to this is the need to deploy the soldierly body as an instrument of violence and of ensuring obedience in the face of the risk of being a casualty. So while heterosexual men might align themselves with 'hegemonic masculinity' through misogyny or homophobia, when they occupy subordinate positions in such social formations as the military, such men may find themselves oppressed. Novels set in war or in the military can therefore be expected to represent the masculinity of their characters in relation to complex and contradictory circumstances.

These approaches to masculinity and violence and aggression suggest why discourses in mid-century America were a site of contestation. What is at stake is how masculinity is to be defined and defended in ways that retain established structures of power. Mailer's and Jones's novels certainly attracted considerable critical and public attention on publication – they were fresh literary voices, and seemed to offer insights into the experience of the war and soldiering.[5] It seems that the importance of providing an authentic account of war explains why they were written in broadly a realist or naturalist style.[6] Significantly, these novels of war and soldiering were accounts of a singularly male domain, and, at a time when there was considerable concern about the roles of men and women, the behaviour of men at war had resonance as an index of masculinity in American culture. Yet the contradictions inherent to the construction of what might be called the ideology of a military masculinity may be revealed by the reality of modern warfare. One aspect of this, which will be considered below, is how these novels represent the inevitability of soldiers' bodies being injured by violence. The reality of a wounded, passive, abject masculinity is incompatible with the aggressive, violent masculinity required by the military.

In the post-war period Freudian psychoanalytic theory had become pervasive in the United States, and American interpretations of Freud emphasised gender difference and strongly demarcated sex roles.[7] Moreover, in relation to masculinity, there was a further level of concern that had arisen from the extensive involvement of psychoanalysts and psychologists with the military during the war. In his survey *The Rise and Crisis of Psychoanalysis in the United States*, Nathan Hale describes how the Second World War brought psychoanalysis into prominence (Hale 1995: 187). Psychological assessments were carried out on all recruits and between 1942 and 1945, 1,875,000 men were rejected as unsuitable. During the same period 1,100,000 servicemen were admitted for neuropsychiatric disorders and of these 6 to 7 per cent were suffering from mental illness or psychosis; the remainder were diagnosed with psychoneurosis, commonly designated as combat fatigue (Hale 1995: 187–8). One significant aspect of these figures was that they were proportionately higher than for the other Allied military services. For example, while 50 per cent of all medical discharges from the American services were for neuropsychiatric reasons, the equivalent figures for the British and Russian services were respectively 30 per cent and 17 per cent. These are significant differences, although such figures are not directly comparable, as psychiatric definitions and policies differed (Hale 1995: 203–4).[8]

Such statistics, coupled with the direct experience of psychoanalysts working with the military, led to an extensive debate that offered different analyses of men's behaviour. Some speak from within the dominant ideological discourses of masculinity, seeking explanations for what was regarded as deviant masculine behaviour – those men who did not conform to normative expectations of a male response to war and combat. Yet there were also voices challenging such assumptions and criticising the actions and attitudes of the authorities during the war. A key question was why men did or did not behave courageously. Others considered how to persuade, induce or force men to expose themselves to the risk of death or maiming.

In tracing the manifestations of these varying perspectives, what emerges is a tension between an idealised expectation of male behaviour and a recognition that in reality, men's behaviour is commonly far from the ideal. Some writers explain this disparity as arising from some corruption of men's natural instincts, by society or by their mothers, for example. In the context of the army as an institution, efforts are made to impose the correct form of behaviour. Joanna Bourke points out the change of attitude between the two world wars – from a 'slightly more understanding attitude' for those who broke down in combat, to a greater emphasis on an instinct for aggression and a corresponding view that the inability to act aggressively was itself a sign of psychiatric disorder (Bourke 1999: 248). For example, in 1941 Franz Alexander argues that 'anyone who is blind to the ubiquitous manifestation of human aggressiveness in the past and present can be rightly considered a man who does not face reality' (1941: 505). It is such attitudes that Bronislaw Malinowski appears to be challenging in an article also published in 1941, 'An Anthropological Analysis of War'. Malinowski discusses war and aggression, arguing that '[. . . a]cts of violence are culturally, not biologically determined' (Malinowski 1941: 527). Such analysis evinces differences between particular views of core 'human' characteristics and expectations of how humans might behave collectively.

Approaching the practical issue of men's commitment to fighting in *Men against Fire* (1947), S. L. A. Marshall argues for the continuing importance of infantrymen in modern warfare and discusses how to ensure the successful deployment and engagement of the foot soldier. He acknowledges that 'fear is general among men' on the battlefield, arguing that a major motivation for soldiers in overcoming their fear was to avoid doing anything 'which their comrades will recognise as cowardice. The majority are unwilling to take extraordinary risks and do not aspire to a hero's role, but they are equally unwilling that they should be considered the least worthy amongst those present' (Marshall 1947: 149).

Marshall's view is that socialisation imbues individuals with strong taboos against aggression and the taking of life.

> The fear of aggression has been expressed to him so strongly and absorbed by him so deeply and pervadingly – practically with his mother's milk – that it is part of the normal man's emotional make-up. This is his great handicap when he enters combat. It stays his trigger finger even though he is hardly conscious that it is a restraint upon him. (78)

He claims that Medical Corps psychiatrists studying combat fatigue cases 'found that fear of killing, rather than fear of being killed was the most common cause of battle failure in the individual, and that fear of failure ran a strong second'.[9]

What is notable about Marshall's analysis is a lack of clarity about who is the object of his discussion. On the one hand, he generalises – all men feel fear – on the other, it seems that it is the soldier, not the officer, who is vulnerable. So for example:

> The unit commander soon comes to realize that one of his difficulties is to get men to leave cover because of enemy bullets and the fear they instill. [. . .] When the infantryman's mind is gripped by fear, his body

is captured by inertia, which is fear's Siamese twin. [. . .] The man afraid wants to do nothing; indeed, he does not care even to think of taking action. (Marshall 1947: 71)

Marshall seems to assume that a commission immunises a soldier from fear. This reveals a recurrent theme, which is that of class and the ways in which supposedly universal characteristics of men are inflected by class expectations.

In Irwin Shaw's *The Young Lions* (1948), the respective representations of Captain Colclough and Lieutenant Green explore such issues.[10] Colclough is shown early in the story to be a bully and a racist (Shaw [1948] 2000: 285). When, much later, his company prepares itself for the Normandy invasion, he is full of bravado as he lectures his soldiers, telling them that they are 'going to kill more Krauts than any other Company in the Division and I'm going to make Major by July fourth, and if that means we're going to have more casualties than anybody else, all I can say is: See the Chaplain' (449). As the invasion gets underway, Colclough appears on the landing craft with a pearl-handled forty-five in a 'fancy leather holster', wearing it 'dashingly, low on his thigh, like a sheriff on the cover of a Western magazine' (449). Yet when it comes to disembarking, Colclough baulks, claiming that there is a mine on the beach. An impasse develops during which Noah, one of the three principal characters of the novel, notices that Colclough's holster has a 'little rawhide fringe on the bottom of it, like the holsters that come with cowboy suits little boys get at Christmas' (450). Once disembarked, Colclough proves disastrously inept, getting lost on several occasions and finally managing to get his company surrounded and under attack. At this point he appears to withdraw into a 'private dream' (456) and Lieutenant Green takes command, commenting ironically: 'The Captain has retired for the season. He will be ready for next year's invasion' (459). Colclough's humiliation is completed by one of the privates, Jamison, whose companion has been seriously wounded. He berates Colclough, saying that he was 'a big man with a speech when nobody was shooting', throws away the pearl-handled pistol and slices off the holster with his bayonet. Colclough is left lying on the floor (460–2).

Lieutenant Green, on the other hand, is a 'frail, girlish-looking man', who is made fun of through training because of 'his mincing walk and high voice'. Yet when they come into combat, despite the fact that his voice is 'no more manly than usual' and he 'giggled', he is authoritative, competent and reassures the soldiers (446, 459). In these episodes, then, the novel deconstructs certain assumptions about manliness, mocking macho pretensions associated with American cowboy imagery and exploiting the common trope of the cowardly bully. Colclough is particularly vulnerable to such mockery given the common expectation that officers should not show fear, yet at the same time the novel decouples courage from conventional markers of manliness. Ultimately, however, proper manliness still requires the manifestation of courage in the test of battle.

Psychoanalytic analysis sought a deeper understanding of individual behaviour as it was manifested in the war. The high levels of psychoneurosis discussed by Hale were given an explanation in *Psychiatry in Modern Warfare* (1945) by Edward Strecker and Kenneth Appel, on the basis of their experience as military psychiatrists.[11] They believed there was a particular issue of morale for American servicemen: 'Our soldiers are fighting on foreign soil, where there is no immediate threat to their homes and loved ones. Anger and aggression are therefore not so actively mobilized. The threat to the homeland is not easily visualized' (Strecker and Appel 1945: 55–6). Strecker and Appel also argue that 'guilt over killing' is much rarer than fear, and that the tension between the 'traumatic experience and the conflict about showing fear' is the cause of neurosis and regression.

Although Streker and Appel do not specifically discuss war neurosis in relation to masculinity, it is possible to see in their analysis certain expectations of men. Defending the 'homeland' and 'loved ones' is an element of the warrior myth. Similarly, the conflict caused by showing fear is symptomatic of the dominance of a form of masculinity that requires bravery and fortitude of men. Also intrinsic to their analysis is the view that aggression and destructiveness, together with the overcoming of a natural fear of death and disablement, are forms of behaviour that need to be inculcated, and that this is done through military regimentation and discipline (63).

Yet there were sometimes tensions between psychiatrists and the military authorities; some of the latter viewed the 'flood' of neuropsychiatric cases as a disgrace, and ordered courts martial to deal with the situation (Hale 1995: 189). Joanna Bourke emphasises the dilemma faced by psychiatrists trying to distinguish between servicemen who were a liability and those who were acting out medical symptoms to escape from combat (Bourke 1999: 240–1). However, many medical and psychiatric officers shared the view of regular army officers that psychological breakdown was a form of cowardice, and that this was associated with a lack of masculinity. Bourke cites, for example, the American psychiatrist Philip S. Wagner, who in 1946 disparaged 'socially and emotionally immature soldiers' who 'shrunk from combat with almost feminine despair and indignation'; such men were narcissistic 'poseurs' who were excessively dependent on mother figures, and Wagner recommended they should be sent back to the battlefield (Bourke 1999: 242; Wagner 1946: 356). Wagner also discusses a category of soldiers with problems of 'morale' – 'the "burned out" veteran campaigner' (1946: 356). These are often 'men who had suffered the most grievous battle experiences, who had borne a main responsibility in their unit for months, and were recognized for their courage and professional skill and often had many decorations' (Wagner 1946: 357). Wagner's view of these men is that 'their resources had been expended' (357). Certainly, Wagner's approach was in general sympathetic to military needs: '[psychiatric] *staff preferred to err on the side of not permitting the reluctant soldier to evade duty*' (359–60). Wagner largely internalises an army perspective, and psychiatric authority becomes intertwined with and reinforced by the army's power structures. In this way, an authoritarian psychiatry becomes another means for enforcing the imposition of certain standards of masculinity on soldiers.

In another article in *Psychiatry*, published a few months before Wagner's, William Needles, like Wagner a psychiatrist who had served with the US Army, specifically identifies and criticises authoritarian psychiatrists. Needles argues that for such psychiatrists, it is 'a point of special pride' that 'they return a large number of patients to duty' (Needles 1946: 171). He describes how a 'dynamic, chest-thumping psychiatrist, who had never been exposed to anything more devastating than a toy pistol, embarked on "pep-talk number three" and harangued a combat-ridden soldier about the necessity of "standing up like a man"' (173). He maintains that not all men are suited for combat: 'not everyone [can] throw over law-abiding, peace-respecting mores for those in which killing effectively is the highest good' (179).

These debates were continuing in 1953 when Eli Ginzberg, John L. Herma and Sol W. Ginzberg published *Psychiatry and Military Manpower Policy*. They invited the views of a number of psychiatrists who had treated soldiers, seeking to establish a consensus in retrospect. They argue that the consensus amongst psychiatrists is that breakdown in combat is caused less by a predisposition than by precipitating factors. They maintain that there has been a shift from the view that there can be a differentiation between the 'weak and the strong' to the 'current opinion that "every man has his breaking point"' (Ginzberg et al. 1953: 23–4). Moreover, psychiatrists who had acquaintance with men in combat learned that:

> ... many of the outstanding combat soldiers were hostile, emotionally insecure, extremely unstable personalities who might well be termed clinically 'psychopaths', whatever that may imply, who fully enjoyed the opportunity of taking out hostilities directly in a socially acceptable setting of warfare and who in the absence of such an outlet not infrequently end up in penitentiaries. (Quote from a psychiatrist's submission; Ginzberg et al. 1953: 24)

The conclusion is that: 'there are a good many instances where men have been heroes on the basis of a neurotic or even of a psychotic disorder'. This inverts the view that a lack of aggressiveness in men is a sign of psychiatric disorder (see page 79). Their investigations also suggested that 'over and above all the other factors of stress, fear of death was considered most important'. One psychiatrist emphasised the significant effect of 'the conflict between the fear of death and the social urge to remain part of the group and do one's duty' (Ginzberg et al. 1953: 28). One element of this is straightforward – an individual's manliness and self-esteem was put at risk if he did not quell his fear. What is also evident is the importance of homosocial relationships within the military – relationships that sit uneasily alongside institutionalised homophobia.

In his book *Their Mothers' Sons* (1946), Edward Strecker places his wartime experiences in a wider context, and, as his title suggests, makes connections with the broader American cultural discourse of 'momism'. Like Wagner, Strecker distinguishes those who suffer honourably from combat fatigue:

> All in all, true combat fatigue comprises a group of upstanding young men who could not be broken until great hardships, deprivations, exhaustion, and soul-searching emotional experiences were loaded upon them. They were as honorably wounded as though they had been struck down by enemy fire. (Strecker 1946: 17)

These are 'mature men', who 'can and are willing to meet life'.

> Not so with most of the 500,000 men who tried to evade service to their country – draft dodgers who resorted to any device, however shameful, even to the wearing of female clothing. Not so with the

majority of the 1,825,000 men who were rejected at induction for various neuropsychiatric causes. Not so with a large proportion of the 600,000 more that had to be discharged from the service for similar reasons. (18)

The latter are defined by Strecker as sick; their sickness is a manifestation of inner emotional conflict – 'self-preservation versus soldierly ideals', the latter of which are defined as:

instilled complex behavior patterns – realistic considerations such as the fear of being shot for cowardice in battle; practical considerations, like the desire to finish 'this dirty job and get home as soon as possible'; more idealistic drives, 'this is my duty and I am going to do it well'. Various higher levels may be attained and sometimes summits are reached, such as the determination to fight and, if need be, die for the preservation of democracy. (19)

Strecker's diagnosis is that there is frequently an unhealthy relationship between mothers and their sons in America which creates immature young men. In particular he maintains that such men are unsuited for military life, which is one of contention with characteristically 'energetic, argumentative discussions, vigorously upheld and vehemently attacked. Men are on edge, and words may be readily enough enforced and punctuated with fists'. Boys who come from the 'pollyanna home' are likely to be regarded as '"soft", or "queer" or "high-hat"' (60). It is clear from Strecker's subtitle – *The Psychiatrist Examines an American Problem* – that he regards this as of national significance. In an introduction, Eugene Meyer, chairman of the National Committee on Mental Hygiene, characterises Strecker's work as 'a warning which he [Strecker] felt should be given to the nation' (Strecker 1946: 7). At the end of his book, referring back to the number of psychoneurotic young Americans revealed by the war, Strecker asserts that 'The threat to our security must not be allowed to go farther' (220).

I have so far discussed broadly psychoanalytic discourses, but there were in addition related contemporary assumptions about masculinity and military behaviour that foregrounded the male body. According to the authors of 'Personnel selection: a short method for selection of combat officers', published in 1943, the 'male body build varies from the strong, rugged, well-muscled, angular, masculine type toward the softer, rounder, less muscled, feminine type. This is true even within the normal range of men in which one does not suspect actual endocrine abnormalities' (Heath et al. 1943: 422).[12] They suggest a 'four-fold scale comprising strong, medium, weak and very weak masculine component'. They list the characteristics of strong masculine component as:

> (1) general angularity and ruggedness of body outline and good muscularity; (2) relatively narrow hips to shoulder breadth; (3) flatness of mammary area; (4) flatness of abdominal area; (5) interspace between thighs; (6) prominence of inner curvature of calves; (7) pubic hair running towards navel. In making actual judgments these are also observed: lack of hyperextensibility of elbows and good muscle tonus. (422)

They differentiate these characteristics from those of young men with a weak masculine component, but who are still

> well within 'normal' range. Note: (1) roundness and softness of body outline, without prominent musculature; (2) relatively greater hip breadth to shoulder breadth; (3) fullness in mammary area; (4) feminine abdominal protuberance; (5) approximation of thighs; (6) greater outer curvature of calves; (7) lateral distribution of pubic hair. In making actual judgments there are to be observed also the arms carried with an angle at the elbow (hyperextensibility), and poor muscle tonus. (422)[13]

The authors also provide a graph that shows those with higher ROTC (Reserve Officers' Training Corps) officer ratings as having a stronger masculine component (425). There is a parallel here with Heath's later publication *What People Are: A Study of Normal Young Men* (1946). Not only are 'people' assumed to be male, 'normality' is to be found in the population of Harvard undergraduates. Heath claims that there is a correlation between what he has identified as 'sound' men in his survey and their resistance to weaknesses: 'There have been no neuropsychiatric casualties in this series' (Heath et al. 146: 100). Heath concludes: '"Soundness" in basic personality and good integration or balance of traits have seemed to be the important factors in enabling a young man to meet problems which confront him, including the acute ones of the present day' (1946: 108). Here there seems to be a circularity of expectation and evidence that leads inexorably to linkages between the body, class and 'normal' masculinity. The social hierarchies of the American class structure are seen to be explained and justified in the research on 'normal young men'.

What is perhaps most revealing about these contemporary analyses of the responses of American men to the demands of the Second World War is the divide between an essentialist assumption of a natural masculine predisposition to courage and military aptitude and a recognition that such characteristics may have to be instilled. There is a tension here between the ideology of hegemonic masculinity that normalises the expectations of men in wartime and the evidence of actual men's behaviour. In fact, the two are closely intertwined and explanations of men's behaviour are often grounded in normative expectations. For example, for Strecker, men would behave appropriately if they were not subverted by inadequate mothering. On the other hand, in *What People Are*, Heath and his cowriters are deterministic in locating a primacy in the body: '. . . physical structure and appearance [. . .] are integral parts of the individual's personality' (1946: 56). Certain expectations of men have become 'common sense'[14] and in the contemporary discourses of masculinity, this common sense is revitalised and reinflected through 'modern', scientific explanations of human behaviour and physique.

Norman Mailer, *The Naked and the Dead*

Let me turn now to Norman Mailer's *The Naked and the Dead* (1948). This was Mailer's first novel and, as mentioned above, enjoyed significant popular and critical success. For example, in the *New York Times*, David Dempsey argues that it is '[u]ndoubtedly the most ambitious novel to be written about the recent conflict [and] also the most ruthlessly honest', and he describes Mailer as 'a new and significant talent among American novelists' (Dempsey 1948). In *Commentary*, Raymond Rosenthal notes that Mailer's novel 'has the value of the authentic inflection, the undeniably accurate feel and shape of what happened' (Rosenthal 1948). A claim to authenticity was important to the reception of *The Naked and the Dead* and rested on the fact that Mailer had seen active service in the war. The publisher, Rinehart, emphasised this point for readers, who were told in ads that the author was 'a young rifleman named Norman Mailer' (Schoenvogel nd).

The Naked and the Dead has been considered a novel about the character of American culture as reflected through the power and command structures of the US Army.[15] In its focus on male relationships within the circumscribed homosocial environment of an army, it is specifically about power as an exercise of masculinity. The novel can therefore be seen to engage with the social construction of masculine identity within power relations. Mailer's novel draws on realist modes of description in seeking to represent the sensory experiences of war, and this realism is given authority through the use of an omniscient narrator. Yet the novel also aims at providing some insight into the psychological condition of the soldiers, in particular through the flashbacks to civilian life of the 'Time Machine' episodes. In this the novel can be seen to engage with the contemporary psychoanalytic discourses discussed above.[16]

The Naked and the Dead is set on the Pacific Island of Anopopei, and, from the perspective of American soldiers, describes the military engagement with the Japanese occupying forces. The structure of the novel has a double focus. On the one hand, there are the officers, led by General Cummings, and on the other the Reconnaissance platoon. In the first phase of the narrative, Sergeant Croft, who is a very experienced soldier and has seen much combat, is in command of the platoon. An episode involving Croft describes a Japanese attack on the platoon across a river at night.

The events are focalised through Croft, and the exchange begins with him – convinced that the Japanese soldiers are preparing an attack – peering across the river in the dark. He is described as 'unbearably tense, but the sensation was not wholly unpleasant' (Mailer [1948] 1993: 155). Eventually, one of the Japanese soldiers calls out:

> 'We you coming-to-get, Yank.'
> Croft felt as if a hand had suddenly clapped against his back, travelled up his spine over his skull to clutch at the hair on his forehead. [. . .] He had the agonizing frustration of a man in a nightmare who wants to scream and cannot utter a sound. [. . .]
> He shivered terribly for a moment, and his hands seemed congealed on the machine-gun. He could not bear the intense pressure in his head. (156)

The Japanese then attack, with a machine-gun firing at Croft:

> [. . .] it spat a vindictive white light like an acetylene torch, and its sound was terrifying. *Croft was holding himself together by the force of his will.* (156; italics added)

As the attack begins in earnest, Croft switches to a different mode; first he becomes like a machine: 'he could not have said [. . .] where his hands ended and the machine-gun began' (159); then Mailer uses a human simile: 'Croft fired and fired, switching targets with the quick reflexes of an athlete shifting for a ball' (159). As it becomes clear that the Japanese attack has faltered, other emotions surface and Croft fires at a dead soldier, feeling a 'twitch of pleasure as he saw the body quiver' (160).

When the attack has finished, Croft realises 'with a pang of shame that for the first time in his life he had been really afraid' (161). He responds to this realisation with 'a terrible rage working through his weary body' and whispers aloud, 'One of these days I'm gonna really get me a Jap' (161). Given that the narrative has just had him shooting numerous Japanese soldiers with his machine-gun, what this might mean is unclear to the reader, but is revealed in a subsequent episode.

Three of the platoon, led by Croft, have walked back from the platoon's advanced position on the line to collect supplies. As they return, they come across four Japanese soldiers resting in a clearing in the jungle. They kill three of the Japanese soldiers with a grenade and take the fourth prisoner. Croft and one of the other soldiers, Gallagher, stay with the prisoner. Gallagher assumes that they will dispose of him promptly: 'Let's get rid of him and get back.' He regards delay as 'torturin' the poor bastard' (198). Before throwing the grenade, Croft is described as tense: 'a small lump of cartilage beneath his ear quivered once or twice' (194). This tension continues as the 'clump of cartilage under his ear kept pulsing' (199). The writing here sexualises Croft's emotional state:

> [Croft] was bothered by an intense sense of incompletion. He was still expecting the burst that Red's gun had never fired. Even more than Red, he had been anticipating the quick lurching spasms of the body when the bullets would crash into it, and now he felt an intense dissatisfaction.[17] (199)

Croft then proceeds to put the prisoner at his ease, giving him first a cigarette, getting Gallagher to give him some chocolate, and then giving him a drink and a further cigarette. As this goes on, Croft remembers the night the Japanese had tried to cross the river: 'He felt a shiver work its way through him, and he stared for a long time at the prisoner. He felt an intense emotion towards him that made him clench his teeth. But what it was, he could not have said' (200).

In contrast, Gallagher's emotions fluctuate. First, he is impatient, then annoyed when the hungry prisoner devours his chocolate.

However, as the prisoner relaxes and produces a photograph of his wife and child, Gallagher makes an emotional connection with him because he is reminded of his wife, who is pregnant and due to give birth. There is an identification here between Gallagher and the prisoner that asserts their common masculinity, and in fact this is the only passage in which the novel itself allows any human identity to a Japanese soldier. Croft then gives the prisoner the second cigarette and, as he draws on it, his eyes close and there is a 'dreamy expression on his face' (201). It is at this moment that Croft shoots him in the head. There is an extraordinary sexuality, or eroticism, in this exchange, with Croft transformed by the shooting: 'His pulse was slowing down and he felt the tension ease in his throat and mouth.' But he is also amused by the smile on the dead man's face and, thinking again of the Japanese attack across the river, he 'prodded the body with his foot. "Goddam," he said, "that Jap sure died happy"' (201).

There are several conclusions to draw from these passages. First, it is important to note that although the novel was intended at least in part to represent the experience of combat in the Pacific, it goes beyond a simple account of the 'truth' of war. Mailer's representation of Croft is an element of a larger political analysis, to which I return below. This may be seen perhaps in the novel's critical representation of Croft's behaviour as a perversion of the ideals of warrior values. Yet it is also the case that the description of Croft aligns with the view quoted above that 'heroes' in combat may in fact be individuals with psychological problems (see page 84 above). Certainly, Croft's fear, despite his considerable experience of being under fire, makes clear that courage is not a natural attribute of masculinity, but a learned response. Yet in other respects, Croft's behaviour does indeed match with conventional expectations of men. He feels a 'shame' at his fear, and it is this anxiety that motivates him. The shoring up of his masculinity is achieved through the power and mastery that flows from an expression of violence in the murder of the prisoner. Croft's self-esteem feeds off those connections between subordination and power that Connell identifies as central to hegemonic masculinity. It is not surprising, therefore, that the descriptive language is notably sexualised, especially given the earlier description of Croft's attitude to women. He is violent towards women and regards them all as whores (167–9), but he also regards himself as 'an old fuggin machine' (167) and cannot bear to be touched (152). Although Croft is described as relieving his tension through violence, it is significant that the primary markers of sexual orgasm are transferred to his victims. First, the dead body in the river 'quivers' as he shoots it and then he anticipates the 'quick lurching spasms' of the soldier that Red should have shot. Finally, he shoots the Japanese prisoner when he has a 'dreamy expression on his face'. Croft's grasping for mastery and subordination of the Other is the corollary of his inability to achieve the abandonment and vulnerability of emotional sexual contact.

Sergeant Croft is one of three central characters in *The Naked and the Dead* whose relationships create a triangular narrative pattern in the novel. The other two are Lieutenant Hearn and General Cummings. In Part 3 of the novel, 'Plant and phantom',[18] Hearn, who has been Cummings's aide, is banished from the General's entourage and takes command of the platoon as it seeks to carry out a solo operation.

The title of this chapter ('Everything in him had come undone') refers to Lieutenant Hearn's response to combat as he leads the platoon on their mission.[19] Hearn has no practical experience to draw on in leading the platoon, nor has he been in combat. Moreover, since the episodes discussed above involving Croft, he has taken control of the platoon from Croft, who deeply resents the situation. It is this rivalry for authority and power that frames the narrative as Hearn comes under fire for the first time.

> Hearn lay prone behind a rock, his limbs twitching, sweat running into his eyes. He stared for long seconds at the granite veins and tissues of the rock before him, looking with numb absorption, without volition. *Everything in him had come undone.* The impulse to cover his head and wait *passively* for the fight to terminate was very powerful. He heard a sound trickle out of his lips, was dumbly surprised to know he had made it. With everything, *with the surprising and unmanning fear was a passionate disgust with himself.* He couldn't quite believe it. He had never been in combat before, but to act like this . . .
>
> [. . .] All the water in his body had rushed to the surface. Perspiration dripped steadily, automatically, from his chin, the tip of his nose, from his brow into his eyes. The skirmish was only fifteen or twenty seconds old and he was completely wet. *A steel band* wrenched at his clavicle, choked his throat. His heart pounded like a fist beating against a wall. For ten seconds he concentrated only on knitting his sphincter, roused to a pitch of revulsion by the thought of soiling himself. [. . .]
>
> [. . .] Why didn't Croft do something? And abruptly he realized that he had been waiting here for Croft to take over, waiting for the sharp voice of command that would lead him out of this. *It roused a vivid rage.* He slid his carbine round the side of the rock, started to squeeze the trigger.
>
> (510–11; italics added)

During the course of these paragraphs, Hearn moves from passivity ('lay prone'; 'without volition') to action ('started to squeeze the trigger'). So how is this represented? In the first place the passage presents a set of contrasts that relate primarily to Hearn's body. It begins with the hard granite of the rock metaphorically related to Hearn's immobility; however, the hardness of the rock contrasts with the incoherence of Hearn's body, which is picked up in the second paragraph. Here the emphasis on the watery flow from his body suggests a softness that is contrasted with the imagined steel band around his throat. That all this relates to Hearn's sense of masculine identity is made explicit in the reference to 'unmanning fear'. I believe the key notion here is that of 'coming undone', which suggests both losing emotional and psychological control and coming apart physically, losing bodily coherence. As Hearn's performance removes from the masculine ideal, his body dematerialises. Hearn is finally spurred to action because he is disgusted by his fear and the apparent dissolution of his masculinity, but he is also provoked by a 'vivid rage' (511). This anger is not directed at the Japanese troops who have been trying to kill him. It arises partly from his self-disgust, but it is motivated by a need to assert himself in relation to Croft.

In these paragraphs one can read Hearn's negotiation with the dominant expectations of masculinity in particular relation to fear and power. Again, like Croft, resistance to fear comes not as a natural concomitant of maleness but has to be strived for. However, it is significant that Hearn is an officer and his reconstruction of his masculine identity aligns with the codes of hegemonic masculinity. So he restores his masculinity not only by dispelling the signs of feminised behaviour, but particularly by reaffirming his hierarchical position in the homosocial world of the army.

As General Cummings's aide, Hearn had a close relationship with the General and it is to their side of the triangle that I now turn. While Hearn was close to being Cummings's confidant, there is constant tension that leads eventually to a falling out – to Hearn's appointment as platoon leader and ultimately his death. Hearn is 'partially convinced the General was a great man' and sees his particular attribute as being able 'to extend his thoughts into immediate and effective action' (85). Yet Hearn resists Cummings's authority and for Cummings, this contest for power is a matter of masculinity: 'The average man always sees himself in relation to other men as either inferior or superior. Women play no part in it. They're an index, a yardstick among other gauges, by which to measure superiority' (328). His perspective may be that of the homosocial world of the army, but it points to the wider intertwining of power and masculinity in contemporary American culture. In the hierarchy of the army, of course, Cummings has the authority to impose himself on Hearn.

Cummings is proud of being a reactionary and expresses racist views in relation to both Jews and African Americans (90–2). He accuses Hearn of being a liberal and claims that 'this is going to be the reactionary's century, perhaps their thousand-year reign. It's the one thing that Hitler said which wasn't completely hysterical' (92–3). Cummings's fascist sympathies are made more explicit in a later conversation with Hearn:

'Historically the purpose of this war is to translate America's potential into kinetic energy. The concept of fascism, far sounder than communism if you consider it, for it's grounded in men's actual natures, merely started in the wrong country, in a country which did not have enough intrinsic potential power to develop completely.' (327)

Morality in the future is to be determined by power, and that power 'can only flow from the top down'. 'When there are little surges of resistance at the middle levels, it merely calls for more power to be directed downward, to burn it out' (329).

Some analyses of the novel have argued that Mailer encounters problems with his characterisation in that he makes Cummings the most powerful character and then has to deploy a rather inelegant plot device at the end of the novel to undermine Cummings and his fascistic ambitions.[20] In contrast, I want to suggest that by focusing on the representation of masculinity in the novel's characterisation, a rather different emphasis emerges. Mailer has to manipulate the plot because the novel struggles to represent a male character whose masculinity can be contained within acceptable social boundaries. While, for example, the novel makes clear the contradictions between the expectations of men with regard to courage and the realities of war (see the descriptions of Croft and Hearn discussed above), it remains enmeshed in dominant narratives of masculinity.

In his analysis of warrior values discussed above, McCarthy makes the point that the warrior code is 'aspirational and normative'. It follows that in practice, breaking the code is 'commonplace', and McCarthy gives such examples as the wilting of courage and the torture, rape and murder of non-combatants (1994: 106). McCarthy, it seems, here makes relatively uncritical assumptions about aspiration and reality when one might argue that this relationship is inverted, with the warrior code being an ideology that misrepresents reality. Cummings certainly adopts a cynical posture in consciously rejecting any notion of honour as necessary to the codes of masculinity. In anticipation of Croft's later shooting of the Japanese prisoner, he claims that it is a 'ridiculous idea' to think someone is a 'dastardly person' to shoot a 'defenceless man' – 'The fact that you are holding a gun and the other man is not is no accident' (91).

It is this disjuncture between warrior values and the exercise of power and the imposition of force by men that is exposed in Mailer's narrative. Cummings tends to match dominant notions of masculinity – he is intellectually acute, courageous, forceful and assertive, wields power effectively – almost 'a great man', in Hearn's view. In the environment of the army and combat Cummings operates successfully, setting goals that he seems likely to achieve. He is certainly represented as flawed, but in terms of the novel's narrative outcomes, it is not his psychological flaws that lead to his lack of success, but chance. At the strategic level of the military campaign where Cummings operates, Mailer's narrative shows him as manoeuvring successfully against the Japanese general. His plan of campaign requires air strikes, which he has difficulty in obtaining from his military superiors. While he is away from Anopopei making his case for this air support, the situation on Anopopei suddenly shifts and Cummings's lumbering second-in-command, Major Dalleson, achieves victory by default.

At a lower level than Cummings, Croft also shows fascist tendencies in his attempts to accrue power and assert himself over others, while embodying key aspects of masculinity – in his courage and leadership, for example. Croft is also defeated. He attempts to lead the platoon over the mountain dominating Anopopei to reconnoitre behind the Japanese lines. This gruelling expedition, which has led to the serious wounding of one soldier and the death of Hearn and another soldier, ends in farce as the soldiers are chased off the mountain when Croft accidentally disturbs a hornet's nest. Croft's obsession with climbing the mountain may be seen as a matter of his masculinity, because any military logic to the expedition has evaporated. Croft has manipulated Hearn into a situation where he was exposed to the Japanese and shot dead, and the remainder of the platoon will not be able to carry out their objective as they become exhausted and demoralised. Croft, nevertheless, is determined to impose his will on the platoon and in so doing achieve a personal goal of conquering the mountain. The mountain is constantly described in phallic terms, and Croft's striving exemplifies his endless struggle to renew his masculinity.[21]

Croft and Cummings seem to aspire to a hypermasculinity that is characterised in terms of power and control, and at best an indifference to others, at worst a sadism. The novel links these characteristics with their sexuality. The turning point in Cummings and Hearn's relationship comes when Cummings lets slip a personal confession – '[M]y wife's a bitch' (187). The statement echoes the consistently misogynist views expressed by the male characters, but it is followed by a homoerotic moment when Hearn wonders whether Cummings might 'touch his knee' (188).[22]

On the one hand then the novel represents Cummings and Croft as the most masculine characters, on the other it shows them as flawed and organises their defeat. Politically, they are of the right, Cummings consciously so. What seems inherent (and inescapable) to Mailer's narrative is a connection between strong masculinity and a will to power on the right. The character most obviously positioned to resist Cummings is Hearn. Yet he is flawed both politically and as an effective male. Cummings attacks Hearn as a liberal but he is politically disengaged. He also lacks the desire to exert the power that is necessary to a true masculinity. After he has taken command of the platoon he realises that his experiences in doing so have ignited a genuine desire to lead the platoon and that he wants to continue. He associates this desire with Croft – 'He could understand Croft's staring at the mountain through the field glasses' (578). However, Croft is determined to reassert his power over the platoon and manages to orchestrate Hearn's death. So Hearn suffers a double defeat at the hands of first Cummings and then Croft.

Similarly, the men of the platoon are defeated by Croft. They stand individually and collectively for a variety of American male proletarian or blue-collar identities – rural southern, Irish, Jewish, Polish, leftist, racist and so on. Each stands as some form of Everyman and the 'Time Machine' episodes, in which their civilian lives are described, provides Mailer with a means of inserting everyday America into the war narrative. These episodes are extensive, and there is not space to analyse them fully where the emphasis here is on violence and masculinity. (Further discussion of the novel in relation to sexuality may be found in the following chapter.) One question is whether through the characters of the platoon Mailer questions the expectations of masculinity and exposes its contradictions. For example, in *Understanding Norman Mailer* Maggie McKinley argues that Mailer 'crafts the inner lives of the individual soldiers' with sympathy and correspondingly allows the male characters 'more vulnerability' (McKinley 2017: 15).

McKinley also picks out an episode late in the novel when one of the soldiers, Roth, finds a small bird with a damaged wing (528ff). The initial focus is on Roth, who is physically ill-suited to being an infantryman and originally was a clerk in headquarters on the island. He is older than the other soldiers, missing his wife and child, lonely, self-pitying and unable to establish any lasting relationship in the platoon. He responds emotionally to the bird: 'all the frustrated affection he had stored for months seemed to pour out toward the bird' (529). This takes place after one of the platoon has been seriously wounded and Croft is involved in making a stretcher to carry him off the mountain. Croft's pent-up impatience with Roth and his engagement with the bird, which has diverted the attention of half the platoon, enrages Croft, who demands the bird and then crushes it in his palm. McKinley argues that in this scene Mailer 'is able to subtly allude to the pratfalls of a violent performance of masculinity, to the cruelty and corruption of leadership in the military, to the impotence of the individual enlisted soldier, and to the repression and redirection of a soldier's grief, tragedy and guilt' (17). The ambiguity of Croft's initial response to the sensation of the bird in his hand – 'He wavered between compassion for the bird and the thick lusting tension of his throat' (530) – certainly reflects contradictory impulses. Croft is driven by anger to carry out the violent act and for him this is a more acceptable emotional expression for a man. In contrast, the appalled reaction of the other men – Goldstein compares it to 'killing a baby' – marks the significance of an affective connection for soldiers who have been emotionally deprived and oppressed for months. So while at points the narrative, as here, marks the contradictory pressures of masculinity, the men are eventually faced with an existential test of individual strength or weakness. This episode therefore turns into an issue primarily of power and potential violence. There has been ongoing hostility between Croft and one of the soldiers, Red Valsen, who sees this as a 'propitious time' to challenge Croft and tells him 'You bit off a little too much this time' (531). The potential physical engagement between the two men is halted by Hearn, who forces Croft to apologise to Roth. Hearn is amused by provoking Croft, but in humiliating him has further stoked his resentment, with fatal consequences for Hearn himself.

The unresolved conflict between Croft and Red Valsen re-emerges later. Croft has driven the remains of the platoon up the mountain, but the men are in shock and mutinous after Roth has fallen to his death the previous evening. It is clear to the soldiers in their depleted state that even if they could ascend the mountain and reach the rear of the Japanese lines, there is nothing useful they could achieve. When Croft orders the men to move out in the morning, Red challenges him. Croft responds by pointing his rifle at Red, and Red realizes what has happened to Hearn and that Croft 'wanted to shoot him' (694). He backs down and the march up the mountain continues, with each man in the platoon defeated and embarrassed, 'trying to forget the way he had been tempted to shoot Croft and had failed' (694).

The divisions between the ordinary soldiers of the platoon and their lack of resistance, both in their civilian lives in America, and in the army, could be seen as a critique of Marxist notions of collective class action. However, Mailer's narrative consistently presents crisis as an existential issue for the individual and links weakness in confronting a crisis to a weakness in masculinity. For the men of the platoon this is frequently expressed through the vulnerability of their bodies. Yet the narrative is trapped by its contradictions – a 'true' masculine identity seems to require the grasping of power and leads to an authoritarianism, while male characters who fail to develop a conventional masculine identity end up defeated. The narrative is only resolved through contrived plotting that undermines both Cummings and Croft.[23]

James Jones, *From Here to Eternity*

Let me move now to *From Here to Eternity* (1951), which is set in an army camp in Hawaii in the early 1940s and concludes with the attack on Pearl Harbor. Both *From Here to Eternity* and *The Naked and the Dead* were very successful novels in terms of critical reception, and sales, and both derived an authenticity from the wartime experience of their authors. However, there were some interesting contrasts in two editorials in *Life*, respectively in 1948 and 1951. When *The Naked and the Dead* hit the top of the bestseller lists, *Life* described this as 'none too reassuring', although the novel is also described as 'good, even excellent, of its kind'. The *Life* editorial expressed concern particularly with the passages in the novel that deal with the soldiers' lives in America and argued that *The Naked and the Dead* makes it seem that Americans only have 'two diversions, liquor and sex. And when they aren't a-drinkin' and a-hellin' around they are talking about it with an obscenity that is utterly and hopelessly unimaginative and monotonous' ('Fiction in the US' 1948: 24). Mailer's novel is criticised for suggesting that life in

America is 'meaningless'. In contrast, the later editorial in *Life* praises James Jones's *From Here to Eternity* for its 'vigor, its sincerity, and a fundamental understanding and respect for the Army' ('From Here to Obscenity' 1951: 40), although it is criticised for its 'obscene' language, as the title of the article makes clear. The criticism of Mailer seems to lie in a deeper worry about the state of American society and the writer argues that *The Naked and the Dead* is not typical of Americans, who, 'despite the Kinsey report and pamphlets of Alcoholics anonymous', do have 'various joys'. The article may be seen as echoing some anxieties and contradictions relating to the boundaries of contemporary American masculinity. On the one hand, social analysts expressed concern about the incapacity of many American soldiers and the feminising influence of their mothers; on the other, the masculine pursuits of soldiery – drinking, swearing and copulating – need to be reined in.

There is a question about why *Life* could regard *From Here to Eternity* as having a 'fundamental understanding and respect' for the army, unlike *The Naked and the Dead*, when it is possible to argue that Jones's novel is in fact more critical of the army as an institution.[24] It's possible that in 1951 the writer's perspective was influenced by the fact that American troops were in action in Korea. It is also the case that the novel's reception gave greater emphasis to an association between Jones's experience fighting in the Pacific, the 'naturalistic' or 'realistic' style of the writing, and the perceived authenticity of the text, than had been the case with Mailer. Compare, for example, the emphasis of David Dempsey's 1951 review of *From Here to Eternity* with his review of Mailer's novel (see page 87 above). Dempsey emphasises that Jones 'has obviously written out of his own experience', having 'served five years in the Army, fought on Guadalcanal, where he was wounded' (Dempsey 1951). While there 'have been more subtly written books about the American soldier', there are 'none that have been written with more integrity, or with a surer grasp of its material'. Dempsey describes Jones as 'an original and utterly honest talent' who 'has restored American realism to a pre-eminent place in world literature'. Moreover, 'the book's extreme naturalism gives it a special importance at this time when much of our serious literature has turned introspective and somewhat effeminate in quest of psychological rather than social relationships'. This is 'in every sense a work of heroic proportions'. Here naturalism (and realism) is associated with an elided American and masculine identity. In his biography of Jones, Frank MacShane argues that Jones consciously adopted an 'insensitive' approach to style which he defended by explaining that it was 'a direct reaction against the hyper-sensitive esthete attitude of the Bowles-McCullers, Vidal, etc axis which, at least I feel, is destroying itself and its ability to communicate' (Jones's correspondence, 23 November 1953; quoted in MacShane 1985: 118). At the historical moment of its publication, *From Here to Eternity* seems, through the associations of style and content, to have been identified with the recuperation of an idealised American masculinity, one that challenges the anxieties manifested in the post-war discourses about the performance of American servicemen.

Jones himself was moreover presented as embodying an unambiguous, heterosexual masculine identity. An article in the *New York Post* – 'Rough, Tough Jimmy Jones' – described Jones as 'like a lonely rock; he is stubby, tough, with a craggy jaw, jutting eyebrows, and there's something rocklike too in the hard fix of his narrow eyes' (Wembley Bald, *New York Post*, 18 April 1951; quoted in MacShane 1985: 107). Scribner's publicity photographs of Jones reinforce this image. In these photographs he is wearing a striped T-shirt, an item of clothing with complex significations at the time (see Barber 2004). The T-shirt became popular after its adoption by the US Navy as the standard-issue undergarment for sailors. It was taken up by men working in heavy industries and therefore acquired connotations of male strength and working-class identity, reinforced by its close-fitting style, which emphasised body shape. Yet it was also taken up in gay and bohemian circles and thus signified a resistance to conventional sexual and bourgeois values.[25] In the caption to the publicity photograph of Jones reproduced in his biography, MacShane notes that Jones was dramatically introduced as 'a new kind of writer, quite different from the usual, tweed-clad novelist' (MacShane 1985: photo section between 116–17). In addition to the assertion of masculinity that has already been noted, Jones's adoption of the T-shirt for the publicity stills emphasises the class perspective of the novel, which is discussed below.

It is possible that the *Life* reviewer's comments were particularly informed by the latter sections of the novel and the soldiers' response to the attack on Pearl Harbor. That episode contrasts with the novel's more problematical representations of army life and masculinity. The novel is organised around two principal characters, Private Robert E. Lee Prewitt, and Sergeant Milt Warden, and their relationship with the microcosm of the army that is G Company. Prewitt is an individualist and, put simply, the novel shows that whatever his commitment to the army, which is genuine, the army cannot cope with him. Indeed, at the end of the novel, Prewitt is shot by the soldiers of his own regiment. Warden, on the other hand, is a strong leader – G Company's sergeant – with a robust male view of life and the army. In certain ways, however, he trims to the requirements of an authoritarian and hierarchical institution. Although the story is told by an omniscient narrator, the narrative is focalised from different perspectives, most commonly that of Prewitt's, but the Japanese attack is shown from Warden's viewpoint.

The narrative impact of the description of the arrival of the Japanese aircraft over Hawaii is considerable and can be read as a conventional celebration of combat as exciting and pleasurable. The attack happens on a Sunday morning while the non-commissioned officers and soldiers of G Company are having breakfast. Warden has been up all night drinking and gambling, some of the company are still in bed and others have not yet returned from their Saturday night revelries – none of the soldiers 'was less than half tight'. No officers are present, as they have been at a 'big shindig dance at the Officer's Club' the night before (J. Jones [1951] 1952: 741). The breakfast is a scene of masculine rowdiness, with 'drunken laughter and horseplay and the clashing of cutlery and halfpint milk bottles' (741). There is the sound of an explosion, which is dismissed as 'dynamitin down to Wheeler Field', but after a second explosion, someone says, 'This is it' (742). This anonymous and therefore universal recognition of the momentous shift from peace to war is immediately followed by a passage of mystical homosocial identification:

> Warden found that his eyes and Stark's eyes were looking into each other.[26] There was nothing on Stark's face, except the slack relaxed peaceful look of drunkenness, and Warden felt there must not be anything on his either. He pulled his mouth up and showed his teeth in a grin, and Stark's face pulled up in an identical grin. Their eyes were still looking into each other. (742)

The Japanese aircraft fly over and strafe the company's barracks, but there is identification too with the enemy: 'The plane flashed past, the helmeted head with the square goggles over the slant eyes and the long scarf rippling out behind it and the grin on the face as he waved, all clearly visible for the space of a wink [. . .]' (744) Warden organises some resistance with machine guns and automatic rifles and the celebratory atmosphere of the breakfast continues:

A V of three planes came winging over from the southeast firing full blast, and the waiting shooters cheered happily like a mob of hobos about to sit down to their first big meal in years. All the artillery on all the roofs cut loose in a deafening roar and the earth stopped. [. . .]

'Holymarymotherofgod,' Chief Choate boomed in his star basso that always took the break-line of the Regimental song uncontested. 'I aint had so much fun since granmaw got her tit caught in the [w]ringer.' [. . .]

Warden lowered his BAR [Browning automatic rifle], his belly and throat tightening with a desire to let loose a high hoarse senseless yell of pure glee. This is *my* outfit. These are *my* boys. He got his bottle from between his knees and took a drink that was not a drink but an expression of feeling. (751–2)

These brief extracts give a flavour of the atmosphere created by Jones. It is one that draws on the ideology of combat – these men are brave and infused with something akin to the berserker spirit. From the moment of recognition that passes between Warden and Stark, the language and images are insistently masculine. The image of the Japanese pilot with his long scarf draws on an iconography that goes back to knights on horseback – he indulges in a complicit grin that is reinforced by the 'wink', a form of communication associated with men. Chief Choate's basso boom emphasises his masculinity at the same time as his 'fun' comes at the expense of a woman's pain – the mangled 'tit' signifying the rejection of motherly and female discipline. Warden's bottle – between his legs – is a phallic signifier, linking with the guns as markers of the masculinity of combat.

Yet this masculinity is not simply aligned with the warrior values as laid out by McCarthy. There is in Jones's account an anarchistic, subversive aspect to it. It is evident in the drunken state in which the soldiers take action and in Warden's command of the company in the absence of officers. Warden leads the break-in to the supply room to get hold of the live ammunition that the supply sergeant has told him cannot be passed out without a signed order from an officer (748–9). Later on, when Lieutenant Ross does arrive and tells Warden to come down off the roof, Warden replies, 'Goddam it, I'm busy' (756). In this anarchic confusion they shoot down two planes, one of which is American.

After these heady events, the narrative switches to a more sober description of the consolidation of the defence of Hawaii and the changed circumstances of the soldiers – somewhere between peacetime preparation and actual combat. It may be surmised then that the 'fundamental understanding and respect for the Army' uncovered by *Life* may in part derive from these final episodes in the novel. They articulate a comforting view of the ordinary rambunctious American soldier acting in an unhierarchical military setting, a representation appropriate to the ideology of the populist myth of American democracy. One element of the story is an unproblematic masculine courage, which obliterates those awkward statistics of fear and anxiety.

Yet, the novel as a whole is a far more complex and critical account of the army. It is one of its attributes that it represents the perspective of the enlisted men and non-commissioned officers rather than that of the officers. This is significant in that the main characters in the book negotiate the codes of masculinity in relation to their class background. Jones problematises the army as an institution primarily through the experiences of Private Prewitt. I turn now to Prewitt and focus on how violence and aggression function in relation to masculinity in the narrative. As the novel begins, Prewitt is transferring to G Company as an ordinary soldier. The company has a sporting reputation, in particular for boxing. In this emphasis on boxing, with considerable practical rewards for the successful fighters, one can see the army as naturalising violence as both an inherent element of its organisational structure and as an expectation of its soldiers' masculine identity. Boxing is both a substitute for actual combat and the inculcation of a dominant mode of masculinity, one that produces the aggressive body. Yet this form of masculinity is inflected with class hierarchies, in that it is organised and led by the officers and performed by and on the bodies of the enlisted men.

Through the novel the ordinary soldiers negotiate the codes of masculinity produced as intrinsic to army life – courage, strength, loyalty, heterosexuality, sport, drinking, gambling – and constitute a male identity that strives for the hegemonic ideal. However, the relationship between this ideal and the American ideology of individualism produces contradictions. In reality, the army as an institution removes any choice from the individual, taking utter control of the soldierly body and disposing of it as suits its purposes. It was certainly James Jones's own view that the army's training was designed to break down 'the sense of the sanctity of the physical person'; the soldier becomes a 'chattel of the society he serves' (J. Jones 1975: 54).[27] Ultimately, this control may be imposed by force – a force that reveals the aggression and violence that produce and underpin the ideologies of masculinity.

Such contradictions are represented most vividly and brutally when Prewitt is sentenced to three months' hard labour in the camp's prison, the Stockade. The nature of the regime in the Stockade is made apparent during Prewitt's initial meeting with the officer in charge, Major Thompson. Thompson claims that 'the quickest, efficientest, least expensive way to educate a man is to make it painful for him when he is wrong, the same as with any other animal' (534). What this brutal behaviourist approach means in practice is demonstrated to Prewitt throughout the interview: for every minor infraction – speaking out of turn, turning his head, not responding when expected to – he is physically assaulted: 'The butt of a grub hoe handle thudded into the small of his back above the kidney on the left side and he was afraid for a second that he would vomit' (534).[28]

Yet there is resistance to this regime, which may be seen as drawing on the ideology of masculinity. This is to display a refusal to break down as an individual, despite the physical punishment one receives; collectively it involves a loyalty to one's fellow oppressed. Prewitt explicitly makes this connection when he is preparing to provoke the authorities into transferring him to Number Two barracks in the Stockade, where he can join the 'tough boys' (541). He has to carry this through 'if he wanted to keep calling himself a man' (561). The inhabitants of Number Two barracks play a game that dramatises the basis of this resistance while simultaneously parodying the physical violence inflicted on them by the authorities.

> Then one man [. . .] would stand with his back to the mattress and the rest would line up at the far end of the aisle according to size with the smallest first and, one at a time, run at the man against the mattress and hit him in the belly with their shoulders. [. . .] It was a rough game. But then they were hard men in Number Two, they were the toughest of the tough, they were the cream. (631)

The situation in the Stockade culminates with a brutal assault on one of the prisoners, Blues Berry, who has defied Major Thompson and his senior NCO, S/Sgt Judson. The other men are taken to the gym to observe the assault by Judson and other Stockade guards.

> Blues Berry stood against one of the side walls in his GI shorts under the lights, still trying to grin with a mouth that was too swollen to do more than twist. He was barely recognizable. His broken nose had swollen and was still running blood in a stream. Blood was also flowing out of his mouth, whenever he coughed. His eyes were practically closed. Blows from the grub hoe handles had torn the upper half of both ears loose from his head. Blood from his nose and mouth, and the ears which were not bleeding much, had spotted his chest and the white drawers. (656)

Berry dies the next day.

Prewitt vows to kill Judson once he is released from the Stockade. His motivation is an attempt to restore the shared masculine codes of the enlisted men in place of the 'illegitimate' use of violence by Judson.[29] Prewitt does this in a knife fight that again foregrounds violence as the masculine mode for resolving matters. In a reiteration of the violence inflicted by Judson on Berry, the novel recounts the cutting and penetrating of Prewitt's knife:

> His knife went into Fatso at the diaphragm, just under the ribs, an automatic counterpunch right-cross to the solar plexus. [. . .] Prew [. . .] pushing and twisting the knifeblade probing in the fat until the haft was buried in it gouging searchingly in the opening [. . .] (671)

This description overtly sexualises violence and in so doing feminises Judson's body – a matter I will return to.

After his murder of Judson, during which he has been wounded himself, Prewitt reflects on how manhood is inscribed on his body:

> He was going to have a nice scar there, he thought with a giggle. The scars on a man's body were like a written history of his life. Each one had its own story and memory, like a chapter in a book. And when a man died they buried them all with him and then nobody could ever read his histories and his stories and his memories that had been written down on the book of his body. (675)

So, for the soldier, a sense of individual masculine identity is produced through the histories of his body. In the narrative, Berry's grinning response and the violent traceries on Prewitt's body represent a form of resistance. Yet that resistant masculine identity has profound contradictions, in that it can only be constructed within the ideology of hegemonic masculinity. And, ultimately, these men's bodies are subject to the power of the institutions of hegemonic masculinity, such as the army.

Abjection and the Male Body

One striking aspect of the novels by Mailer and Jones is the recurrent representation of the wounded male body. The notion of the abject is one way of considering this. In her account of the production of 'bodies that matter' Judith Butler argues that as part of the reiterative process, 'the heterosexual imperative enables certain sexed identifications and forecloses and/or disavows other identifications'. This foreclosure produces 'a domain of abject beings' which is required to circumscribe the domain of the subject (Butler 1993: 8). Butler's deployment of the abject is related to Julia Kristeva's theorisation of abjection in *Powers of Horror* as a necessary stage in the acquisition of subjectivity. For Kristeva, it is only through the delimitation of the 'clean and proper' body that the symbolic order, and the acquisition of a sexual and psychical identity within it, become possible (see Grosz 1990: 86). However, this subjectivity remains provisional and abjection remains a threat to its relative stability: '[. . .] the abject does not cease challenging its master' (Kristeva 1982: 2). In Kristeva's account, the cultural practices of the taboo and the artistic practice of sublimation are social activities that attempt to contain the threat of the abject.

Butler's deployment of the notion of the abject differs significantly from Kristeva, who sees it as a necessary stage in psychic development, and who Butler criticises for accepting a normative account of gendered and heterosexual subjectivities. Butler, on the other hand, emphasises that the abject domain is constitutive of the regulatory norms of identity, arguing that in its discursive relationship with the normative the subjectivity of the abject has a disruptive potential. Now Butler is particularly interested in the disruption of the dominant heterosexual discourse and Kristeva designates the abject as feminine, like the semiotic. So there is a question about how these conceptualisations of the abject might relate to heterosexual masculinity.

A powerfully written description of a wounded body occurs in *The Naked and the Dead*. In the same exchange of fire that I discussed in relation to Hearn, another of the platoon, Wilson, is shot in the stomach. Wilson's wound and his condition are represented both from his perspective and from that of the soldiers trying to rescue him. From the perspective of his fellow soldiers, he is shown as immobile, passive and dependent; and it is arguable that he is represented as abject. Here is the view of his fellow soldier, Roth:

> [Wilson's] face had been white, and his uniform was covered with blood. [. . .] [H]e had looked dead when they had brought him in. [. . .] Ooh, the wound was like a mouth, it was horrible looking. To add to his misery [Roth's] stomach began to churn, and he lay on his bed, retching feebly. (571–2)

There are several aspects of this description that fit with Kristeva's definition of the abject. First is the breaching of the boundary between inside and outside the body – in this case, the blood leaked out on the military uniform. Then there is the ambiguity and sexuality of the wound, like a mouth, misplaced on the body, and the uncertainty of Wilson's condition. For Kristeva the corpse is 'the most sickening of wastes' because it exists on the borders of life and death (1982: 3). Wilson is not a corpse, but he looks dead. In addition, Kristeva describes the reaction to the abject as visceral, which is how Roth reacts.

As the effect of Wilson's wound progresses he becomes delirious. He imagines that the profuse bleeding is in fact caused by urinating and he expects to be scolded by his mother. Then he imagines his wound as 'roiled and twisted flesh, curling about itself, writhing. It kept squeezing the blood out. "Looks like a pussy," he heard himself murmuring' (535). Later his wound throbs 'and in his mind he saw a horn boring into his stomach, pausing and then boring forward again' (624).[30]

In these passages there is a twin focus on abjection – the subject, Wilson, is falling into the abyss of abjection, while his body/corpse is abject in the eyes of his comrades. This abjection is not simply a matter of death and dying, however. What is also crucial to the representation of this abjection is the feminisation of Wilson's body. His wound is sexualised as a mouth/vagina and he perceives himself as penetrated by a phallic object. In this Wilson's wounding echoes that of Judson's knifing by Prewitt, described above. There is then a correlation with Kristeva in that this horror of abjection is inseparable from a horror of the feminine – of falling into the abyss of the feminine. Roth's body expresses this terror in his vomiting – an unsurprising reaction given this is one of the points in the narrative that foreshadows Roth's own later fall to death from a mountain ledge (Mailer [1948] 1993: 663).[31]

The phallic male body, that ideal 'strong, rugged, well-muscled, angular, masculine type' (see page 86 above), is then constantly threatened with abjection and the feminine. Significantly, of course, this threat is most acute when the male body is called on overtly to demonstrate its manliness at the same time as being under threat, as in war. In terms of Butler's analysis, the reiteration of regulatory discourse ensures that heterosexual male bodies do 'matter'. When the male body becomes wounded and vulnerable, it signifies as feminised; boundaries become ambiguous and the feminised male body is culturally abjected, thus restoring the borders of 'sex'.

Mailer's and Jones's novels confirm certain aspects of contemporary discourses that sought to analyse and explain the behaviour of men at war. For example, the deeply embedded expectation that men should behave in certain ways when faced with combat is frequently represented as an incontrovertible truth in the novels. However, it seems that in their depiction of violence, the novels draw attention to an additional dimension lacking in the analytical prose of the experts. It might be argued that this silence in the analytical discourses is an aporia that conceals what has the potential to destabilise the ideology of masculinity and its warrior codes. Both *The Naked and the Dead* and *From Here to Eternity* graphically represent the brutalities of the military and combat. McCarthy raises the issue of why men continue to submit to the conditions of war and these novels suggest why men continue to do so. The internalisation of a normative violent male subjectivity through hegemonic social formations – in this case the military – provides these men with codes of behaviour through which to negotiate an acceptable masculine subjectivity. In particular, the markers of the proper masculine body may be inflected by class in ways that allow individual men a sense of self-esteem, even if they might be relatively oppressed within the structures of gender and power. So for example, the marks of the violence inflicted on Prewitt's body, which might be seen as the consequence of his lack of social status and wealth, are transformed by him into signifiers of a masculine subjectivity.

This chapter has explored whether violent and aggressive behaviour was viewed as intrinsic to masculinity in this period. Clearly the anxiety about the feminisation of American culture was manifested in concern about men's ability to perform according to conventional assumptions about masculine courage and a willingness to use violence in war. The necessity of maintaining one's courage in the face of physical threat is a recurrent theme in the war fiction of the period and is shown to be an essential requirement of manliness. The loss of manliness through wounding is a complementary threat to masculinity – the risk of violent injury threatens both body and mind and this fracturing of masculine identity may be associated with the feminine. At the same time resistance to the overbearing repression of hegemonic structures of power can be channelled through the manifestation of masculine tropes of violence. So in *From Here to Eternity* the glorification of the marks of violence transform humiliation and wounding into a form of masculine assertion. Aggression may also be a form of control – a shoring up of gendered hierarchies – and a protection against a threat to status. This can be seen in the behaviour of Croft in *The Naked and the Dead*, and of Lou Ford in *The Killer Inside Me*. Thompson's novel associates a damaged psychological subjectivity with masculine violence and sexuality. Such an association is also made with the character of Croft in *The Naked and the Dead*. In the case of Croft and Ford, a violent sexuality is accompanied by extreme misogyny. For Ford violence is a lone pursuit, but in the war novels circumstances may be a catalyst for male bonding, as in the description of the Pearl Harbor attack in *From Here to Eternity*. The issue of homosocial connections recurs in the following consideration of masculinity and sexuality.

Notes

1. Norman Mailer [1948] 1993: 510.
2. Women, of course, may also inflict violence and murder (see the discussion of Ann Petry's *The Street* in Chapter 5).
3. Stanley Kubrick has described Thompson's novel as 'probably the most chilling and believable first-person story of a criminally warped mind I have ever encountered' (see Polito 1997: 11).
4. The soldiers in Mailer's *The Naked and the Dead* consistently express the view that female sexuality is uncontrollable; see Chapter 3.
5. *The Naked and the Dead* sold about 200,000 copies in its first year of publication, including book club sales (Schoenvogel n.d.). *From Here to Eternity* was published in February and had become the best seller in America by April, with 163,000 copies sold by May (MacShane 1985: 107). *From Here to Eternity* was of course published at a time when America was at war again in Korea.
6. This is a generalisation about the writing style, which seeks to convey the immediacy of experience. Structurally, Mailer's novel is complex, and he uses devices like the 'Time Machine' sections to develop the characterisation.
7. Mari Jo Buhle provides a comprehensive analysis of the unfolding development of psychoanalysis in America in *Feminism and its Discontents* (1998).
8. See also Joanna Bourke's analysis in *An Intimate History of Killing*, which emphasises the importance of economic and administrative factors weighing on psychiatric assessments, especially in relation to the financial benefits ensuing from discharge (233–4).
9. Joanna Bourke discusses Marshall's book and explains that his statistical analyses have subsequently been discredited. Marshall claimed that many soldiers did not use their weapons even when under fire and discusses how this lack might be countered. Bourke's broad argument

is that, on the contrary, soldiers in the twentieth century were not reluctant to use their weapons and kill – indeed, that pleasure in killing was common.
10. Further discussion of Shaw's novel follows in Chapter 4.
11. Professor Edward Strecker was an eminent American psychiatrist with a national reputation.
12. This article's notion of the 'masculine component' is discussed by Bourke (1999: 99). The analysis in the article was derived from research that Heath was involved with at Harvard before the war began – the Grant Study. This was a longitudinal research project which aimed to answer such questions as: 'What are the characteristics of healthy young men? How are these related, and how do they come about? What further methods can be developed, what wisdom gained, which will better direct people to suitable training and careers? What can we learn that will help people to live happier, more successful lives?' (Heath et al. 1946: 7). The research was based on interviews with Harvard students and first findings were published in Heath et al. 1946.
13. Such views conformed to contemporary views on sexuality, which associated heterosexuality with a 'masculine' physique and homosexuality with the attributes of a 'feminine' body; these are discussed in Chapter 3 below.
14. 'Common sense' is here used as it was developed by Gramsci in his analysis of ideology and hegemony.
15. See for example Tony Tanner ([1971] 1976) 349–50, and Peter G. Jones (1976): ch. 3, 'The literature of command', in which he analyses General Cummings's role in the novel (87–96).
16. There is further discussion of *The Naked and the Dead* in relation to sexuality in the following chapter.
17. Red was the third of the soldiers and had been instructed by Croft to 'finish off' any of the Japanese soldiers who were not clearly dead. His gun jammed as he did so and he was then attacked by the Japanese soldier who is being held prisoner by Croft and Gallagher.
18. The title refers to Friedrich Nietszche's *Thus Spake Zarathustra* (1883–91: 3).
19. The description of Hearn's experience and reaction corresponds to Marshall's analysis referred to above (80–1).
20. See for example Wenke 1987: 8–9.
21. There is an echo here of Mailer's claim in *Advertisements for Myself*: 'being a man is the continuing battle of one's life, and one loses a bit of manhood with every stale compromise to the authority of any power in which one does not believe' ([1959] 1961: 199–200).
22. Mailer makes clear in 'The homosexual villain' (reprinted in *Advertisements for Myself* [1959] 1961: 200–5) that a sinister element of Cummings's character was the homosexuality at the 'core of much of his motivation' (200).

23. Josh Cohen makes the point that the success of Major Dalleson and the demise of General Cummings are connected with the supersession of an authoritarian, masculine perspective by the new hegemony of mass culture (the novel concludes with Dalleson considering the use of a pin-up 'to jazz up the map-reading class' and the final words of the novel are his '*Hot dog!*' (717). Mailer's view was later articulated as the 'womanisation' of America (see Cohen 1998: 28).
24. Some of the elements that may have led *Life* to its conclusion were probably the core elements that were extracted from the novel in the making of the film in 1953. The film significantly misrepresents the novel's account of the army.
25. The erotic and subversive significations of the T-shirt can be seen in Marlon Brando's publicity stills for the film of *A Streetcar Named Desire* (1951) and his performance in *The Wild One* (1953), and in James Dean's character in *Rebel Without a Cause* (1955).
26. Stark is the non-commissioned officer responsible for the company's food.
27. This text was written to accompany a selection of images about World War II.
28. See page 657 for a detailed description of the grub hoe handle and its effectiveness in the assaults.
29. See A. Campbell on the conventions of the 'fair fight' (1993: 60ff).
30. There is a further dimension to these images, because Wilson has also been ill with venereal disease, and at moments he also imagines that the pain is caused by this and that his stomach is full of pus.
31. Roth's masculinity and his relationship with the other men are intricately bound up with their perception of his 'Jewishness'.

Chapter 3

Representing Sexualities and Gender

– Just wait, said the pfc with the horn-rimmed glasses, everything we know is going to be swept under.
– But sex is here to stay, the mess sergeant said, chewing on a toothpick.

(Burns, *The Gallery* [1947] 2004: 156)

John Horne Burns's *The Gallery*, set during the Second World War and published in 1947, articulates parallel visions of the wartime threat to masculine mental and bodily integrity and the vitality of the erotic life force. The geographical centre of the novel is Naples in 1944 and in its representation of the collisions and negotiations of American and Italian culture, the novel offers a critique of American culture and, in particular, male American sexuality. A year later, in 1948, Alfred C. Kinsey published *Sexual Behavior in the Human Male*, a professedly scientific work that stormed American public consciousness and stimulated a national debate about American sexuality. In *American Sexual Character*, an analysis of the reception of Kinsey's work, Miriam Reumann shows how it resonated with contemporary concerns about American identity. She argues for a reading of the 'various crises of American sexuality as responses to post-war worries about the stability and strength of the nation and its population' (Reumann 2005: 3). In this context, the Kinsey Reports 'were received not only as collections of statistics but also as important statements about gender difference, social change, and American identity' (5). In certain respects, such concerns about American national identity in relation to sexuality echo those discussed in the previous chapter in relation to courage and the American male character. The discourses relating to the sexuality of the American male are complex and contradictory. For example, anxieties about male sexuality encompassed both a fear of rampant and immoral behaviour and the perception of a decline in male sexual vitality, ensuing from the supposed feminisation of American culture and the deconstruction of traditional gender roles.

As Reumann's analysis makes clear, the representation of sexual attitudes and behaviour should be regarded as embedded in broader discourses about identity and culture. For example, Paul Robinson's analysis of twentieth-century sexual theorists, including Kinsey, in *The Modernization of Sex*, first published in 1967, proposes a particular perspective, which is, as suggested by the title of the book, to register the emergence of a progressively enlightened view of sexuality during the twentieth century. Robinson judges Kinsey favourably as 'an attractive, even a heroic figure in our intellectual history' ([1967] 1989: 119). Yet, as Robinson himself later acknowledges in the Introduction to the 1989 edition of this book, his conceptualisation of a simple 'modernisation' of sex has subsequently become more problematical (vii–xii). This is in part the consequence of Michel Foucault's genealogical analysis of sexuality and its discourses in *The Will to Knowledge* (1976), in which he challenges the 'repressive hypothesis' – the notion of 'modernisation' depending of course on the defeat of such repression. Moreover, as Jeffrey Weeks suggests by titling the opening chapter of his *Sexuality* (2003) 'The Invention of Sexuality', the theorisation of 'sexuality' as an intellectual field is both relatively recent and open to interpretation, and, indeed, contestation. Robinson is sceptical of Foucault's critique of the 'repressive hypothesis', but Foucault and other theorists, such as Weeks, have additionally drawn attention to the relationship between power and sexuality. Social structures organise human sexuality in different ways in particular cultures – producing conventions around reproduction and identifying and forbidding tabooed sexual practices, for example. In America in this period McCarthyism constructed and exploited putative correspondences between male homosexuality, communism and un-Americanism as part of political discourse.[1] Discourses on sexuality criminalised homosexuals, but such discourses also regulated power relations between men and women, primarily in the context of the institution of marriage.

The focus of this chapter is on male sexuality and the body, analysing how their fictional representation relates to varying constructions of masculinity in post-war America. The novels are, however, intricately entwined with other contemporary discourses about sexuality, and the chapter therefore begins with an account of such discourses. The chapter will argue that while the novels inevitably relate in some respects to conventional attitudes, there are ways in which, as works of fiction, they may challenge or reveal contradictions in the dominant ideology. Undoubtedly, the most significant publications on American sexual practice in the post-war period were Kinsey's two publications *Sexual Behavior in the Human Male* (1948) and *Sexual Behavior in the Human Female* (1953). Writing in *Partisan Review* in 1948, the literary critic Lionel Trilling registered the significance and impact of the first Kinsey Report:

> By virtue both of its intrinsic nature and its dramatic reception, the Kinsey Report, as it has come to be called, is an event of great importance in our culture. As such an event, it is significant in two separate ways, as symptom and as therapy. The therapy lies in the large permissive effect the Report is likely to have, the long way it goes toward establishing the *community* of sexuality. The symptomatic significance lies in the fact that the Report was felt to be needed at all, that the community of sexuality requires now to be established in explicit quantitative terms. (1948: 184)

On the other hand, it is important to note that there was already considerable critical discourse about sexuality and marriage. In fact, responding in 1948 to the Kinsey male Report, Margaret Mead claimed that the findings of the Report were not unique, although she acknowledged that the publication of the Report was a 'cultural phenomenon' (1948: 59). In *Desiring Revolution* (2001), Jane Gerhard traces the longer-term vagaries of intellectual fashion and moral exhortation in relation to female sexuality. She notes that Theodore H. van de Velde's *Ideal Marriage: Its Physiology and Technique* went through thirty-two reprintings between its first publication in English in 1928 and 1957. This book drew on the Kama Sutra and emphasised the importance of the female orgasm, while maintaining the authority of the male as the initiator of women's sexual pleasure (Gerhard 2001: 23–4). As its title overtly declares, sexual pleasure was expected to be channelled through marriage. Gerhard goes on to argue that a more conservative trend developed in the 1930s and 1940s, fuelled by the emerging dominance of American psychoanalytic models. This trend had two principal and related characteristics. First was an emphasis, derived from Freud, on successful vaginal intercourse as the signifier of mature womanliness. Second was the essentialising of heterosexuality through an emphasis on women's role as mother (Gerhard 2001: 31ff). Such views had consequences for notions of male sexuality. Helen Deutsch in *The Psychology of Women* (1944) stated:

> The 'undiscovered' vagina is – in normal favourable instances – eroticised by an act of rape. [. . .] This process manifests itself in man's aggressive penetration on the one hand and the 'overpowering' of the vagina and its transformation into an erogenous sexual zone on the other. (quoted by Gerhard 2001: 36)

Parallel to this was Ferdinand Lundberg and Marynia Farnham's view in *Modern Woman: The Lost Sex* from 1947:

> The rule therefore is: The less a woman's desire to have children and the greater her desire to emulate the male [. . .], the less will be her enjoyment of the sex act and the greater her general neuroticism. (1947: 265)

These views relate to the widespread identification of women as 'frigid' by Freudian psychoanalysts. One of the most widely published writers on female sexuality, Edmund Bergler, defined frigidity as 'the incapacity of woman to have a vaginal orgasm during intercourse' (Bergler and Kroger 1954: 70).[2] The quotation from Deutsch inscribes, in psychoanalytic terminology, a focus on genital penetrative heterosexual practice, with the male figured as virile and aggressive, indeed with violence sanctioned. Lundberg and Farnham imply the same without such explicit or violent expression, but additionally relate sexuality to a differentiation of male and female social roles.

These attitudes to sexuality, reproduction and gender roles echo the dominant Christian morality of the United States. The taboo against forms of sexual behaviour beyond heterosexual vaginal intercourse was commonly a legal prohibition in many states, articulated in relation to the catchall of sodomy. Kinsey himself identified the oppressive nature of contemporary American legal codes in relation to sexual acts:

> However it is labelled, all intercourse outside of marriage (non-marital intercourse) is illicit and subject to penalty by statute law in most of the states of the Union, or by the precedent of the common law [. . .] In addition to their restrictions on heterosexual intercourse, statute law and the common law penalize all homosexual activity, and all contacts with animals; and they specifically limit the techniques of marital intercourse. Mouth-genital and anal contacts

are punishable as crimes whether they occur in heterosexual or homosexual relations and whether in or outside of marriage. Such manual manipulation as occurs in the petting which is common in the younger generation has been interpreted in some courts as an impairment of the morals of a minor, or even as assault and battery.

There have been occasional court decisions which have attempted to limit the individual's right to solitary masturbation; and the statutes of at least one state (Indiana Acts 1905, ch. 169, §473, p. 584) rule that the encouragement of self-masturbation is an offense punishable as sodomy. (Kinsey et al. [1948] 1968: 263–4)

It is clear that the moral and legal codes seeking to control the sexual body were highly restrictive and driven by a primarily Christian ethos of marriage, reproduction and the family.

It was in such elements of Kinsey's approach that Robinson saw a more liberal and humane attitude to sexual activity. Yet Kinsey's reports must be regarded as contributing to a set of contested discourses about sexuality, rather than simply as a free-standing, true statement about human sexuality. This was recognised by Kinsey's contemporaries.[3] For example, Lionel Trilling asserted that the male Report 'is full of assumption and conclusion; it makes very positive statements on highly debatable matters and it editorializes very freely' 1948: 186). Trilling is critical of Kinsey and an element of his critique is alluded to in his reference to the 'quantitative' nature of Kinsey's analysis (see page 113).[4] In certain respects, Trilling also calls on Freud in repudiating Kinsey, and the reception of the Kinsey Reports needs to be seen in the context of the pervasiveness of Freudian psychoanalytic theory as an explanatory discourse in America, both in academic and popular fields.[5] In considering contemporary American attitudes to sexuality, it is important therefore to take account of the two approaches – Kinsey's broadly biological and behaviourist analysis of the sex drive and Freudian notions of the vicissitudes of desire and object choice. To generalise, one might argue that both of these were *potentially* radical approaches, challenging official American social and legal attitudes to sexuality.

Certainly, Kinsey's widely circulated evidence of a large gap between how American males were supposed to behave sexually and his revelations about such activities as masturbation, extramarital intercourse and homosexuality provoked an outcry from the guardians of American morality, who perceived a threat to family life, and thus to the nation's values (see Reumann 2005: 26–7). Concern about the morally subversive potential of Kinsey's work was expressed by

J. Edgar Hoover, then Director of the Federal Bureau of Investigation; he was cited in the *Reader's Digest* as criticising Kinsey as anti-American and warning, 'Whenever the American people, young or old, come to believe there is no such thing as right or wrong, normal or abnormal, those who would destroy our civilisation will applaud a major victory over our way of life' (quoted in Reumann 2005: 27). Margaret Mead asserted that 'the publicity that has been given to this series of facts about extra-marital and abnormal and unusual forms of sex satisfaction, has upset the balance in our society between ignorance and knowledge'. She considered that American 'virtue' had in large part depended on not knowing what other people were doing (Mead 1948: 60). At the same two-day conference at which Mead spoke, organised by the American Social Hygiene Association[6] in 1948 in response to the publication of the male Report, the sociologist Carle C. Zimmerman launched a scathing attack on the Report. Zimmerman's view was that the Report embodied a particular view of sex – that it was really 'just another drink of water', and was a further contribution to the 'revolutionary anti-family behavior of our times' (1948: 83–5). It was clearly Zimmerman's view that Kinsey's biological and behaviourist approach to sexuality would lead to unbridled male sexual activity: the 'domestic womb' would become 'just another place for the sexual relaxation of the uninhibited male' (98). Zimmerman's argument was that cultural stability depended on the family, and that the maintenance of the family depended on sanctions that could 'channel the sex drive of the male' (97).[7]

Although Kinsey and Zimmerman apparently have little in common, in fact Kinsey's approach does seem to embed conventional attitudes about male sexuality. His behaviourist and statistical approach implied a straightforward connection between sexual performance and the individual. Yet, when he came to analyse the statistics in relation to women's sexual behaviour, he found significant differences between men and women. The pattern of sexual activity across a lifetime showed women's rate of orgasm increasing to a peak in middle age, compared to the male teenage peak. However, what Kinsey found hard to account for was the significantly lower *overall* rate for women, given his argument that physiologically there were no significant differences between men and women.[8] Kinsey's decision to use rate of orgasm as his measure of sexuality therefore has a number of consequences, in particular a distinct approval of higher levels of men's orgasmic output.[9] Embedded within this are his culturally conditioned expectations of masculine virility and the male body (echoed in Deutsch's psychoanalytical theorisation). Kinsey also found class differences in sexual practice, with men with higher levels of education more likely to experience sexual intercourse later but to include greater variety in their sexual practices. Kinsey is ambivalent about these differences, admiring the direct move to heterosexual penetration, which was supposedly an element of the less well educated, while recognising the importance of clitoral stimulation for female sexual satisfaction. Indeed, Kinsey directly challenged Freudian orthodoxy on vaginal orgasm (see Kinsey et al. 1953: 582–4).

The connection between masculinity and sexuality is mirrored in other discourses about sexuality. Margaret Mead, writing in *Male and Female*, sees heterosexual performance as a key signifier of masculinity:

> For the man, the demon to be avoided at all costs is lack of potency, defined in a number of quantitative ways – frequency, time, interval before rearousal, accuracy in judging the strength of his own impulse. There is an implicit assumption for males that if one copulates one is happy. (1949: 293)

However, the urgency implied by this account is mitigated by cultural expectations. Mead argues that while sexual contact between adolescents and young men and women is less circumscribed than before, pregnancy outside marriage is severely disapproved of. Yet abortion and birth control are not accessible, so the answer to the 'dilemma' is 'petting'. As Mead points out, 'petting' requires complete control of the boundaries of sexual contact to avoid pregnancy. This control is the responsibility of the girl: 'the boy is expected to ask for as much as possible, the girl to yield as little as possible' (1949: 290).[10]

Mead argues that the effects of this pattern of sexual contact carry over into adult and married relationships with deleterious results, with many women unable to make 'complete sexual surrenders' (291). Mead sees a new emphasis on sexual pleasure for women as emerging at the time of the First World War: 'Good women became women who should enjoy sex, and enjoy it in a way that is definitely analogous to male enjoyment' (293). After marriage there is a shift from petting to copulation, so women were expected to have orgasms 'from the simple act of copulation' and, if they didn't, were 'voted as frigid by a psychiatry in which a European male version of sex differences was very influential' (294). Any return by spouses to the techniques of 'petting' that might have been more conducive to female sexuality were ruled out by the ideological privileging of copulation. Mead's analysis confirms how male sexuality – and masculine identity – in the period is heavily invested in a notion of potency associated with penetrative vaginal sex. This involves significant expectations of the performance of the male body as intrinsic to male sexuality and masculinity.

A more radical approach to sexuality, informed by both Freud and Marx, was Herbert Marcuse's *Eros and Civilisation* (1956). Although Marcuse's ideas were influential later in the 1950s and 1960s, *Eros and Civilisation* is clearly intended to be an intervention in the debates of the early Fifties. This may be seen particularly clearly in the Epilogue, titled 'Critique of Neo-Freudian Revisionism', in which Marcuse argues that American psychoanalytical theorists have simplified Freud and moved to the endorsement of social conformism in their practice (for example, see [1956] 1998: 256). Marcuse's purpose is to interrogate Freud's theories about repression and civilisation. He seeks to challenge Freud's argument that the development of society and culture is necessarily dependent on the repression of the instincts. (Zimmerman echoes Freud in his view of the necessary repression of male sexuality.) Marcuse sees Freud's repressive theory of sexuality as directing a large 'quantum of energy and time' into 'non-gratifying labor' and perpetuating 'the desexualization of the body in order to make the organism into a subject-object of socially useful performances' (199). Freud's view was that if repression was ended, the body would be resexualised and all erotogenic zones reactivated. Socially, the institutions in which private interpersonal relations have been organised would disintegrate. Marcuse sums this up as an expectation that instinctual liberation can 'lead only to a society of sex maniacs' (201). He counters that such a consequence would only arise from the release of repressed sexuality, and would not be the effect of a 'transformation of the libido' (202). Marcuse sees the 'primacy of the genital function [as being] broken'; the 'organism in its entirety becomes the substratum of sexuality' (205). Marcuse thus articulates the liberatory potential of Freud's theories of sexuality, imagining alternatives to the male-dominated, heterosexual genital emphasis of other contemporary discourses. In so doing he also subverts normative models of masculinity and femininity, derived from biological essentialism, and hints at other possible gender identities. In turning now to a selection of novels from the period, I will consider how they relate to normative models of sexuality and gender and whether they imagine more radical possibilities.

Robie Macauley, *The Disguises of Love*

Robie Macauley was an established fiction writer and literary critic when *The Disguises of Love*, his first novel, was published in 1952.[11] *The Disguises of Love* is discussed by Ihab Hassan in *Radical Innocence* in a chapter titled 'Contemporary scenes', where he describes the novel as a 'tragi-comedy', written with a 'lively, witty sensuousness' (1961: 74). Macauley's novel was thus still sufficiently regarded ten years after its publication to have been deemed worthy of the attention of a notable critic.

Hassan situates Macauley's novel in relation to current discussions of sexuality, marriage and divorce – including a specific reference to Kinsey – diagnosing America with an 'erotic distemper' (1961: 75; 74–6). Relating Macauley's novel to such discussions is not surprising given that it is an account of a married man's sexual affair. The novel is set on a college campus and describes the ramifications of a sexual liaison between a married academic, Howard, and one of his students, Frances. Howard is married to Helen, and they have a teenage son, Gordon. The novel alternates between the perspectives of Howard, Helen and Gordon, and the jacket from the novel's first edition refers to the three views of life represented as the sentimental (Helen), the satiric (Gordon) and the romantic (Howard). Significantly, however, Frances, Howard's lover, does not have a voice except within the sections focused on Howard. Evidence for the 'wit' Hassan finds in the novel might be exemplified by the epigraph, which is a quotation from Francis Bacon, and its relationship to the plot. This suggests that humans find it difficult to deal with the 'naked and open day light' of 'Truth', preferring a 'mixture of a lie' that 'doth ever add pleasure'. These 'disguises' of the title are the self-deceptions of the three members of the family, for which they are all satirised.

There is no doubt, however, that Howard is the both the principal character and object of attack. The mocking of Howard begins on the dust jacket: 'Howard Graeme, a moderate, commonplace man, a dull husband, an indifferent father, a pedantic teacher, just lapsing into middle age, suddenly finds himself in a hotel room one night in the midst of a headlong affair with one of his students.' In terms of the novel's relationship to current debates about sex and marriage, it can be argued that, whereas Hassan connects Macauley's novel loosely with the debates around Kinsey's research and publications, there are much closer correspondences. The novel's critical attitude to Howard may be read as broadly aligned with conservative critiques of Kinsey. In particular there are grounds for seeing Howard as evincing considerable similarities to Kinsey. One element of this is Howard's academic subject area – he is an academic psychologist and, following the dominant current of the period, is a behaviourist (Macauley 1952: 33). Moreover, Howard's son, Gordon, describes his father as

> being something like a bottle with nothing inside him. He is sensitive to changes of temperature, light, moisture, sound, touch, and that's all. I never imagined that he could have such a thing as an *emotion*. (53)

Gordon's perception is analogous to criticism of the lack of attention to emotional response in Kinsey's analysis.[12] Moreover, the novel makes fun of Howard's behaviourism. In Howard's description of himself as a behaviourist, he describes his training as teaching him to regard psychology as 'approaching a truly objective science'. Within this discourse, Freudian psychoanalytic approaches are regarded as 'Witchcraft! Witchcraft!' (33).[13] Yet the behaviourist titles on his shelf are satirised: *The Educability of the Perch* and *A Study of the Knee Jerk*, for example. Howard does read Freud and Jung but ends up with 'a feeling of hopelessness and confusion' (34). The novel immediately goes on to 'quote' a case history read by Howard (35). This case involves a middle-aged married man who regularly visits a prostitute, but whose libido can only be aroused by acting as if he is a child again. Howard reacts to this as an 'evil fantasy', yet not only does the novel's representation of Howard's sexuality connect with this case (in breaking ethical codes in having an affair with a student), it also suggests that without a psychoanalytic understanding of human sexuality, Howard has no insight into himself and his motives. In this reference to a sexual case study, the novel alludes to the case studies on which Kinsey's research was based. Furthermore, by implication, the novel suggests that behaviourist explorations of sexuality are likely to be one-dimensional.

My analysis so far suggests therefore that the novel is broadly situated within the camp that was critical of Kinsey. However, there is a further relevant contextual dimension to Macauley's novel. As Frances Saunders has demonstrated in *The Cultural Cold War* (1999), Macauley combined his literary career with another as a CIA officer, and he can therefore be seen to represent the attitudes of a certain influential element of American society. He was recruited in autumn 1953 as a CIA case officer to work with Michael Josselson and the Congress for Cultural Freedom in Paris (Saunders 1999: 240).

The Congress for Cultural Freedom was central to the American policy of recruiting the anti-communist left in the Cold War campaign against the Soviet Union (see Saunders 1999: 63). Saunders claims that the ranks of the CIA were filled with the scions of a hundred or so wealthy families concentrated in Washington who 'stood for the preservation of the Episcopalian and Presbyterian values that had guided their ancestors': 'Trained in the Christian virtues and the duties of privilege, they emerged believing in democracy but wary of unchecked egalitarianism' (36). The cultural cold war engaged the American liberal literary tradition and this involved the recruitment of Ivy League academics to the CIA – it was via Kenyon College that Macauley was recruited.

The cultural campaign that Macauley was involved in promoting received some of its covert funding through the Rockefeller Foundation. The Foundation's funds were crucial to the maintenance of the intellectual publications sponsored by the CIA, but they were also vital to Kinsey's research.[14] For Kinsey, it was the withdrawal in 1954 of the Rockefeller funding after the publication of *Sexual Behavior in the Human Female* that contributed to his decline.[15] However, as Jones recounts in his biography of Kinsey, some members of the Rockefeller Foundation Board of Trustees were opposed to further funding of Kinsey as early as 1951, following the publication of the *Male* volume (James H. Jones 1997: 648ff). Jones argues that although the ostensible reason for questioning Kinsey's research was his statistical methodology, it was in fact a matter of the moral propriety of his subject (649). Leading the attack was John Foster Dulles, Secretary of State and Chairman of the Board; for Jones, 'the same unerring moral compass that had told this Cold War Warrior to contain communism abroad made Dulles alert to any threat to public morality at home' (650). Dulles's views are consistent with those that Saunders describes as permeating the CIA and, indeed, his brother, Allen, was a CIA officer and director of the CIA from 1953 to 1961.

Macauley is intimately bound into this network of conservative discourses,[16] and *The Disguises of Love* may be read as a critique of Kinsey and a moral intervention on the side of marriage. The characterisation of Howard's lover, Frances, is central to this. The novel shows Frances as an object of sexual fantasy created out of Howard's romantic delusions. In terms of the literary effectiveness of the novel the fantasy is only sustainable by representing Frances from Howard's perspective – in other words, the illusion would collapse for the reader if Frances became a character in her own right. Although the plot of the novel requires her to be an agent in the relationship, any explanation of her motivation is lacking, and she is no more than a sexual cipher. The gender and sexual economy of the Frances–Howard–Helen triangle is broadly conventional. So, for example, Howard perceives Frances as 'domestic only insofar as it was necessary to be', whereas Helen is 'a kind of sanitary engineer', who thus produces 'monotonous and largely tasteless food' from a big modern kitchen. On the other hand, Frances cooks 'marvelous delicacies' from a 'messy cubbyhole of a kitchen'. Helen looks 'dowdy' in expensive clothes, whereas Frances always looks 'beautifully dressed' even in old clothes (117). Yet Frances's sexual allure is not merely passive – she is the instigator of the affair with Howard. Frances's overt sexuality and her conscious sexual display are apparent from Howard's recollection of her first appearance in his class. She comes in late, wearing 'a green wool dress, stockings and high heels' rather than the 'customary uniform of the college girl – sweater, skirt, socks, and saddle shoes'. '[N]obody could help but look at her' and she disturbs Howard (59–60). The sinful sexuality of 'Woman' is made explicit in Howard's reporting of a conversation with Frances in which she expresses her view that life without 'history' is boring and that in Paradise 'Eve saw her chance' to begin history (114–15).

The promiscuous nature of Frances's sexuality is made clear when Howard discovers that she has apparently been off pursuing another liaison instead of studying one weekend. The key metaphor for her sexuality is the hotel ceiling. On the morning after her first sexual encounter with Howard, Frances remarks on the ceiling, commenting that she has never seen one like it before (97). Later, after Howard has berated her for her apparent infidelity, she tells him about 'some more hotel-room ceilings' – claiming to be 'a Goddamn expert on hotel ceilings' (129). In this the novel makes a clear moral statement: Frances is sexually promiscuous – crudely, on her back for various men in various hotels – but it is clear that she finds this unfulfilling. The sophisticated reader, with an understanding of contemporary American psychoanalytic theory, could infer from Frances's attention to hotel ceilings that in fact she was not emotionally engaged during sex – and, from that and other aspects of her behaviour, that she is therefore sexually 'frigid' and immature. She can be seen therefore as failing to fit the ideal type of woman as wife and mother. As Jane Gerhard argues in *Desiring Revolution*, the contrast here is between 'sexual order and gender chaos':

> The long-standing conflation of female sexuality and women's social identities by sex experts essentialized a specific set of traits for women that by the 1940s tightly associated women with motherhood, sexual

dependency, and men. [. . .] Antifeminists based their logic on a set of ever widening assumptions, moving outward from the opposition between the clitoris and the vagina, between feminine women and masculine women, between mothers and feminists, and ultimately between sexual order and gender chaos. Female sexuality bore the freight of social order or social breakdown. (2001: 48–9)

This dichotomy is played out in the plot of the novel. At the end Howard's affair has become public knowledge and he believes he is about to fly off with Frances, yet at the airport she refuses to allow him to come (281). The nuclear family reassembles at the airport, and with Gordon noticing that 'From one of the engines of the plane grew a slim feather of black smoke' (282), there is the promise of Frances's demise. This then is a conventional patriarchal narrative, contextualised in post-war America. Frances is independent and sexually active; her supposedly dysfunctional female sexuality is the primary agent of the disruption of a typical, dull but stable American middle-class family. The destructive effect of her sexuality is not only on those around her, but on herself as she meets an inevitable doom. Frances is thus not only refused a voice in the novel, but silenced by its plot. Macauley's novel may therefore be read as aligned morally with conservative discourses about sexuality and the family.

Yet novels cannot simply function as polemic and the narrative of *The Disguises of Love* also represents some of the contradictions in conservative attitudes to male sexuality. If Frances occupies a masculine role in their affair, what are the implications for Howard's masculinity? Howard certainly seems to embody an active masculinity in his virile heterosexuality. However, as an adulterer, he is an exemplar of those men who operated outside the conservative boundaries of accepted moral behaviour. Howard's masculine sexuality is difficult to contain within conservative discourses. To do so, the novel mocks him for his romantic delusions and seeks to code his sexuality as passive by projecting an active sexuality onto Frances. This passivity is represented grammatically in the jacket blurb, where Howard 'suddenly finds himself . . .' The unresolved contradictory representations of Howard's masculinity and sexuality in the novel reflect contradictions in wider discourses about male sexuality. Through the projection of Howard's desire onto Frances as the Other, male sexuality may be disavowed. Yet the price to be paid is an undermining of Howard's masculine identity. The narrative suggests therefore a potential incompatibility between conservative approaches to male sexuality and the desire to recuperate traditional masculine values.

Conservative formulations of masculinity required sexual partnership with a passive female Other who is focused on mothering. However, such partnerships do not fit easily with the sort of heterosexual adventurism that might mark out the truly masculine man.

Macauley's novel is therefore revealing of the problems of establishing a consistent narrative of male sexuality within the context of marital fidelity. I turn now to MacKinlay Kantor's novel, *Glory for Me*, which raises another aspect of sexuality and the family in exploring the common concern about how servicemen would readapt to civilian life when the war drew to a close.

MacKinlay Kantor, *Glory for Me*

MacKinlay Kantor was the prolific author of forty-three novels and won the Pulitzer Prize in 1956 for his Civil War novel, *Andersonville*. He worked as a war correspondent in the Second World War and experienced combat flying with US Air Force and RAF pilots over occupied Europe. His novel *Glory for Me* (1945) was an elaboration of a story written by John Hersey, 'Joe is Home Now', which appeared in *Life* in 1944.[17] Kantor's novel was the basis for the film *The Best Years of Our Lives* (1946), which was directed by William Wyler and the winner of eight Academy Awards, including Best Picture. The principal themes of the novel evidently had considerable cultural resonance. The novel deals with the effects of war on male bodies and minds, and in exploring the return to civilian life for these men, it focuses on their sexual relationships with women.

The novel has three male principal characters: Al Stephenson, an army sergeant, who fought in Germany; Fred Derry, a bombardier in the air force; and Homer Wermels, a sailor who was seriously injured when his ship was torpedoed and who is 'spastic'. Homer is evidently physically damaged by the war, but the novel also makes clear the mental effects of war on the three men, in particular on Fred Derry. All three men come from Boone City in the Midwest; they fly back there together, and as a result their lives become intertwined.

This is an unusual novel in that it is written in blank verse. This aesthetic decision has several effects. It allows Kantor an alternative to the dominant realist mode of most contemporary fiction. Kantor uses 'poetic' language and rhythm to create effects that are not possible in prose. There is an omniscient narrator, but the verse form also allows the narrative voice to slip unobtrusively from the narrator to each of the three men. For example, the following passage reflects Fred Derry's perspective when he is finally flying home.

> What could you do against this patterned world beneath?
> What could you do that men might pay you well?
> That men might cheer your name in inky print,
> And hang applause upon your chest –
> An oak-leaf cluster for each several missions?
> What might you do in life that needed not
> The plunging weight of all the destiny you held?
> Six thousand pounds of destiny,
> So well encased, kicked loose from cocking shackles,
> To plummet down on Lille and Kiel
> And Bremen and the rest. (19)

Derry's peacetime worries echo a number of passages where he relives a traumatic night raid on Germany. He is anxious and ill-equipped to succeed in civilian life, as this passage suggests. The rhythms, the repetition and alliteration here do contribute some effectiveness to the narration, but while there are some strong poetic images and phrases in the novel, on the whole the versification is workaday and subservient to the need to tell the story. Indeed, Kantor's occasional use of somewhat archaic 'poeticisms' such as 'plaint' (218) or 'fain' (239) combine with the limitations of the verse to create a generally sentimental effect. In fact, Kantor has himself confessed to a strong element of 'sentimentality which has infected me through the years' (quoted by Judy Alter 1980: viii).

In this, the literary form of the novel matches the tone of the narrative, which fails to give real weight to the difficulties of adaptation faced by many of the men returning from the war. These problems are discussed by William M. Tuttle in *'Daddy's Gone to War'*, in which he focuses particularly on the effect of the disruptions to parenting on America's children in the war. He draws attention to the difficulties faced by servicemen on their return, quoting Anna Wolf and Irma Black, who were writing in 1946: 'Domestic life, so longed for in foxholes, may seem in the first difficult days to be a woman-dominated, intricate array of trivialities in which a man has neither the wish nor the power to find a real place. The pattern of life for his wife and children seems to be complete without him' (quoted in Tuttle 1993: 224). Tuttle also claims that by 1950 a million veterans had been divorced (220). From this it is clear that a straightforward reinstatement of traditional gender roles was problematical after the experiences of wartime. In contrast, the novel offers a superficial resolution of such difficulties, despite initially appearing to be a relatively innovative articulation of them. The narrative therefore fits with those discourses of the post-war period in America that reasserted family values, pressed for the return of women to a domestic ideal and a requirement on men to settle down and forget the war. Yet, if one considers the relationship between sexuality and masculinity in the novel, it is apparent that, as with *The Disguises of Love*, the novel struggles to strike a balance between representing these men's masculinity while containing their sexuality in a pattern of domestic relations.

In the case of Homer Wermels, his masculinity is already impaired. He is physically incapacitated and it is made clear in the response of Al Stephenson and Fred Derry that he is less than a man should be:

> '[. . .] Who is this, wearing cloth
> Worn only by the strongest and the best,
> The straightest and the ruggedest,
> The fine?' (14)

And his 'bright' eyes are like

> [. . .] a twist
> Of ribbon on a girlie's lingerie:
> Pale blue, and rather soft and feminine and kind. (15)

These metaphors echo the connections between the wounded male body and the feminine discussed in the previous chapter, and they show that Homer's masculinity is compromised. This loss of masculinity is most evident in his loss of sexual authority and in his envy of 'worthless men' with obedient bodies, who can

> Wrap their arms around . . . the girls
> Recoiling never at their touch,
> As if a mauling dog
> Had slobbered all too close. (93)

Neither he nor his family can deal with his disabilities and he begins to drink heavily. One of the motives for his drinking is that it provides an adult masculine identification that he can no longer claim sexually with his body in view of his anticipated rejection by women.[18] His perception is that because his injuries have disabled him, he will be infantilised by women rather than seen as a sexual being:

> Oh, I must run away
> Before those women overcome my soul
> With any kind solicitation –
> Yes, dress, by Jesus Christ!
> I'm not a baby . . . dress myself . . . (94)

He therefore rejects Wilma, his fiancée, on a number of occasions – 'She can go to hell' (94).

Homer's circumstances are brought to a crisis when, opportunistically, he tries to commit suicide using Fred Derry's revolver (241). Wilma and Homer are subsequently reconciled, with Wilma figured straightforwardly as maternal. She has sought to understand Homer's disability and makes plain her desire to help him recover. Her speech comes from the depths of an idealised, naturalised womanhood:

> Pool . . . the ice-blue water of her hardihood,
> A strength of mountains, pine, and rocky shore.
> For she was speaking now, not as child to child,
> But with a nursing passion in her heart.
> In whitest purity she offered up her breast to him,
> And let him drink his nourishment.
> He put his shaking lips
> Around the nipple of her life,
> And deeply took the milk she gave. (252)

Wilma's metaphorical nursing of Homer reflects the text's refusal of masculinity to Homer; despite the narrative's apparent sympathy for his plight, his physical disability renders him infantilised. He is, then, brought into a scene of domestic harmony, but at the price of desexualising both him and Wilma.

Fred Derry returns home expecting to find his wife, Marie, who had been living with his father and stepmother. However, she is not at home. When he does find her, she is with another man, and Fred finds evidence of further sexual relationships. Fred and Marie are represented as having a strong sexual relationship (48), but her expression of this sexuality while he is away is condemned. She accuses him of having 'had a hundred girls', and while he admits to 'nine', he also invokes a version of the double sexual standard:

> 'I've had girls,
> Just like I said. Most people have.
> It ought to make me feel a little different,
> But it don't. See – if our wives at home
> Had men, we never want to know it. [. . .]' (55)

Clearly, Marie is not the wife that the returning warrior deserves and it seems that this is because of her uninhibited sexuality. This sexuality is connected with class and dirt in the description of Marie's background:

> The dirty house, the mother tired of the dirt,
> The poverty, the skating rink,
> The older sisters with their kids,
> And Dad who cut the people's hair. (56)

Fred divorces Marie and gradually his romantic trajectory becomes aligned with Peggy, Al Stephenson's daughter. Although Fred experiences an awakening sexual desire for Peggy, it is significant that their first encounter is in Al and Milly Stephenson's kitchen, the night after Al, Fred and Homer have all got drunk together. Fred and Peggy talk in the kitchen over breakfast:

> The warmth of domesticity
> Was golden all around them. (99–100)

In this, their initial conversation, Peggy reveals that she works for the Red Cross, a role that emphasises the conventional feminine attributes of care and compassion, in marked contrast with Marie. In representing Fred and Peggy's relationship the novel channels male sexuality towards an idealisation of Woman. So for example, in Fred's eyes Peggy is perceived in the following way:

> She shone
> More beautiful, more charged with limpid life
> Than all the courtesans of history . . .
> More fruit within her bosom, sun in hair;
> She was the mistress every mortal wants,
> The mother who would comfort him,

> The nurse who'd feed, the Sister
> Who would talk to him of Light,
> And make him feel a Peace and hear a Voice. (202)

Fred's sexuality and relationships with Marie and Peggy are inflected with class. Fred appears to repudiate a less inhibited but 'dirty' sexuality by projecting it onto Marie, while simultaneously securing his economic and social advancement. The idealisation of Peggy correspondingly intertwines class and sexuality. The novel finishes with Fred taking up the opportunity for pursuing higher education through the GI Bill.[19] His masculinity and sexuality are thus simultaneously channelled into an appropriate respectability. However, the sentimental writing, as in the passage above, weakens the narrative outcome.

Al Stephenson's return appears to be a more straightforward reinvigoration of his marriage to Milly. That his masculinity is not open to question is shown when he has to dress again in a suit for work. He finds that his body has changed so that his suits are now ill-fitting.[20]

> He'd changed his body
> As he'd changed his soul
> He weighed around two hundred when he left
> And now he weighed one-eighty-two.
> His hips were thin, his belly flat
> And there was room he needed now
> Throughout his shoulder surface
> That he didn't need before. (105)

The narrative here emphasises that the experience of war has changed Al; in marked contrast with Homer, his body now signifies as ultramasculine. At the end of the day that starts with him trying on his suits, Al is drunk and being helped to bed by Milly. Despite Milly telling him he is 'much too drunk to think of *that*!' (91), in a match with his bodily masculinity, Al's sexuality is equally powerful:

>   He lay entranced
> And yielded up the pulsing joy
> Which, drunk or sober,
> He could always give to her. (92–3)

Al's ill-fitting suit both signifies his masculinity and his corresponding rejection of the corporate and conformist world of the bank where he has resumed work. He resigns from the bank, and will go into partnership running a plant nursery. Al's narrative therefore contrasts with both Fred and Homer in involving an uncomplicated sexuality, satisfied within marriage, and a masculine independence in the world of work.

The novel is consistent, though, in seeking to stabilise male sexuality within a suitably domestic arrangement. This containment of male sexuality, however, is achieved unexceptionably through a projection of sexual voracity onto women or through a representation of women that idealises and desexualises them. Yet there is another dimension of male sexuality in the novel, and it suggests a different energy behind male desire. In the air force Fred has pinned up a photo of Marie with pictures of other women, such as Lana Turner, with 'satin skin/And slinky gowns' (37). His comrades – 'the boys he flew with' – declare Marie to be the best, and name her 'Derry's Diamond-studded tail'. When Fred goes to track her down, he declares 'I'm between/Your legs tonight,/Or I'm unworthy of the 3-0-5th' (51). This determination to sleep with Marie is a repetition of an earlier avowal:

> I'll sleep with her tonight,
> Or I'm no credit to the 3-0-5th.
> I've got to take up slack,
> And do some double sack-time for some other guys
> Who'll never do their own. (39)

Taken together with the shared lusting after Marie, whose photo is pinned up by Fred with other women, the text here suggests that male heterosexuality is a matter of a relationship with other men as much as with an individual woman. This is also made explicit in the first-person account of Al's response to Milly on his first return:

> I feel the thigh of her I love
> Snuggled against my bomb-explosive body
> (And fit to have the time-fuse set it off
> Without the ordinary wait for arming!) [. . .]
>   But other men
> Eat at my board; I cannot order them away. [. . .]
> They occupy my chair.
>   And other men
> Are here to purify my bed . . . they would defile it
> Were they of the flesh.
> Sit down to eat,
> My children, with the best condemned platoons

That ever met the enemy in rain and mortar spray.
Open your limbs, my love,
To half a battalion at a time.
I am forever They,
And They are I. (46)

The text here represents male sexual embodiment, in a conventional metaphor, as needing to be discharged; and with that need particularly urgent after a period of abstinence. The military metaphor also coincides with the masculinisation of Al's body in the military, discussed above. But particularly notable is the association of Al's sexuality with the dead soldiers of his platoon and battalion. Male heterosexual desire is represented here not as an individual and private matter but as gaining intensity and meaning through a collective imagining.

Al's imagined possession by the ghosts of his comrades during sex with his wife may be seen as a means of discharging and neutralising the homoerotic risks prevalent in the masculine environment of the army. Certainly, the communal dimension to male heterosexual desire can be related to Eve Sedgwick's notion of the homosocial continuum and is a theme considered further below. Despite the heterosexual imperative and the complementary hostility to homosexuality, which were a pronounced feature of contemporary American culture, there were writers willing to represent homosexuality in sympathetic ways, and the next section is focused on such examples.

Homosexuality and Queer Sensibility

This section begins by considering two novels, which, like Kinsey's *Sexual Behavior in the Human Male*, were published in the United States in 1948: *Other Voices, Other Rooms* and *The City and the Pillar*, written respectively by Truman Capote and Gore Vidal, who were both regarded as outstanding emergent writers in the post-war period. The section subsequently examines Patricia Highsmith's *The Talented Mr Ripley* (1955), which, it can be argued, reflected the extreme hostility to homosexuality that developed with McCarthyism.

Given that Kinsey, Vidal and Capote all published in the same year, there is no causal relationship here. However, the fact that they were published at the same time is indicative of Estelle Freedman's point that 'Social historians have recently identified the 1940s as a critical period in the formation of a public homosexual social world in the United States' (Freedman 1987: 103). She is referring to historians such as John D'Emilio and Allan Bérubé, who have described the liberating effects of the Second World War for young homosexuals. Yet the same period is notable for an extreme social and political antipathy towards homosexuals. Freedman's article 'Uncontrolled desires' contextualises this in relation to changing discourses around sexuality from the 1920s – discourses that began to register both heterosexual practices that were not aimed at reproduction and the possibility of female desire. Her focus is on legal attitudes to sexual psychopaths, and she argues in particular that 'At times it appeared that a major motive of the psychopath laws was to prevent the contagion of homosexuality from spreading from adults to youths' (1987: 103). Such attitudes were reinforced by American psychoanalytic theory, which pathologised homosexuality and connected gender and sexuality. The choice of a same-sex partner was linked with the inversion of gender characteristics, so male homosexuality signified a 'failure' of masculinity. In the 1940s Sandor Rado argued that the male–female pairing was the 'standard pattern', that homosexuality was an illness based on fear of women and that it could often be cured through psychoanalysis (see Bayer 1981: 28). Indeed, Hoover's worries about the normal and the abnormal, quoted above, may be read as primarily aimed at homosexuality.

The three texts considered here are resistant to these discourses and the discussion will focus particularly on how they engage with them in relation to the notion of a homosexual identity and the relationship between gender, sexuality and the body. In such a consideration, Judith Butler's discussion in *Bodies that Matter* is relevant. She warns that although the act of self-naming in the use of the term 'queer' is challenging as an act of disidentification with the regulatory discourses of sexuality and gender, such an act is not straightforwardly subversive.[21] The novels discussed here may 'queer' normative accounts of gender and sexuality, but they cannot entirely escape from them in a simple act of agency.

There are a number of strands in Kinsey's representation of homosexual behaviour. First, he questioned the common use of the term 'normal' in relation to humans. He argued that sexual behaviour varies significantly but that those variations may be mapped out on a continuous curve, which, he says, 'raises a question as to whether the terms "normal" and "abnormal" belong in a scientific vocabulary' (Kinsey et al. 1948: 199). He concluded that many aspects of human sexual behaviour which are labelled abnormal, or perversions, in textbooks, prove upon statistical examination to occur in as many as 30 or 60 or 75 per cent of certain populations (201). In particular, it was of course his statistical findings in relation to the incidence of homosexual orgasm that were so startling for many of his contemporaries. In summary, his statistics seemed to show that 'at least 37 per cent of the male population has some homosexual experience between the beginning of adolescence and old age' (623).

Kinsey also took issue with American psychoanalytic theory and its characterisation of homosexual males as a personality type. In the following quotation Kinsey is paraphrasing such attitudes, and points out that there is a close correlation here between psychological measures of masculinity and femininity and assumptions about sexuality.

> [Homosexual males] are rarely robust physically, are uncoordinated or delicate in their movements, or perhaps graceful enough but not strong or vigorous in their physical expression. Fine skin, high-pitched voices, obvious hand movements, a feminine carriage of the hips, and peculiarities of the walking gait are supposed accompaniments of a preference for a male as a sexual partner. It is commonly believed that the homosexual male is artistically sensitive, emotionally unbalanced, temperamental to the point of being unpredictable, difficult to get along with, and undependable in meeting specific obligations. (637)

What is particularly notable is the way in which these defining signifiers of homosexuality are inscribed on the body. These discourses thus construct and make visible the 'other' male – not heterosexual and not masculine – simultaneously, of course, also defining and constituting the supposed 'real' man.

Kinsey moves on to criticise such terminology, in particular the term 'inversion', which he sees from a biological perspective as describing situations where a female behaves actively and a male passively. Although Kinsey here adopts a conventional perspective on masculine and feminine types of behaviour, his principal point is to establish that 'inverted' human behaviour may be apparent in either heterosexual or homosexual relations:

> [. . .] there are a great many males who remain as masculine, and a great many females who remain as feminine, in their attitudes and approaches in homosexual relations, as the males or females who have nothing but heterosexual relations. (615)

In a radical move, Kinsey goes on to contradict the conventional belief in a homosexual identity (637).

> It would encourage clearer thinking [. . .] if persons were not characterized as heterosexual or homosexual, but as individuals who have had certain amounts of heterosexual experience and certain amounts of homosexual experience. (617)

Kinsey supports this point by challenging the view held by scientists and laymen that most people are either inherently heterosexual or homosexual and that there are insignificant numbers of bisexuals (636). Kinsey uses the evidence of his questionnaires to demolish such views. This shows that

> only 50% of the population is exclusively heterosexual throughout its adult life, and since only 4% of the population is exclusively homosexual throughout its life, it appears that nearly half (46%) of the population engages in both heterosexual and homosexual activities [. . .] (656)

On this basis, Kinsey argues that the pattern of sexual activity across individuals' lives is complex and that a simple division into heterosexual, bisexual and homosexual is inadequate. He advocates the adoption of a seven-point 'Heterosexual-homosexual rating scale' (638). Of course, the distinctions that Kinsey draws are perhaps more graphic than substantive, but his aim is primarily to deconstruct conventional notions of sexual identity and their linkage with gender characteristics.[22]

In a number of respects Gore Vidal's perspective parallels that of Kinsey. In an Afterword to a revised version of *The City and the Pillar* published in 1965, Vidal states: 'Despite current usage, [homosexual] is an adjective describing a sexual action, not a noun describing a recognizable type. All human beings are bisexual' (1965: 207). Kinsey and Vidal both resist the identification of unconventional sexual behaviour as neurotic. With typical satirical humour, Vidal dismisses such views: '[. . .] it was a conventional part of American folklore that homosexuality was a form of mental disease, confined for the most part to interior decorators and ballet dancers' (1965: 208).

Both Vidal and Kinsey argue that social mores and consequent anxieties about discovery are the likely causes of any neurosis. Here is Vidal, again writing in 1965: 'When legal and social pressures against homosexuality are particularly severe, homosexual-ists can become neurotic [. . .] Yet a man who enjoys sensual relations with his own sex is not, by definition, neurotic' (1965: 207). He claims that in writing the novel he wanted to examine the homosexual underworld and show the 'naturalness' of homosexual relations (207).[23]

The City and the Pillar is therefore clearly intended to challenge conventional views of male sexuality. The novel centres on Jim Willard and his developing self-awareness as a 'homosexual-ist'. It begins with his initial adolescent experience of sex with Bob, a fellow high school student. Bob leaves to become a merchant seaman. Jim idealises and romanticises their sexual encounter and the novel describes his quest for Bob in order to realise a fantasy of physical and psychic completeness. In the process of his quest, Jim has sexual encounters and relationships with other men. The extent and pattern of these coincide with Kinsey's findings.

It is through his description of Jim's experience that Vidal seeks to demonstrate the naturalness of homosexuality. For example, in his representation of Jim's longing for Bob, Vidal renders the male body as the object of scopophilic desire:

> [. . . Bob stood] flexing his long muscles and admiring himself in the green smooth water. Though slim, he was strongly built and Jim admired him with a strange different emotion that had no envy in it. [. . .] Jim undressed, watching Bob as he did, fixing his image in his mind. He [. . .] always memorized [Bob's] wide shoulders and the slim legs. (Vidal 1948: 39)[24]

What is key to the normalisation of Jim's sexuality is the association of desire and pleasure with a conventional masculinity, not only in his preferred partner but in himself. Unlike the stereotyped homosexual, both Bob and Jim are star sportsmen in their high school and Jim later develops a career as a tennis coach. Jim is represented as an ordinary, athletic young male, who continually passes as straight; to propose that such a man was gay was to contradict the conventional linkages between gender and sexuality and the body.[25] Jim embodies the apparently contradictory combination of gay sexuality and conventional masculine signifiers, and as a character, he has internalised this contradiction and it blocks his self-knowledge.

Vidal has identified a further theme in the novel which is alluded to in its title, taken from the Biblical myth of Lot and his wife, who is turned to a pillar of salt for her disobedience in looking back on the destruction of Sodom and Gomorrah. In his Afterword Vidal makes it clear that Jim Willard is analogous to Lot's wife, in that his fixation with a false idyll in his past is destructive. Vidal describes this as the 'romantic fallacy' (1965: 210). Yet the fate of Sodom and Gomorrah is regarded as a punishment for homosexual desire and is presented as an anathema on homosexuality.[26] On the one hand, therefore, the 'City' of the title invokes the biblical destruction of the cities of the plain, while the 'Pillar' draws attention to the fate of Lot's wife.[27] By normalising Jim's masculinity, Vidal attempts to neutralise the homophobic overtones of the 'city' and to shift the emphasis of the narrative to his anti-romantic theme – a critique applicable to heterosexuals as much as homosexuals. Indeed, one of the principal characters in the novel, Maria Verlaine, endlessly and fruitlessly pursues the perfect and complete heterosexual relationship.

The title also alerts us to the condition of Lot's nameless, silent and punished wife. The connection here is that the narrative's assertion of Jim's gay masculinity comes at some cost to women and effeminate homosexual men. Initially, Jim's alienation from effeminate men ('affected womanish creatures', 101) is a mark of his refusal of his sexuality, but the novel repeats such denigration in the voices of other characters. Early in the novel, while he regards himself as incomplete without Bob, Jim also imagines himself having sex with women. This leads to an episode where an opportunity for heterosexual sex arises. However, when the woman undresses,

> [. . . Jim] found himself comparing her with Bob. He thought of Bob; for the first time in months he thought of the cabin and the river and he knew it was not like this; it was not dirty like this; it was not unnatural like this. He didn't care now if he *was* different from other people. He hated this woman and her body. (81)

Again Vidal inverts normal expectations, rendering heterosexuality dirty and homosexual desire as pure. At the same time, though, the narrative views the women involved in this episode with some distaste.

Yet this masculinised homosexuality is still not proof against the name-calling of normative sexual expectations. As Jim rejects the possibility of a heterosexual encounter, his male companion, Collins, shouts: 'Let the queer go; don't mind him. I'll take care of you' (81). This naming interpellates Jim in the normative discourses of sexuality and gender. It opens him to the public shaming of a forbidden sexuality as it simultaneously emasculates him. So long, therefore, as the credibility of a gay masculinity is derived from an association with hegemonic heterosexual masculinity, that credibility is vulnerable to revocation.

The epithet 'queer' is repeated much more dramatically and disastrously at the end of the novel, after Jim has finally met up again with Bob. Bob's reaction to Jim's sexual advance is stunning: 'You're a queer, [. . .] you're nothing but a damned queer!' (306). Jim responds with fury and strangles Bob as they wrestle in an ironic and melodramatic repetition of their earlier love-making. This violence clearly symbolises the breaking in of reality to Jim's fantasy, but it is unfortunate in the light of Vidal's professed desire to represent the 'naturalness of homosexual relations'.[28]

Truman Capote's novel *Other Voices, Other Rooms*, like *The City and the Pillar*, is a narrative of self-discovery. It begins with Joel Harrison Knox, aged thirteen, travelling from New Orleans to Skully's Landing, located in the rural South. After his mother's death, he is seeking his father, unknown to him since infancy. The trajectory of the narrative draws Joel into the orbit of 'Cousin Randolph', and it is in the nature of their relationship that the novel provokes controversy and contradictory readings. Some initial hostility to the novel can be read as a predictable response to its homosexual theme; on the other hand, recent readings of the text have sought to position it as a positive and radical intervention in narratives of male homosexual becoming. For example, Brian Mitchell-Peters reads the text as 'queering the gothic' through a camp style (2000). Yet responses to the novel are not uniformly sympathetic. For example, in his survey, *Gay Fictions: Wilde to Stonewall*, Claude J. Summers dismisses the novel in a few pages, criticising it as a piece of writing. Crucially, he also attacks the novel for its representation of homosexuality:

> [. . .] its stereotypically negative depiction of homosexuality works against the narrative thread that culminates in Joel's recognition of his gayness. The result is a muddle: the novel's positive theme of progress toward self-knowledge is contradicted by its subliminal message that homosexuality is a retreat from real life into a ghostly death-in-life existence. (Summers 1990: 132)

Evidence for Summers's view might be taken from the conclusion of the novel, which is considered below. However, it is possible to argue that the novel does challenge heterosexual narratives of adult awakening and gives voice to a different experience of masculinity and male sexuality; yet, in certain respects, as we have seen with *The City and the Pillar*, it remains entangled in conventional perspectives on sexuality and gender.

It could be argued that if Vidal's project, like Kinsey's, was to normalise gay male sexuality, Truman Capote sought to queer and marginalise normality in *Other Voices, Other Rooms*. As does Highsmith in *The Talented Mr Ripley*, Capote uses the word 'queer' frequently in the novel and it is apparent that Capote intends a *double entendre* in using it. However, usage now must also take into account the recent emergence of 'queer theory' and it is from within such discourse that Brian Mitchell-Peters describes the novel as 'queering the gothic'. Capote's contemporary usage may suggest that the novel brings into public discourse in a lightly coded language a sexuality that is conventionally obscured and denigrated. Joel's developing self-awareness through the novel could then be read as a representation of a developing homosexual identity. On the other hand, to read the novel in relation to queer theory would be to suggest that in its narration of subjectivity, gender and sexuality, its focus is less on representing a 'gay' identity than on disrupting and resisting what Lynne Segal refers to as 'the central binary divisions of male/female, heterosexual/homosexual' (1994: 188).

In order to make strange, or queer, the landscape and characters of the novel, Capote draws on the literary tropes of American 'Southern Gothic'. As Joel nears Skully's Landing, the surroundings are described as '[. . .] lonesome country; and here in the swamplike hollows where tiger lilies bloom the size of a man's head, there are luminous green logs that shine under the dark marsh water like drowned corpses' (3). Skully's Landing itself is a mysterious destination that the locals will not discuss. Joel arrives there late at night, remembering the next morning 'stumbling through an odd chamber of a hall where the walls were alive with the tossing shadows of candleflames' (41).

In his book *Gothic*, Fred Botting explains that in Gothic fiction from the nineteenth century: '[. . .] the family became a place rendered threatening and uncanny by the haunting return of past transgressions and attendant guilt [to] an everyday world shrouded in strangeness' (1996: 11). For Joel, the family that he encounters at Skully's Landing as he seeks his identity seems dangerous and uncanny. The next day, looking up at the house from the garden, Joel sees 'the queer lady', whose 'sudden appearance seemed to throw a trance across the garden' (67). While the 'queer lady' certainly signifies strangeness, it also becomes evident that 'she' is Cousin Randolph.

In this queer ambience the reader is estranged from conventional representations of the body, identity and sexuality. This may be exemplified by reference to one recurrent metaphor, that of the mirror and reflection. Fred Botting has identified mirrors as a stock device of later Gothic; he argues that they marked the alienation of the human subject from the culture in which she or he was located (1996: 11). In *Other Voices, Other Rooms* this alienation is coupled with an indeterminacy of identity. So to return to Joel's vision of the 'queer lady' and her 'marshmallow features', these remind him of 'his own vaporish reflection in the wavy chamber mirror' (67). This reflection is described as

> floating on the watery-surfaced lookingglass; his formless reflected face was wide-lipped and one-eyed, as if it were a heat-softened wax effigy; the lips were a gauzy line, the eyes a glaring bubble. (64)

The words 'watery', 'wax', 'gauzy' and 'bubble' here create an image of softness and lack of definition. The image is one that emphasises Joel's identity as feminised, indeterminate and fluid. This condition is not merely a reflection of Joel's adolescence; a similar effect is described in relation to Randolph, and such descriptions build the narrative linkages between Joel and Randolph, in anticipation of the final scene of the novel. In these ephemeral reflections of Joel, the conventional signs of the masculine body are absent.

This absence is made apparent from the opening of the novel, where Joel is described through the eyes of Sam Radclif.

> [Radclif] had his notions of what a 'real' boy should look like and this kid somehow offended them. He was too pretty, too delicate and fair-skinned; each of his features was shaped with a sensitive accuracy, and a girlish tenderness softened his eyes, which were brown and very large. (4)

Randolph is similarly feminised in descriptions of his physical appearance:

> [his face] seemed composed now of nothing but circles: though not fat, it was round as a coin, smooth and hairless; two discs of rough pink coloured his cheeks, and his nose had a broken look, as if once punched by a strong angry fist; curly, very blond, his fine hair fell in childish yellow ringlets across his forehead, and his wide-set, womanly eyes were like sky blue marbles. (78–9)

In addition, Randolph's room is a feminine space with its 'faded gold and tarnished silk reflecting in ornate mirrors' (137). In these descriptions Randolph embodies and occupies femininity. In this association of implied homosexuality with the feminine, it might be argued that

Capote colludes with dominant representations of male homosexuality. However, Randolph, with his cross-dressing, is more complex and elusive. Joel observes as Randolph,

> posturing somewhat, studied himself in a mirror; while duplicating him in all essentials, the mirror [. . .] seemed to absorb his colour, to pare and change his features: the man in the mirror was not Randolph, but whatever personality imagination desired him to resemble [. . .] (139)

Here identity is not simply reflected back and fixed in bodily appearance, but open to reconstruction and change in the play of the imagination.[29] Randolph asks, 'whatever became of me?' (136). Insofar as this question relates to his sexual identity, which the novel leaves open, Randolph might be seen as exemplary of the openness and fluidity of queer theories of identity.[30]

In varying ways then Kinsey, Vidal and Capote seek to challenge the dominant understandings of homosexuality. Indeed, they can be seen as representing the radical opportunities produced in the few years between the opening up of new freedoms for gay men and women in World War II and the witch hunt against homosexuals and communists instigated by McCarthy in 1950. However, these texts were not free from the antagonism intrinsic to contemporary discourses. Although Kinsey proceeded to produce a volume on women's sexuality in 1953, as noted above, the controversies surrounding his work led to the removal of the most of his funding by the Rockefeller Foundation in 1954. The anxiety about men's susceptibility to homosexual acts may be seen in critical responses to Vidal's and Capote's novels. For example, John Aldridge, writing in 1951, is negative about both the novels. He criticises *The City and the Pillar* as 'journalistic' and suggests that Vidal contrives the plot 'to make a sociological point': 'The characters are nothing more than allegorical shells designed to illustrate the plight of the sexually abnormal in modern society' (Aldridge 1951: 177). Aldridge ostensibly makes an aesthetic judgement about *Other Voices, Other Rooms*: Capote's achievement is of 'the skilled use of metaphor rather than symbol' and 'such an achievement is necessarily of lesser scope than, for instance, Conrad's in *Victory*' (216). He goes on to argue that 'The characters and the devices produce a world, [but] they do not produce a world of external significance' (218). He is arguing that Joel's development is of no universal significance and it seems that this is because for Joel, 'the door leading to the real world, to manhood and the love of woman is closed forever'. Joel is 'changed from a living thing with a free existence in a real world into a dead prisoner in an unreal world' (206).

Furthermore, despite the radical impulses of Gore Vidal and Truman Capote, their novels may be seen to contain traces of the oppressive discourses that they challenged. The main narrative of *The City and the Pillar* is enclosed within a scene set in a New York bar. Jim at both the beginning and end of the novel is drinking himself to oblivion after his final encounter with Bob – a narrative circularity that suggests the 'hopelessness for the invert' for which Donald Webster Cory criticised *The City and the Pillar* in 1951 in his ground-breaking and polemical book *The Homosexual in America* (Cory 1951: 94).

The final scene of *Other Voices, Other Rooms* finds Joel again in the garden looking up at Randolph's window, where 'a face trembled like a white beautiful moth, smiled. She beckoned to him, shining and silver, and he knew he must go' (231). This has been read as Joel's acceptance of his homosexuality. However, it is also significant that this reading involves Joel's absorption into the uncanny family space, shut away from the world. In this the novel dramatises the continuing exclusion of gay men and women from public visibility.[31] To conclude, while the texts rehearse the pleasures of sexuality and agency for gay men, they also exemplify the representational limits of homosexuality in 1948. This analysis of Vidal's and Capote's novels therefore reveals the dominance of models of gender and sexuality that privilege heterosexuality as one of the key attributes of masculinity.

If the enlarged experiences of gay men and women fostered by the conditions of war might have generated a more optimistic frame of mind, by the early 1950s negative psychiatric attitudes to homosexuality were so deeply intertwined with McCarthyism that public discourse about homosexuality was extremely hostile (see Introduction, page 13; Corber 1993: 8). It was in this environment that Patricia Highsmith wrote and published *The Talented Mr Ripley*, and the novel cannot be considered outside such a context. Indeed, Andrew Wilson's biography of Highsmith shows how her reading and experience reflected contemporary preoccupations with sexuality, and she underwent Freudian psychoanalysis in the hope that she might learn to enjoy sex with a man. The psychological complexity of the character of the protagonist, Tom Ripley, can be seen in Patricia Highsmith's own assessment:

> [. . . H]e could be called psychotic . . . a bit sick in certain areas. But I would not call him insane because his actions are rational . . . He's not so psychopathic that he has to kill someone. I consider him a rather civilized person who kills when he absolutely has to. He kills reluctantly. [. . .] He's rather shy of [his sexual nature], not very strong emotions and a little bit homosexual I would say, not that he has ever done anything about that. (quoted in Wilson 2010: 190–1)[32]

Ripley's relationship to his creator can be seen in some interpretations of the novel. For example, Edward A. Shannon has suggested that Ripley might be seen as a transgender *femme fatale*, and Slavoj Žižek has referred to Ripley as a 'male lesbian' (Shannon 2004; Žižek n.d.). For Shannon, Ripley's 'desire for objects transcends simple avarice, taking the form of a fetishism that defines his very sense of self' (2004: 24). In *Queer Gothic* George Heggarty argues that Ripley is not able to acknowledge his desire for Greenleaf, instead transferring it into an intense identification with Greenleaf (Heggarty 2006). It is Heggarty's queer reading of *The Talented Mr Ripley* that will be taken up here and developed.

Key issues about Tom Ripley's masculinity centre on gender and sexuality and his past is informed by Freudian ideas about the way family relationships might foster homosexuality. Ripley's parents died when he was very young and he was brought up by his dominating and cruel aunt, who claims that both he and his father were sissies (Highsmith [1955] 1999: 34). Yet, as Highsmith herself makes clear, Ripley is not sexually active despite being a 'little bit homosexual'. Despite this, questions of sexuality are at the front of Ripley's mind from the very beginning of the novel, when he is approached by Dickie Greenleaf's father as a supposed friend of Greenleaf, and wonders whether Greenleaf's father could be a 'pervert' (2). Then in Italy Ripley puts on a camp performance for Dickie Greenleaf that he calls 'Lady Assburden on the New York subway'. On a number of occasions Ripley is confronted with the accusation that he is 'queer'. The first of these occurs after Ripley – in a fit of jealousy after seeing Greenleaf kissing Marge Sherwood – has thrown some of Greenleaf's painting equipment out of the window and dressed himself in Greenleaf's clothes. As he is posing in front of the mirror noting how much like Greenleaf he looks, Greenleaf discovers him, accusing him of being crazy. Greenleaf goes on to maintain that he is not 'queer', but that Marge Sherwood thinks that Ripley is. Ripley's reaction is that 'Nobody had ever said it outright to him, not in this way' (70) and then asserts to Greenleaf, 'I'm not queer either.' The interchange prompts Ripley to cast his mind back to New York and people he knew there who were queer. He had turned down sexual invitations and regards himself as 'one of the most innocent and clean-minded people' (71). He remembers one of his lines in New York: 'I can't make up my mind whether I like men or women. So I'm thinking of giving them *both* up' (71).

Ripley's masculine identity is therefore compromised in conventional terms as he is not perceived as heterosexual, but rather as 'queer', with its implication of homosexuality. However, Ripley is not sexually active and this behaviour further marks him as 'queer' in the sense of being strange. He regards himself as 'innocent', but it is others' perception of his queerness that is a crucial element of his motivation in the two murders. Greenleaf cools towards Ripley after the dressing-up incident, but they go to Cannes and San Remo together. Ripley has an insight into his relationships – that he could never know people, and that now, 'Dickie has been snatched away from him. They were not friends' (78). In Cannes Ripley intently watches a group of acrobats in yellow g-strings on the beach. Greenleaf's comment – 'Ten thousand saw I at a glance' (a reference to Wordsworth's 'Daffodils') – causes a 'sharp thrust of shame' in Ripley and he remembers the accusations of Marge and his aunt. It is this further exposure to shame that finally induces Ripley to think seriously about killing Greenleaf. Ripley's violent action echoes Jim's attack on Bob in *The City and the Pillar*, but although both are shamed by other characters, Ripley's considered murder of Greenleaf in a small motorboat in San Remo bay differs from Jim's spontaneous assault on Bob.

> Tom swung a left-handed blow with the oar against the side of Dickie's head. The edge of the oar cut a dull gash that filled with a line of blood as Tom watched. [. . .] Dickie gave a groaning roar of protest that frightened Tom with its loudness and its strength. Tom hit him in the side of the neck, three times, chopping strokes with the edge of the oar, as if the edge of the oar were an axe and Dickie's neck a tree. [. . .] Tom got a bayonet grip on the oar and plunged its handle into Dickie's side. Then the prostrate body relaxed, limp and still. (91)

The description of the violence is gruesomely similar to the language of Thompson's novel *The Killer Inside Me* (see Chapter 2), and includes sexualised imagery of penetration. The brutal violence of the murder and its sexual overtones reflect Ripley's angry response to his association with queerness.

Violence and sexuality are connected in Thompson's, Vidal's and Highsmith's novels but with markedly different connotations. In Vidal's novel Jim's angry violence marks the closures of hegemonic masculinity, which exclude gay men. Lou Ford's murders of women can be seen as a dysfunctional assertion of a heterosexual masculine identity. Ripley's murder of Greenleaf is a repudiation, internally and outwardly, of a queer identity. Moreover, the murder enables him to cast off his own identity through his impersonation of Greenleaf. His self-disgust is relieved after he has taken on Greenleaf's identity; he leaves San Remo on a sleeper train, and as he settles into the 'luxury' of the sheets he feels 'happy, content, and utterly confident as he had never been before in his life' (97).

After murdering Greenleaf and taking on his identity, Ripley hides himself away in Rome. Freddie Miles comes looking for Greenleaf, and tracks down Ripley in his apartment. Ripley is unprepared and wearing Greenleaf's clothes and jewellery, which makes Miles suspicious. Ripley's anxiety about queerness resurfaces and he fears that Miles is 'the kind of ox who would beat up somebody he thought was a pansy, especially if the conditions were as propitious as these' (123). At a practical level Ripley kills Miles because he feels his fraud is about to be exposed, but as he waits to dispose of Miles's corpse, he considers how Miles had sneered at Greenleaf because he suspected him of sexual deviation, and concludes that Miles was a victim of his 'own dirty mind' (127). Moreover, Ripley reflects on how Miles had found the apartment through a young Italian man. He shamefully imagines how a 'dark, panting young face' must have followed him home, and he walks faster, 'as if he were fleeing a sick, passionate pursuer' (131). Shame and anger prompted by challenges to his sexuality are therefore key factors in impelling Ripley to murder Miles. He is also frustrated by such challenges because he is 'innocent' – as he asks Miles's corpse, 'Where was the sex?' (127). Ripley's perception of his own innocence is a signifier of his internal denial.

Later, when Greenleaf comes under suspicion of the murder of Freddie Miles, Ripley has to revert to himself: 'He hated going back to himself as he would have hated putting on a shabby suit of clothes, a grease-spotted, unpressed suit of clothes that had not been very good when it was new' (164). The attractions of being Greenleaf are about the wealth and possessions Ripley could thus obtain, but it is also about being able to lose his own identity, and his sense of grubbiness, which is a mark of people's perception of him as 'queer'. His repudiation of his self can be seen as a response to the cultural context in which to be a homosexual was to be a pervert and un-American. George Heggarty points out that once Ripley moves reluctantly back into his own identity he is in fact able to reinvent himself, and he has learned that emotions can be faked. 'If you wanted to be cheerful, or melancholic, or wistful, or thoughtful, or courteous, you simply had to *act* those things with every gesture' (165). Heggarty argues that in repudiating desire and actual emotion, Ripley has acquiesced to the demands made of the queer in the 1950s (2006: 177).

Ripley's actions fit with the view that masculine behaviour turns to aggression to exert control. Ripley's murders of both Greenleaf and Miles are angry but futile attempts to control perceptions of him as 'queer'. His need to control such perceptions, and, indeed, to repress his queerness arises from the extremely hostile environment for homosexuals in the 1950s. Yet the paradox of the murders and the unforeseeable consequences of his actions are that Ripley is liberated by this violence. Not only is he free to pursue his ambitions for travel, but in forging Greenleaf's will he has acquired a large inheritance with which to satisfy his expensive tastes. In this Ripley evades the punishment that might be the expected consequence of both his violence and his queerness.

Military Masculinity and Sexuality

The previous chapter considered the representation of masculinity in novels about the Second World War. The war and military life was inevitably a significant literary theme in the immediate post-war period, and I return now to novels set in a military environment to discuss their treatment of masculinity and sexuality. Not surprisingly, perhaps, given the inevitable foregrounding of conventional masculine traits in the military, such novels demonstrate the importance of heterosexual identity to contemporary military masculinity. Such an identity necessarily involves an emphatic repudiation of homosexual activities, but the homosociality of military life complicates the aspiration for such a simple divide. I will begin by returning to Mailer's *The Naked and the Dead*.

Given that *The Naked and the Dead* focuses on a military engagement between American and Japanese forces taking place on a Pacific island – Anopopei – during the Second World War, it is perhaps paradoxical that the novel is infused with sexuality. This presence is layered in the narrative, embedded in the interactions and discussions between the main characters; the representation of their memories by the narrator; and in the retrospective 'Time Machine' passages. These various representations of sexuality are mediated in the dramatic present of the novel, which is the masculine environment of the army at war. So, however vivid the recollections of the men's sexual activities may be, as memory erupts in the present, there are no women characters who speak for themselves. The sexual and marital relationships of the male characters are therefore constructed within the homosocial circumstances of the situation on Anopopei and may be seen primarily in relation to the construction of masculine identities within those circumstances. In addition to these uniformly heterosexual experiences, the narrative includes implicit and explicit homoeroticism, and there is frequent sexualisation of the landscape.

Although the variety of heterosexual experiences filtered through the different characters of the men appears to provide a complex representation of sexual relationships, in fact the novel repeats some predictable attitudes towards female sexuality. In the first place there is the constant repetition of a narrative that involves young men, usually driven by unfulfilled desire, falling into a romantic trap set by women. For example, two members of the platoon, Wyman and Red Valsen, an older man who has struggled through the Depression and always moved on from relationships to avoid commitment, are talking after a batch of mail has reached the island. Wyman has not received a letter from his girlfriend since being posted overseas. The narrative is focalised through Red, who has sympathetic impulses but finds that 'Wyman's emotion was embarrassing him' (Mailer [1948] 1993: 260). However, he prompts Wyman to describe how he met his girlfriend. He anticipates Wyman's description and then thinks: 'It happens to all the fuggin kids [...] and they all think it's something special' (261). Despite Wyman's assertion that 'It was really something special' (262), Red cynically imagines Wyman's possible future with this girl or another – a marriage that would contain 'arguments, the worries over money, the grinding extinction of their youth' (262).

Red's understanding of Wyman's sense of emotional contact comes from his past and a summer evening conversation with his girl, Agnes – an evening that 'had had a beauty which he had never felt in exactly the same way again' (261). In the 'Time Machine' section describing Red's past, this scene and the rejection of a possible future with Agnes has already been described in relation to his father's death in a mining accident and his determination that 'A man's gotta get out where he don't owe nobody nothing' (228). Later, Red settles into another relationship with Lois, but when her implied offer of marriage coincides with America's entry into the war, he signs up. His attitude is that 'if you stop and quit moving you die' (239).

This brief interaction between Red and Wyman is cast as one between youth and experience, if not quite father and son. Red is cynical about long-term relationships with women but gives Wyman relatively gentle advice: 'There's lots of women, kid' (260); 'Naw, she didn't lie, but people change, you know' (262). The underlying assumption here is that there is a fundamental contradiction between masculine identity and permitting or expressing emotion, which needs to be recognised as sentimentality. Clearly, such an emotional connection invokes a dependency that subverts individual masculinity – proper heterosexual masculinity requires one to be able to keep moving on – there is always another woman.

There is another dimension to this exchange, which is Red's embarrassment at Wyman's emotion. This may be read in the light of Eve Sedgwick's discussion of the 'homosocial continuum' and erotic 'triangles' in *Between Men*. Sedgwick argues that a continuum between 'men-loving-men' and 'men-promoting-the-interests-of-men' (1985: 3) is impossible in Western culture, where patriarchal power structures depend on the banishment of homosexuality. The triangle here is between Red, Wyman and 'Woman' as construed in contemporary American culture. Red and Wyman are not heterosexual rivals in a specific way; indeed, in the context of their wartime situation they might be thought of as having an interest in promoting each other's well-being. On the one hand, emotional dependency on a woman is regarded as 'death' to one's masculinity; on the other, an emotional connection with another man is 'embarrassing'. The prohibition on homosexuality in the construction of normative masculine identity, which is a particularly powerful discourse in the military, thus blocks even a minimal emotional relationship between these soldiers.

The representation of sexuality in the novel is almost without exception heterosexual. The exception is General Cummings, whom Hearn feels has sexual desire for him: 'He had an intuition that if he remained motionless long enough the General would slowly extend his arm, touch his knee perhaps' (188). The significance of this lies in Mailer's representation of Cummings as fascistic and representative of an extreme right-wing thread in American culture. As mentioned in Chapter 2 (95n), it seems that the suggestion that Cummings might have homosexual desire is for Mailer an incontrovertible signifier of his character flaws. Cummings, however, is married, and the novel describes the early part of his marriage as marked by intense sexual activity. Cummings's heterosexuality is troubling in its sadistic overtones.

> Their love-making is fantastic for a time:
> He must subdue her, absorb her, rip her apart and consume her.
> [...]
> I'll take you apart, I'll eat you, oh, I'll make you mine, I'll make you mine, you bitch. (419)

Although Margaret, his wife, is described as initially responding to this, eventually she comes to see that 'he is alone, that he fights out battles with himself upon her body' (419). The trajectory of Cummings's marriage is largely consistent with the marriages of other men represented in the novel, and in the moments before Hearn's intuition about Cummings, the general has claimed that it is in women's 'nature' to cheat, and he describes his wife as a 'bitch'. In the following brief section (one of a number identified as a 'Chorus'), this one on the topic of 'Women', there is a discussion about whether women are inherently unfaithful. Brown argues most vociferously that there is no woman 'you can trust. They all cheat on you' (191). He maintains that women like sex 'just as much as men do, and it's a helluva sight easier for them to get it' (191).

There are a number of points to be drawn from this. There is a significant ambiguity about whether Cummings's initial fantastic love-making is his perception or that of the omniscient narrator. Given that the novel repeatedly represents initial sex in marriage as passionate, followed by a decline and the emergence of a distance between the couple, then it seems that the narrative is endorsing this sex as 'fantastic'. If this is so, then 'fantastic' heterosexual love-making is figured as a form of masculine narcissism. The further implication of the attitude of the soldiers is that while a responsive female sexuality is rewarding for men, once women are sexualised they are no longer controllable by men. The constant stories about sexual encounters recounted by the men in the novel testify to the importance of their sexual performance to their manhood. At the same time, the equally constant denigration of women is evidence of male sexuality as problematical. Male sexual performance needs constantly to be retold for endorsement in a homosocial environment. If male heterosexuality is the lonely act that helps establish masculine identity as suggested by the description of Cummings, then there is a further implication of the General's trajectory. Despite an intense heterosexual performance, these may mask same-sex desires – an echo of contemporary narratives about all men's potential for homosexuality that was an element of the pervasive anxieties about masculinity.

Elements of such attitudes were reported by the sociologist Henry Elkin, writing in 1946 on 'Aggressive and erotic tendencies in army life', an article informed by psychoanalytic theory. Elkin emphasises the importance of the 'values associated with the ideal of virility' in 'molding the soldier's image of himself' (1946: 410). He argues that the use of profanity is also associated with masculinity, and perhaps the most striking feature of army life: '[. . . P]rofanity most perfectly suggests that the user is capable of asserting his will, using his fists, drinking inordinate quantities of alcohol, taking women in contemptuous, domineering stride.' Elkin discusses the most commonly used 'profane term' (presumably 'fuck') as the one that 'most clearly expresses this swaggering masculinity and revengeful, contemptuous (and defensive) attitude towards women'. He argues that the term renders the sexual act '"dirty" and animalistic', suggesting that while such associations do not reflect on men, 'they ineradicably contaminate and degrade the human female' (411). Crucially, Elkin reports a fundamental misogyny at work in these attitudes: '[. . .] the G.I. did not like or desire women other than as means of gratifying his self-respect and his primitive sexual desire. He commonly referred to women by the profane term for vagina and treated them all, even when there could be no ground for confusion with a degree of bluntness and indiscrimination [. . .]' (413).

Related to this are the GI's homosocial interactions. Elkin focuses on the widespread use of the term 'ass', giving such examples as 'to tangle assholes' (argue or fight) and 'asshole buddies' (close friends). He relates such expressions to practices as goosing and 'wearing of pants too tight for comfort' and argues that this represents 'a vital concern with the only major erogenous portion of the human anatomy that does not distinguish male from female'. He argues that the term ass is most suitable 'for expressing asocial and indeterminate erotic tendencies in a socially approved form' (412). These observations are juxtaposed with Elkin's comment that there is a combination of a pervasive joking about homosexuality with an 'apparent total lack of awareness of homosexual attitudes and inclinations, such as were extremely widespread in a latent, and not uncommon in a practiced, but verbally unadmitted, state.' He suggests that these attitudes imply 'strong tendencies and equally strong repressions', arguing that such homoerotic tendencies were managed through the conventions of the pin-up, which minimised the feminine and presented the woman's body as suggestive of 'boyishness and activity', rather than representing a female sexuality of 'all-absorbing intensity and voluptuousness' (412).

Given this analysis, it is perhaps not surprising that *The Naked and the Dead* is suffused with misogyny and evinces little tenderness amongst the men for their wives or girlfriends, although fear of death or wounding produces sentimentality, and there is some feeling expressed for their children. One moment of tenderness in the novel comes after Wilson has been wounded.[33]

> Brown continued to massage Wilson's forehead. In the darkness, Wilson's face seemed connected to him, an extension of his fingers. [. . .] He flinched every time he heard an unexpected sound. But it was more than fear; he was keyed very high, and every quiver, every painful gesture of Wilson's body travelled intimately through Brown's fingers, through his arms, deep into his mind and heart. Without realising it, he winced when Wilson winced. [. . .]
>
> [. . .] Wilson was not wholly real to him at this moment. He existed in this brief duration of Brown's mood as the body, the flesh of Brown's longings. He was Brown's child, but he was also a concretion of all Brown's miseries and disappointments. For a few minutes he was more vital to Brown than any other man or woman had ever been. (536–7)

In this moment, the narrative seems to break through the taboos surrounding the homosocial continuum, not in authorising sexual engagement between the two men, but in expressing an intimacy that would normally be disavowed. In part this is the consequence of a certain romanticisation of the closeness of men *in extremis* in the then exclusively male world of war. In this idealisation, the passage reinforces the priority of male relationships within patriarchal social structures. However, within such relationships it may sometimes be possible to express the same kinds of emotional gestures that are constructed as feminine without prejudicing one's masculinity.

Indeed, in Prudencio de Pereda's episodic novel *All the Girls We Loved*, published in 1948, the possibility of homosexual love between soldiers is offered as both a possibility and as beyond the pale for the military authorities.[34] Two young soldiers on the front line in the First World War are described as 'good-looking cleancut, sensitive kids – and they always hung out together' (1948: 54). These young men were discovered having sex and instead of being court-martialled were told they should walk together towards the enemy lines to '[a]void the disgrace'. When the first soldier is shot he falls to the ground and the other grabs his hand. They continue holding hands as the second soldier faces the rest of the American soldiers in the trench, staring 'with a look of contempt' (54).

John Horne Burns, *The Gallery*

In *The Gallery* (1947), John Horne Burns idealises female sexuality but additionally valorises the notion of a deep emotional connection between lovers – a connection that encompasses homosexuality as well as heterosexuality. *The Gallery* was well received when it was published, described by John Aldridge as 'a fine book which almost everybody read' (1951: 133), with Burns himself identified by Malcolm Cowley as one of the significant young novelists of the war (1954: 25). The novel has numerous characters and an episodic structure, at the heart of which is the Galleria Umberto Primo in Naples (the 'Gallery' of the book's title). The novel is held together by a narrator called 'John', who provides omniscient narration of the various characters' stories. These are interspersed with his first-person accounts of his experiences in the war and the army as well as observations on humanity, titled 'Promenades'. Burns's representation of sexuality is played against a sense of despair in 1944, when the novel is set. For example, in one of the Promenades John describes himself in Algiers 'in a glacial fever of horror and loneliness' (Burns [1947] 2004: 158). Similarly, in a later Promenade in Naples, he declares that his 'heart finally broke' there over the disjuncture between the ideal of 'America' and the reality of American behaviour (259ff). He describes how 'being at war with the Italians was taken as a license for Americans to defecate all over them' and he enumerates the obnoxious face of American masculinity – 'old ladies pushed off the sidewalks by drunken GIs and officers'; propositions to Italian girls 'we wouldn't have made to a streetwalker back home'; 'American MPs beating the driver of a horse and wagon because they were obstructing traffic on Via Roma' (262). A mess sergeant's description of the 'Eyties' is quoted: '[they] ain't human beins. They're just Gooks that's all' (262). The novel is then generally critical of American values and culture.[35]

This critique extends to American men's sexual performance. For example, an Italian woman says that Americans 'made the act of love as sanitary as brushing their teeth or gargling with mouthwash' (284). This criticism is generalised by John in an analysis of American sexual relations. He argues that 'love in America is often divided into the classifications of Having Sex and Getting Married' (303). 'Having Sex' means that 'the two bodies involved never really knew each one another. They just rolled and arose strangers, each loathing the other' (303–4). John remembers double dates in America where there was a 'negation of intimacy and privacy' and American men are described as 'graceless bulls' (304, 305).

In Naples, however, there is an eroticisation of sex in which John discovers the difference between making love and 'Having Sex'; he says, 'There's none of the blind preoccupation with my own body and its satisfaction. The first aim is to please my love. And I end by being pleased too' (306). This pleasure is expressed through a sensual empathy:

> I put my hand out to encounter another hand, already reaching for mine. My mouth went out exploring, only to meet another mouth working toward mine in the darkness. In that kiss I felt as though my tongue had at last articulated a word I'd been striving to pronounce all my life long. (306)

This encounter becomes a 'rising intensity of pain and delight. And for one instant we were in a place where there was no difference between us. We melted into all those who've ever loved and lived at all' (306). This sort of description serves as a critique of American male sexuality with its singular focus on copulation. It involves a mutual delight in bodily pleasures and implies an alternative expression of masculinity. In this, *The Gallery* resonates with Herbert Marcuse's radical imaginings of sexuality and eroticism.

However, there are limitations to Burns's sexual radicalism. The representation of sexuality in *The Gallery* involves a projection of sexuality onto the female Other – both American and Neapolitan women. One example is Louella, an American officer and Red Cross volunteer, portrayed as a narcissistic and snobbish alcoholic, who despite having 'trained in psychiatry in college' (35) has no self-awareness and is in denial about her own sexuality while critical of others'. She considers Italian men as 'too effeminate', 'lacking in spunk' and not 'to be trusted sexually' (32–3). Louella is similarly dismissive of American GIs, whom she regards as 'vulgar' (26), a view confirmed when she is nearly run over by a jeep bearing the title 'Wet Dream' (31). Louella confines her ministrations to American pilots, whom she regards as 'the sort of towheaded fellows who are the backbone of American manhood. Thinking was a pussy disease of modern life, but the fliers of the United States Air Force hadn't caught the contagion' (42). Her attitude to sex is in marked contrast to the dominant erotic voice of the novel. For example, whereas John in the Promenades celebrates the Italian language, for Louella it 'made her think of gooey kisses pressed by some greaser on the neck of his sweating mistress' (32). Moreover, she isn't 'at home in the arcana of love; she preferred the way American men had of laying their cards on the table. They got drunk and threw themselves all over you, and you could either say yes or no' (33). Louella is therefore emotionally cold and lacking in erotic energy. This perception of American women is generalised through the eyes of 'Momma', an Italian running a bar in the Galleria Umberto Primo. This bar is frequented by gay men, but there is one American woman, Rhoda, who comes regularly and confirms Momma's theory that romantic love is on the wane in America because American girls must be 'mighty emancipated and intellectual' since Rhoda was so 'cool and unfeminine' (136).

This generalisation about American women is repeated by John, the narrator, who maintains that the experience of love-making in Naples brings American men to look upon 'Having Sex, this ejaculation without tenderness, as the orgasm of a frigidaire' (303). The metaphor of the refrigerator is strikingly gendered – more so perhaps when one considers that before electrically powered refrigerators, Americans used 'ice boxes' to keep food cool and that this label carried over to fridges. Moreover, as I showed above, female sexual 'frigidity' was a dominant term in American psychoanalytical theory. In other words, although there is criticism of American male sexuality, this resonant phrase projects American sexual dysfunction onto American women. In contrast with its representation of American women, the novel idealises Italians and Naples as the possessors of a feminine and maternal life force – Naples is described as 'a short girl with dark eyes and rich skin and body hair. Motherhood. Huge and inscrutable as the feminine Idea' (206). The American men are taught about making love by the Italian women:

> I caught on fast, with the lessons she gimme [the corporal said]. These babes know something . . . She taught me to kiss slow, to take my time. I useta close my eyes an just jab, hoping for the best . . . Rosetta kisses sleepy like. Sometimes she puts her tongue in my ear. Or just brushes her lips along my throat. Gee . . . (305)

This aspect of the novel is open to different readings. Certainly, in such descriptions the Italian woman is granted a sexual agency, while the American male exhibits a passivity that is distant from the penetrative urgency expected of heterosexual masculinity. Yet in the sexuality, eroticism and fecundity ascribed to the language, culture and women of Naples, there is an idealisation of an exotic Other. This focus inexorably shifts attention away from the sexuality of the American male, rendering it less open to discursive scrutiny. Moreover, Burns's idealisation of Italian women and the nature of sexual relations tends to obscure the extent to which such relationships in Naples in 1944 were also a matter of economic exchange and material needs.

However, there are further layers to *The Gallery*. Recent approaches to identity problematise theories of identity.[36] The complexity of the relationship between Self and Other may be seen in Homi Bhabha's psychoanalytic approach to post-colonial exchange. Bart Moore-Gilbert in *Postcolonial Theory* summarises Bhabha's approach:

> For Bhabha the relationship between colonizer and colonized is more complex and nuanced – and politically fraught – than Fanon and Said imply, principally because the circulation of contradictory patterns of psychic affect in colonial relations (desire for, as well as fear of the Other, for example) undermines their assumption that the identities and positionings of colonizer and colonized exist in stable and unitary terms which are also absolutely distinct from, and necessarily in conflict with, each other. (1997: 116)

Although Burns's novel represents aspects of conservative discourses about sexuality in its representation of female characters, the heterosexual relationships that are articulated in *The Gallery* may be seen in relationship to the notions of Self and Other theorised by Bhabha. In other words, it is possible to see the relationships between the GIs and the Neapolitan women as potentially involving exchange and mutuality as well as exploitation.

Furthermore, while the novel overtly narrates heterosexual encounters, it is notable that in fact descriptions such as those quoted, in which John describes the pleasures of 'making love', are carefully written so as not to specify the sex of John's lover. In Burns's case this was likely to be another man and is indicative of a radical intention to normalise homosexual acts within the erotic narrative of the novel. As I have shown, contemporary discourses pathologised homosexuality and assumed effeminacy as characteristic of gay men, which created difficulties in representing homosexuality as compatible with a positive masculine identity. Homosexual men were thus aligned with the feminine Other, presenting gay authors with considerable difficulties in negotiating such notions of gender and sexuality. The ambition of *The Gallery* to articulate a radical representation of gender and sexuality may perhaps be reflected in its innovative formal structure, which is described by Paul Fussell as follows: 'The result is a plotless book less like a novel than a memoir, or even a travel book, or a collection of sketches illustrating a double theme' (2004: ix). The novel may then be considered as attempting to develop a narrative that challenges and reworks contemporary expectations of gender and sexual identity, of self and other, but without being able to establish a consistent alternative vision.

Male sexuality in the period was highly contested. However, across the spectrum of views, there is a consistent expectation of male sexual performance, in that the virile heterosexual body was seen as an inalienable constituent of masculine identity, indeed of what might be regarded in Connell's terms as hegemonic masculinity of this period. Masculine heterosexual identity can be seen to be defined in relation to a female 'Other', which is consistent with Connell's approach. Yet the narratives do not produce a unified male subject, more the 'fragmented and fractured' subject referred to by Stuart Hall (2000: 17). In fact, the apparently hegemonic heterosexual male identity is infused with contradiction – it should be both rampant and contained. In the novels the projection of sexuality onto the female Other – who may be frigid, or a predator, or idealised – serves less to constitute a secure masculine sexual identity, and more to deflect scrutiny of this identity and its contradictions.

The novels therefore reflect dispute over what constituted a legitimate expression of masculine virility. Conservative writers sought to contain male sexuality within marriage, whereas Kinsey's behaviourism did not make equivalent moral judgements. Kinsey's account in particular opened up a significant public space in which male homosexuality was extensively discussed. That this coincided with changing patterns of behaviour may be seen in the novels by Gore Vidal and Truman Capote, which sought to give voice to homosexual experience, although their fiction and Highsmith's Ripley novel also marked the exclusion of a male gay identity from the discourses of hegemonic masculinity. While Vidal and Capote overtly introduced homosexuality into their fiction, the problem of containing male sexuality within a simple binary structure of heterosexuality and homosexuality is shown in other novels where male sexuality continually bursts the boundaries of the ideal model of the heterosexual marriage partnership. Repeatedly in the novels, male sexuality is given meaning through the imaginative sharing of experience, and indeed of women, within a homosocial network. Where this homosocial contact shades into relationships of intimacy and caring, gender identities are shown to be open to revision. In Burns's novel it is the projection of sexuality onto an exoticised female Other which creates a space for the critique of the 'Having sex' of American male masculinity, and for a homosexual male identity to be represented. These novels suggest therefore that there is less a clearly established and available hegemonic masculinity, but that contestation and instability is intrinsic to the representation of masculinity in this period. Yet, despite such instability, men retained their dominance in the networks of gender relations. In terms of sexuality, it can be argued that this was because contemporary discourses successfully contained the contradictions, despite some fraying at the edges.

Notes

1. See Robert J. Corber, *Homosexuality in Cold War America*, 1997.
2. Bergler described himself as a 'psychiatric' author in the Preface to *Kinsey's Myth of Female Sexuality* (vii). He estimated that between 70 and 80 per cent of all women were frigid (quoted in Mari Jo Buhle 1998: 214).
3. Kinsey's methodology and therefore his statistical analysis were challenged following publication of *Sexual Behavior in the Human Male*. The criticisms were twofold: first that Kinsey's samples were not random, as was required by the then emerging techniques of polling. Kinsey answered this by arguing that investigations into sexual behaviour could never assemble a random sample, since so many individuals would refuse. He believed that by carrying out very large numbers of interviews and by taking 100 per cent samples from groups, for example all members of a society, his findings were robust. The second criticism was that his interviewees were not taken from a sufficiently wide sample of the American population. Kinsey admitted to elements of this point in agreeing that he did not have sufficient interviews with African American males to include them in his findings.
4. Writing sympathetically on the *Male* volume in *Life* magazine, Francis Wickware summarises the criticism it has received. He concludes that most 'provocative' are the criticisms of Kinsey's evaluations, that is, his 'atomization' of sex and emphasis on 'outlet' as the whole of sexuality (Wickware 1948: 94).
5. For a much more acerbic psychoanalytic attack on Kinsey than Trilling's see Bergler and Kroger 1954.

6. The Association was founded in 1914 to respond to the perceived social threat of venereal disease and since 2012 has been known as the American Sexual Health Association.
7. The conservative emphasis on the importance of the family and a consequent concern about perceived threats to the family from non-marital sexual activity, pornography, sex education, abortion, homosexuality and paedophilia remain strongly held and expressed in America. Indeed, Kinsey and his publications continue to fuel controversy in the early twenty-first century (see for example Judith Reisman (n.d.), 'The Kinsey coverup').
8. Kinsey's comparisons between men and women are in Part III of *Sexual Behavior in the Human Female*. He concludes that 'the anatomic structures which are most essential to sexual response and orgasm are nearly identical in the human female and male' (Kinsey et al. 1953: 593).
9. In *Twentieth-Century Sexuality* Angus McLaren describes the male sexual behaviour volume as a 'hymn to virility' (1999: 145).
10. In fact, Mead also suggests that in many cases this 'dangerous and exacting game' becomes played as a 'partnership' (1949: 292). The 'game' is described in Salinger's *The Catcher in the Rye* (see Chapter 1 above).
11. Macauley's literary career included the editorship of the academic journal the *Kenyon Review*, writing for the *New Republic, Partisan Review* and the *New York Times Book Review*, and working as the fiction editor of *Playboy* in the 1960s.
12. See for example Reinhold Niebuhr, who criticises Kinsey for dealing 'merely with the human animal' (1954: 62).
13. Kinsey notably criticises Freudian pathologising of human sexuality (see for example Kinsey et al. 1948: 199–203).
14. For discussion of Kinsey's funding see James H. Jones, *Alfred C. Kinsey* (1997), chs 18 and 19, and Gathorne-Hardy, *Sex the Measure of All Things* (1998), chs 10 and 15. See Saunders 1999: 135ff for a discussion of the Rockefeller Foundation's funding of the CIA's activities. For a specific example of the connections between the Rockefeller Foundation, the CIA and intellectual and literary discourses, see her discussion of the case of *Partisan Review*, 335–9.
15. See Gathorne-Hardy 1998: ch. 21.
16. Indeed, so was Kinsey, and the withdrawal of funding from Kinsey was not simply on account of the intrinsic focus on sex research. Kinsey's research had originally attracted sponsorship as a result of a belief that greater knowledge of human sexuality would strengthen marriage and cohesion of the family. However, as James Jones points out, 'Social hygienists failed to recognise that scientific data could be used to support sexual liberation as easily as social control' (James H. Jones 1997: 418–19).

17. The original article in *Life* focused on one returning soldier whose arm had been amputated. However, the article was 'fiction but based on fact. It is distilled from the actual experiences of 43 different discharged soldiers'. The *Life* story is highly idealised, reproducing clichés of soldierly and wifely duty.
18. It is through a similar association with alcohol that Holden Caulfield also pursues an adult male identity; see Chapter 1 above.
19. The GI Bill of Rights, properly the 'Servicemen's Readjustment Act of 1944', provided ex-servicemen with such benefits as education; a loan guarantee for a home or business; unemployment pay; and job-finding assistance.
20. In the period the suit had a symbolic significance as a signifier of conformity – see *The Man in the Gray Flannel Suit*, discussed in Chapter 1 above.
21. 'If the term "queer" is to be a site of collective contestation [. . .], it will have to remain that which is, in the present, never fully owned, but always and only redeployed, twisted, queered from a prior usage and in the direction of urgent and expanding political purposes' (Butler 1993: 228).
22. In his book *Homosexuality*, Edmund Bergler offers the conventional psychoanalytic view of homosexuality as a 'disease' (1956: 27) and claims that '*psychiatric-psychoanalytic treatment can cure homosexuality*' (9). He also specifically challenges Kinsey's statistics, asserting that Kinsey's 'volunteers' were 'mostly neurotics' (51).
23. In his essay 'Come back to the raft ag'in, Huck honey!' Leslie Fiedler argues that while there is legal and cultural hostility to homosexuality and social prejudice against African Americans, there is in American literature a recurrent motif of 'the mutual love of *a white man and a colored*' (146). Fiedler refers to both Vidal's and Capote's novel in this essay, while Corber argues that Fiedler's inclusion of *The City and the Pillar* is an attempt 'to contain the emergence of a distinctly gay male literary tradition by assimilating it into the dominant paradigms of American literature' (Corber 1997: 137).
24. Unless otherwise stated, all page references are to the original 1948 edition of *The City and the Pillar*. Vidal made significant alterations to the text of the novel in 1965, including changing the ending.
25. Claude Summers suggests that Vidal's choice of tennis was related to the case of the tennis star William 'Big Bill' Tilden, who was involved in a homosexual scandal in 1946, shocking those who thought sportsmen could not be gay (Summers 1992: 58).
26. Genesis 18 and 19.
27. For the 1965 revision Vidal added an epigraph, quoting the verse from Genesis (19: 26) that describes Lot's wife being turned into a pillar of salt. Presumably this was intended to reinforce what Vidal saw as the anti-romantic theme of the novel.

28. This account of the end of the novel is based on the first American edition of 1948. Vidal revised the ending in 1965, with Jim raping Bob rather than murdering him. Vidal claims in the Afterword of the 1965 edition that he rewrote the end of the novel not because the original ending was forced on him by the publishers to make it a 'cautionary' tale, but because he found it 'melodramatic' (1965: 210). Vidal made further revisions and wrote a new Preface in 1994. The English edition, published in 1949 by John Lehmann, also contained revisions, although the outcome of the narrative – the murder of Bob by Jim – remained as in the 1948 American edition.
29. Some critics have advocated a Freudian/Oedipal reading of the novel and in so doing emphasised Joel's search for a father figure (see for example John Aldridge 1951: 194ff). In some respects Capote's novel therefore represents a conventional patriarchal narrative of succession, but in its figuring of the imagination and asethetic sensibility as feminine, it disrupts conventional expectations of masculine bonding.
30. It could be argued that Capote is deliberately evasive about Randolph's sexuality given the circumstances in which he was writing. However, the novel is fairly explicit in narrating sexual and gender identities which are unconventional, so this does not seem to have been the primary reason for the ambiguity.
31. For a more extensive discussion of the queerness of Capote's narrative, see Valente 2013. In his analysis, Hutchinson (2018) makes clear the importance of race to Joel's experience.
32. At the time of this interview, Highsmith had published three further Ripley novels, so her view of his character was likely to have evolved.
33. See also the analysis in Chapter 2 above.
34. De Pereda's novel is primarily about the sharing of male heterosexual experience in the particular context of army life.
35. Gore Vidal was acquainted with Burns and reports Burns claiming that 'to be a good writer it was necessary to be homosexual' (quoted in Kaplan 1999: 54).
36. See for example, Stuart Hall 2000.

Chapter 4

Identity and Assimilation in Jewish American Fiction

Chapter 4 takes a new perspective, relating the representation of masculinity to issues of race and identity in novels written from Jewish American perspectives. Considering masculinity from this perspective, and then from the point of view of African American writers in the following chapter, emphasises the point that male identity takes multiple forms and that hegemonic masculinity may be open to contestation from different cultural traditions. Jewish American fiction of this period is of intrinsic significance because it gave voice to second-generation East European immigrants whose work became central to American literature. For example, the critic Ruth R. Wisse argues that Saul Bellow demonstrated 'how a Jewish voice could speak for an integrated America' (Wisse 205). The four novels considered in this chapter all articulate issues around Jewish American identity in ways that also involve gender. Saul Bellow's third novel, *The Adventures of Augie March* (1953), opens with the straightforward claim of Augie March: 'I am an American, Chicago born'. Augie March's maleness is an essential element of his claim to an American identity, but Bellow's novel continues an interrogation of the expectations of men in American society. The other novels, all published earlier, in the 1940s, explore issues of anti-Semitism and assimilation in relation to American culture. Arthur Miller's *Focus* (1945) deconstructs the logic of anti-Semitic racism and explores how it recruits individuals, but shows that it can be defeated through masculine resistance. Irwin Shaw's *The Young Lions* (1948) articulates an idealised Jewish American masculinity within the context of American anti-Semitism, Nazism and the Second World War. Jo Sinclair's *Wasteland* (1946) focuses on close relationships within a Jewish family and the problems of assimilation, while radically challenging gender roles through the presence of a lesbian character.

The context for the emergence of a Jewish American literary voice was a change in legal and cultural circumstances. This change can be explored through the notion of 'whiteness', which has been developed as a critical concept through which the ideologies of 'white' identity can be interrogated. Like masculinity, whiteness has protean characteristics, constantly being adapted to changing cultural circumstances. As Valerie Babb argues in *Whiteness Visible*: '[W]hiteness is not a term describing an immutable biological content, but rather a term reflecting mutable relationships of social power' (1998: 13). Babb argues that there is a 'white hegemony' in America in which the foundation of national identity lies in the notion of whiteness: 'being white became synonymous with being American' (2). American identity is the consequence of a cultural and historical process and in *Whiteness of a Different Color* Matthew Frye Jacobson explores the changeability of notions of American identity in relation to whiteness. Jacobson argues that through the seventeenth and eighteenth centuries, 'the idea of citizenship had become thoroughly entwined with the idea of "whiteness" (and maleness) because what a citizen really was, at bottom, was someone who could put down a slave rebellion or participate in Indian wars' (1998: 25). The mass immigration of the nineteenth and early twentieth centuries, from Ireland and eastern and southern Europe and Asia, problematised what had previously been a relatively broad definition of 'white'. The 'new' immigrants were regarded as inferior to the original stock of northern Europeans – the Anglo-Saxons or Nordics – and this attitude was accompanied by anti-Irish and anti-Semitic prejudice. Subsequently, this 'hierarchy of whiteness' was given spurious scientific credibility by eugenicists (Jacobson 1998: 41, 82). The 1924 immigration act (the Johnson Act) reflected these views in restricting immigration on the basis of a quota system, which was founded on the proportions of the population established in the 1890 census. The 1924 quotas therefore restricted the numbers of Irish and Jewish immigrants (Jacobson 1998: 83).

Jacobson suggests that one consequence of the restriction of immigration in 1924 was a new focus on the American-born generation and a further shift in which the notion of Anglo-Saxon superiority receded, and the notion of the 'Caucasian' emerged as a more inclusive term for whiteness that included Jews, amongst other groups (1998: 94). The multiple stratification of the white races was replaced by a much broader notion of the 'major divisions', characterised as the Caucasian, the Mongolian and the Negroid (92). The New Deal ideology of the 1930s reflected this reformulation of whiteness as Caucasian, and Roosevelt emphasised the inclusion of immigrants as 'fully American' (Goldstein 2006: 190). During the Second World War Jews and Catholics were integrated into the military and wartime propaganda emphasised 'the American values of tolerance and equality as the antithesis of Nazi racism' (Goldstein 2006: 192). Race came to be erased in relation to the 'minor' divisions of humanity – the culture-based notion of ethnicity took its place and 'the racial characteristics of Jewishness, or Irishness or Greekness were emphatically revised away as a matter of sober, war-chastened "tolerance"' (Jacobson 1998: 96). By the late 1940s, the principal division in America centred on 'colour' difference, with the 'Negro Problem' perceived as *the* primary issue relating to race.

By 1945 then, Jewish Americans were officially regarded as white American citizens, even if popular perspectives on race and identity meant continuing anti-Semitism. Indeed, it is important not to ignore the virulent wartime anti-Semitism in America, and Leonard Dinnerstein makes the point in *Antisemitism in America* that the high point of anti-Semitism was during the Second World War (1994: 128ff). Anti-Semitism had been amplified in the 1930s during political and economic conflict around the New Deal, Russian communism and the Spanish Civil War. A particular contributor to anti-Semitism and sympathy for Nazism was Father Charles Coughlin, a Catholic priest from Boston, who was able to spread his views through radio and print media. Coughlin's anti-communism and anti-Semitism received organised expression through the Christian Front. Such anti-Semitism was largely based on unsubstantiated claims and such 'evidence' as the fraudulent Protocols of the Elders of Zion, but many Christian Americans in the late 1930s and 1940s held Jews responsible for the death of Jesus, as the authors of the Russian Revolution, as controlling the American economy and as 'dirty, lawless, unethical, unpatriotic and un-American' (quoted in Dinnerstein 1994: 115ff). After 1939 anti-Semitism was related to political efforts to keep America out of the war in Europe, but after the Pearl Harbor attack this motivation ceased and in fact Coughlin's propaganda was curtailed in 1942 on the grounds that it subverted the war effort. Even so, anti-Semitism continued, with a widespread belief that the Jews had taken the United States into the war for their own interests and that they refused to join up. Such prejudices against the Jews and the resulting anxiety and oppression are reflected in such fiction as Norman Mailer's *The Naked and the Dead*, Arthur Miller's *Focus* and Irwin Shaw's *The Young Lions*, which all represent circumstances before 1945.

In the immediate post-war period anti-Semitism declined significantly as it became less socially acceptable (see Dinnerstein 1994: 150–1). Dinnerstein finds an explanation for this shift in a number of factors: the disreputable legacy of Nazism and Hitler; general optimism and economic buoyancy; an opposition to intolerance amongst servicemen and women; and the leadership shown by Truman in advocating fair employment and civil rights (150–2). After the Second World War, American Jews showed a new militancy and unity in opposing anti-Semitism (16). For example, 'In 1946 the Jewish Welfare Board published a two-volume work describing the Jewish contribution to the war effort. It listed over half a million Jews who had served in the armed forces, eleven thousand who had died in combat, twenty-four thousand who had been wounded, and thirty-six thousand who had been decorated' (Shapiro 1992: 17). However, it was expected of the Jewish population, as they integrated into white society, that they would 'keep expressions of group difference at a level that would not offend the sense of unity and homogeneity from which whites of the post-war era drew their confidence and stability' (Goldstein 2006: 194). Goldstein goes on to argue that despite the articulation of difference around a notion of ethnic identity rather than race, in post-war America there remained a 'tension between Jews' desire for both integration and distinctiveness' (208).

The changing position of the Jewish population in America was reflected in creative and intellectual production, most notably in the emerging influence of the New York Jewish intellectuals. In *Prodigal Sons* Alexander Bloom considers the claimed shift of cultural authority from Paris to New York after 1945 and the dominance of Jewish intellectuals.[1] Yet such a shift was also marked by a second generation of New York intellectuals – such as Saul Bellow, Alfred Kazin, Leslie Fiedler and Irving Kristol – coming into their own and securing 'positions closer to the heart of American society' (Bloom 1986: 137). However, Bloom argues that the Holocaust overshadowed this development and produced 'a shattering reawakening of Jewish consciousness' (137). The result was an examination of their sense of personal, Jewish identity in contrast with the former dominance of the notion of universalism (138).[2] The debates of these intellectuals were primarily engaged in the pages of *Partisan Review* and *Commentary*. *Partisan Review* broke with the Communist Party in 1936 and, after a hiatus, re-emerged in 1937 with Trotskyist sympathies. *Commentary* was launched in 1945 and was 'self-consciously a "Jewish" intellectual magazine, relating issues of cultural priorities and political analysis to Jewish questions and identities' (Bloom 1986: 158–9). The founding editor of *Commentary*, Elliott Cohen, claimed that 'an American Jewish intellectual could live comfortably in both worlds, that there was no necessary contradiction between Jewish particularism and full participation in American life and culture' (see Wisse 2003: 194). Wisse argues that 'the two magazines reinforced the sense of an emerging Jewish culture that would not only adapt itself to the American mainstream, but transform the larger culture in the process of self-adaptation' (194).

In the post-war period both journals evinced a very strong anti-communist editorial policy. Bloom maintains that this shift is indicative of the New York Jewish intellectuals generally moving towards 'the center of American society, politically and socially' and that one element of this was 'a reassertion of the Western tradition and Western values' (1986: 166). In *The Cultural Cold War* Frances Stonor Saunders argues that after 1939–40, *Partisan Review* began 'creating a counter-language to articulate anti-Stalinism and redefine radicalism in a non-Communist context', and echoes Bloom in seeing this primarily as a newfound 'Americanism' (1999: 160). However, it is also the case, as Saunders shows, that the expression of such views was fostered by the CIA, which sought to recruit the anti-communist left to its Cold War anti-Soviet campaign, and which, through organisations such as the Congress for Cultural Freedom, financially supported *Partisan Review* and *Commentary*. As I argued in the Introduction, the development of Cold War politics in the United States was culturally represented in terms of gender with a feminisation of those who were 'soft' on communism. For Jewish writers engaged in this cultural context, matters of politics and identity also involved the issue of masculinity.

This brief summary provides a context for a number of themes that emerge in Jewish American novels written after the Second World War. Despite an ideological shift that saw the recognition of American Jews as 'white' and therefore as proper American citizens, anti-Semitism remained a significant element in American society. Moreover, the Holocaust cast a traumatic shadow for second-generation American Jews whose families had emigrated from Eastern Europe. For first-generation immigrants, assimilation into American culture was a desirable aspiration in comparison with the pogroms and exclusions Jews had experienced in Eastern Europe.[3] Yet for second-generation Jewish Americans assimilation was a more problematical process. In *Jewish Self-Hatred* Sander Gilman argues that those who are Other might be encouraged to assimilate to the values of the 'reference group' of a culture, but that to abandon difference is an illusion because the Other can only ever be a 'shoddy counterfeit, an outsider'. This creates inherently irreconcilable circumstances, but anyone faced with this 'represses this conflict, saying, in effect, The conflict must be within me, since that which I wish to become cannot be flawed' (Gilman 1986: 2). Such circumstances informed the New York intellectuals' debate about the relationship between Jewish and American identity and was manifested in the theme of alienation. Alienation was seen as an inevitable element of modern life and also as core to the Jewish American experience of double consciousness in which awareness of one's Jewish identity made one not quite at home in America. In these circumstances 'the Jew's alienation was his qualification for telling the story of everybody' (Wisse 2003: 202). In the novels discussed in this chapter the problems of identity and assimilation into American society turn on questions of gender, and in particular on the nature of Jewish American masculinity. The analysis begins with two novels that consider American anti-Semitism: Arthur Miller's *Focus* (1945) and Irwin Shaw's *The Young Lions* (1948).

Arthur Miller, *Focus*

Arthur Miller's novel, set in New York towards the end of the Second World War, is an exploration of anti-Semitism through the experiences of Lawrence Newman, a gentile. At the outset Newman is both anti-Semitic in his habitual outlook, and active as a personnel officer for a corporation that will not hire Jews. Newman begins a journey of greater insight into such prejudice when he begins to wear spectacles that supposedly give him a Jewish appearance, and in fact he begins to be perceived as Jewish. Through the narrative Miller deconstructs essentialist notions of Jewish identity and appearance. In its examination of the amplification of petty anti-Semitism into organised hate and violence, the novel explores the attitudes and motivations of individuals and in so doing foregrounds issues related to masculinity. For Alan Wald, Newman 'finds his manhood by choosing an identity as an ally of the Jew'; he 'becomes a new man [. . .], by defining himself as a Jew' (2007: 231).

Lawrence Newman's character at the opening of the novel fits in many respects with the analysis of the mid-century sociologists who saw American culture as conformist and feminised. Newman is an office worker for the Corporation and is fearful that it will crush him unless he is seen to fit in (Miller [1945] 2009: 20). Similarly, he wants to be accepted by his suburban male neighbours and he thinks of the sameness of the houses on his street as soothing 'his yearning for order' (19). Christopher Bigsby quotes Riesman in arguing that Newman is 'other directed and that passivity pervades the text as it pervades [Newman's] life' (2005: 69). Newman therefore is in many respects represented as the emasculated male much discussed at the time. His desire for order is expressed in a generalised anxiety and a sense of powerlessness. However, his general unease is countered when he reads about the vandalising of a Jewish cemetery – the 'threat of dark deeds and ruthless force [. . .] flowed out to him' (34). Similarly, after he begins to respond to the pressure from his neighbours in relation to the recently arrived Jewish shopkeeper – Mr Finkelstein – he allows his prejudices to express themselves in indignation as he looks at the shop; in return he feels 'a strange power flowing into him, it was as though his very body was growing larger' (66). The next day on the subway, he feels 'able', 'even tough' or 'dashing' (67). Newman is therefore characterised as an anxious and conformist male in ways that seem consonant with contemporary diagnosis of the feminisation of American culture, but the novel suggests that he experiences a sense of masculine reinvigoration in the hostility to the 'Other' generated by anti-Semitism. Ironically, he then begins to suffer from anti-Semitism – first at work and then in his neighbourhood – when he starts wearing the glasses that supposedly make him look Jewish.

The anti-Semitic Christian Front organisation is active locally, and for self-protection Newman attends a local Front meeting (168ff). The narrative describes the arousal of the crowd into a mob and then the identification of Newman by one of the audience as a 'Jew' (176). Newman is set upon and thrown out of the hall onto the pavement despite his protestations. His clothes are torn and he is bruised and bewildered; as he picks his way home he is accompanied by Finkelstein, who was watching outside the hall. Newman feels an affinity with Finkelstein – 'Despite himself he felt drawn to this man' (180). Although he does not see himself as being in the same situation, he sees Finkelstein as 'in possession of a secret that left him controlled and fortified, while he himself was circling in confusion' (180–1).

After this incident, Newman realises that he is waiting to be attacked, and imagines how he might need to use violence to defend himself – 'Did he have the power to knock a man down?' (202). Finally, this wait ends one evening after Newman and his wife have been to the cinema. They are followed by a group of six men, but Newman still hopes that their target is actually Finkelstein's shop. He tries to divert his attackers towards the shop, waving them towards the shop with, a 'silly, feminine gesture' that marks his continued lack of masculine strength and purpose. At this moment Finkelstein emerges from the store, breaking the silence with 'a gigantic monolith of sound from a single throat, a torrential bellowing' (225). He appears with a 'great leap out across the sidewalk, a bat in each hand' fighting off his three attackers. He hands one of the bats to Newman, who now fights back strongly: 'A giant wall seemed to tilt over inside him and a great stream of silver light scoured his body' (225). Finkelstein endows Newman with masculine strength in the symbolic passing of the baseball bat and Newman experiences this as a metaphysical transformation as the silver light cleanses him. Finkelstein and Newman stand together, back to back, fighting off their assailants, who retreat.

After the fight Newman and Finkelstein move into the store, where Newman helps Finkelstein with his bloody nose and then takes him into his home and puts him to bed. Newman stares into Finkelstein's eyes and sees his humanity. Finally Newman feels a deep calm and stillness (229). Newman's identification with Finkelstein is completed when he reports the incident to the police and allows himself to be identified as a Jew.

Focus articulates an intellectual critique of anti-Semitism and its logical absurdities. Yet this critique cannot be separated from the importance of masculine strength in providing physical resistance to anti-Semitism. In this Finkelstein embodies a masculinity that resists the notion of Jewish male effeminacy and provides a model for American men who are repressed and at risk of feminisation in American culture. Miller's novel can be seen then as largely subscribing to contemporary anxieties about feminisation and describing a Jewish masculinity that is rooted in conventional masculine traits of strength and aggression.

Irwin Shaw, *The Young Lions*

In Chapter 2 I briefly discussed Irwin Shaw's *The Young Lions* and the mocking of Captain Colclough's posturing and lack of courage. I return here to Shaw's novel to consider more widely its representation of masculinity from a Jewish American perspective. Irwin Shaw was born in New York, the son of Russian Jewish immigrants, and therefore writes from the perspective of a second-generation Jewish American. *The Young Lions* is a novel about the Second World War, but the narrative begins before the war and describes the circumstances of the three principal characters before they join up and experience war. Noah Ackerman is a second-generation Jewish American. At the beginning of the novel his father dies and it is clear that Ackerman is seeking direction in his life. Michael Whitacre works in the New York theatre business. He has a hedonistic and comfortable life but his marriage has failed, and he feels a deep dissatisfaction about himself (Shaw [1948] 2000: 38). Christian Diestl is a ski instructor and Nazi Party member who believes before the war that if 'wiping out the Jews' is necessary to have 'a decent and ordered Europe' then it should be done (17). All three men are ordinary soldiers, with Whitacre and Ackerman serving in the same company in the US Army. The narrative moves between the experiences of the three men but finishes with them all in a confrontation near an SS concentration camp in Europe at the very end of hostilities.

The over-arching focus of the novel is the experience of men serving as ordinary soldiers during wartime. Yet this experience is set in the context of broader conditions of life in the middle of the twentieth century and in particular the moral implications of anti-Semitism and the Holocaust. The focus here is on the representation of Jewish American masculinity through the character of Noah Ackerman. Ackerman's Jewish identity is of importance to him and closely related to his perspective on the war and military service. For example, he tries to enlist as 'an honourable citizen, as a believer in the war, as an enemy of Fascism, as a Jew' (168). However, he is uncomfortable with an emphasis on his Jewishness and later says to himself, 'Must stop thinking about the Jews' (215). His ambivalence is a reflection of his attitude to his father – an immigrant from Odessa – who looked like a 'Hebrew King' and peppered his speech with quotations from the Bible, but is irreligious and led 'a long, riotous life' of bankruptcies and abandoned women (40–1). Ackerman has never been to a synagogue and his desire is to assimilate.

However, in the context of the 1940s it is clear that whatever his aspirations, Ackerman's Jewish identity cannot be ignored. After his induction into the army, Ackerman is picked on first by Captain Colclough and Sergeant Rickett and then, following their lead, bullied by others in the company. Ackerman's cultural sophistication is signalled by Colclough's objection to his possession of Joyce's *Ulysses* – a 'filthy, dirty book' (286).[4] On an inspection Ackerman is singled out for supposedly failing to clean a window and it is this that triggers virulent anti-Semitism in which he is told by Rickett that he has to keep the windows 'white-man clean, Ikie' (288). Rickett, who has a lisp, also tells him that he has no time for 'Niggerth, Jewth, Mexicans or Chinamen', expressing a racist attitude that refuses the integrationist view that counted Jews as 'white' (288–9). However, the abuse goes beyond this with a beating and the theft of ten dollars that he had been saving for buying a birthday present for his wife. Ackerman's response involves a challenge to whoever stole his ten dollars that he wished to 'take [. . .] satisfaction, in person, with my own hands' (308). The ten biggest men in the company tell him, 'We took it, Jew-Boy' (308). Ackerman fights each of these men, suffering considerable injuries, including broken ribs, and permanent facial disfigurement. He refuses all attempts to dissuade him from continuing in the belief that his 'victory', through 'the complete tour of sacrifice and pain', is 'a demonstration of will and courage that only the best of them could have been capable of' (317). In an echo of the way Prewitt's masculinity is inscribed in the scars on his body, Ackerman believes that the outcome will be his acceptance by the other soldiers. However, as he is warned by another Jew in the company, Fein, the anti-Semitism of some people cannot be changed whatever he does (315). Indeed, after the final fight, which Ackerman wins, the others just walk away, showing no 'spark of admiration or grudging respect' (329). Ackerman's failure emphasises the depth of anti-Semitism remaining in the integrated US Army, but also raises the question of how helpful conventional attributes of masculinity are for Jewish men.

The novel then follows Ackerman's experience of fighting in Normandy. After the company is led into a trap by the incompetent and cowardly Captain Colclough and surrounded by Germans, the soldiers have to escape in small groups under cover of darkness. In these circumstances Ackerman shows qualities of courage and leadership that mark him out as an exceptional soldier. Despite this, when reunited with the remains of his company, Rickett can only greet him with, 'Oh, Christ, oh, Christ, we still got the Jew' (456–88).

Through the representation of Noah Ackerman as a brave and resourceful soldier and leader of men, the novel establishes a Jewish masculinity that aligns with the conventional attributes of manliness. However, despite Ackerman's courage, the reaction of Rickett persuades him that no matter what he did, he would remain beyond the pale to such men (518). He therefore adopts a new attitude, 'a philosophy of aloof detachment' to protect himself (518). Ackerman is wounded, but once recovered and waiting for reassignment, he meets up again with Whitacre. Whitacre notices that although his experiences have left Ackerman frail and coughing, 'he seemed to have found some inner balance, a thoughtful, quiet maturity' (597).

Ackerman and Whitacre find their way to the front line and there in the Battle of the Bulge Ackerman, 'watched out for [Whitacre] with critical, veteran eyes, protected him by word and example, even when it had been a full-time job trying to keep himself alive' (623). Ackerman's care for Whitacre emphasises another dimension to his character and this is reflected in Whitacre's observation of him as he sleeps.

> Michael noticed for the first time that his friend had soft, upcurling eyelashes, full and blond at the tips, giving the upper part of his face a gentle appearance. [. . .] Looking at him now, this way, Michael realized at what cost this frail boy maintained his attitude of grave competence, made his intelligent, dangerous, soldierly decisions, fought tenaciously and cautiously, with a manual-like correctness to remain alive [. . .] (624)

Ackerman's eyelashes are also described as an 'incongruous girlish ornament' and in this the narrative represents a model of Jewish masculinity that seems to fuse the soldierly attributes of manliness with a gentle empathetic masculinity. Here the feminisation of Ackerman's appearance, rather than posing a threat to his masculinity, describes a more complex identity.

The final scenes of the novel bring Ackerman and Whitacre together with Diestl and are set at a concentration camp just before and after its liberation. Inside the camp, Jews have been starved and murdered, and outside the camp Ackerman is 'sacrificed' (Garrett 2015: 92). Diestl has retreated with the German army but has become isolated. He is lurking in the forest outside the camp, having left just before its liberation. He tries to shoot Ackerman and Whitacre, who are having a break and walking in the forest, but only succeeds in hitting Ackerman. Whitacre pursues Diestl and his eventual shooting of Diestl as revenge for Ackerman marks the moment he becomes a proper soldier. This development and his survival against Diestl is the consequence of Ackerman's actions – in the nurturing of Whitacre's capabilities and in the example of friendship.

Ackerman is therefore represented in the novel as an idealised Jewish American male. As Garrett puts it in *Young Lions*, the novel 'suggests to readers that the modern man can be strong *and* emotional *and* intellectual' (2015: 10). In contrasting Ackerman with

American anti-Semitism, with the cynicism and amorality of Diestl, and by foregrounding the racist element of Nazism, the novel constructs a counter-narrative rooted in liberalism and pluralism (see Garrett 2015: 5). The legacy of the Holocaust and Ackerman's sacrificial death is intended to cement these values at the centre of American culture. The moral core of these values is embodied in the figure of a Jewish American male.

Saul Bellow, *The Adventures of Augie March*

Despite critical success with his first two novels, Bellow first established a significant readership with the publication of *Augie March* (1953).[5] *Augie March* also marked a significant shift in Bellow's style that was noted by his contemporaries. For example, Robert Penn Warren, reviewing the novel in the *New Republic*, contrasted *Augie March* with the 'finely wrought' style of *Dangling Man* and *The Victim*, written in the 'Flaubert-James tradition'. *Augie March*, in comparison, is 'a triumph in the apparent formlessness of the autobiographical picaresque novel' (Warren 1953).[6] *Augie March*, therefore, may be seen to have resonated with the reading public at the time of its publication, while the shift in Bellow's style and focus marked a significant intervention in American fiction. Although Zachery Leader emphasises Bellow's reluctance to be cast as a Jewish American writer (2015: 447), there is no doubt that the novel draws heavily on the Jewish American experience, both in its representation of immigrant life and culture in Chicago and in its narrative style. Not only does the novel make regular use of Yiddish words and the inversions of phrasing in English characteristic of East Europeans whose first language was Yiddish, the characterisation is marked by an emotional expressiveness. The novel is also rich in allusion to history, myth and religion; such allusions are juxtaposed with description of the everyday, a characteristic of Yiddish conversation noted by Bellow (see Leader 2015: 445).

The novel is narrated in the first person by Augie March, who describes his account as his 'memoirs' at the end of the novel (Bellow [1953] 1995: 596). As noted above, Augie claims to be an 'American' at the beginning of the novel and this reflects the changes in Jewish American status in the period. Yet there is a question about how he fits with the expectations of American masculinity. James Atlas, in his biography of Bellow, argues that *Augie March* is 'an American *bildungsroman* – a novel of education' (2000: 188). Leader, however, questions this analysis, considering the novel as picaresque and arguing that this form is ill-suited to portray the qualities of development or maturity (2015: 437). He also cites Norman Podhoretz's review of the novel in *Commentary* in 1953, in which he argues that Augie does not 'change in the course of the novel, he doesn't even learn' (quoted in Leader 2015: 439). In another review in 1953 Robert Davies claims, '. . . the book is in a sense unfinished. But if it ends without Augie's either finding or transcending himself, it leaves him with the conviction that both achievements are possible, and that they may be simply different names for the same things' (Davies 1953). Furthermore, Lionel Trilling, in a 1965 introduction to the novel, argues that Augie rejects the trajectory of the subjects of nineteenth-century novels towards 'the world of power and glory' and 'refuses the "heroic" in favor of what he believes the heroic destroys, a complete humanity' (Trilling 1953: 104). However, Daniel Fuchs maintains that the novel has a 'dual nature' in incorporating elements of both the picaresque, in which 'respectability is close to crime' and the *Bildungsroman*, which 'implies more emphatic development, greater moral strenuousness and conclusive self-discovery' (Fuchs 1984: 59). Certainly the traditional form of the *Bildungsroman* emphasises the transition of young men to maturity, with an emphasis on success measured by the conventions of the time. In comparison, Augie March's picaresque account cannot be seen as heroic and although he seeks to assert a 'moral strenuousness', it is debatable whether the novel concludes with 'self-discovery'.

Two other innovative and important mid-century novels – *The Catcher in the Rye*, considered in Chapter 1, and *Invisible Man*, discussed in the next chapter – are also first-person narratives that eschew the conventions of the *Bildungsroman*. Holden Caulfield rejects that 'David Copperfield kind of crap', and, similarly, the *Invisible Man*'s circular narrative – like Caulfield's – and his ambiguity about his present circumstances and his future mark a rejection of any straightforward progression from childhood to manhood. These two novels have in common a primary male character who does not fit the dominant characteristics of American masculinity – Holden Caulfield is an alienated adolescent, and the invisible man is an African American.[7] In their representation of an outsider male voice through first-person narration, together with stylistic and formal innovation, these novels enable the articulation of a critical perspective on the expectations of American manhood.

The examples of *The Catcher in the Rye* and *The Invisible Man* suggest a link between a critical engagement with the genre of the

Bildungsroman, formal innovation and a questioning of the trajectory of male development in the period. In his first novel, *Dangling Man*, Saul Bellow explicitly questions contemporary American masculinity through his principal character, Joseph:

> [T]his is an era of hardboiled-dom. Today, the code of the athlete, of the tough boy [. . .] is stronger than ever. Do you have feelings? There are correct and incorrect ways of indicating them. Do you have an inner life? It is nobody's business but your own. Do you have emotions? Strangle them. To a degree, everyone obeys this code. And it does admit of a limited kind of candor, a closemouthed straightforwardness. But on the truest candor, it has an inhibitory effect. Most serious matters are closed to the hardboiled. They are unpracticed in introspection, and therefore badly equipped to deal with opponents whom they cannot shoot like big game or outdo in daring.
> (Bellow [1944] 2007: 9)

In relation to this critique of contemporary American masculinity, including its allusion to Hemingway, Joseph asks himself: 'How should a good man live; what ought he to do?' (39). In asking this question, Joseph sets the expectations of men in contemporary America in relation to the notion of the *mensch*, the good Jewish man, developed in the Eastern European, or Ashkenazic, Jewish tradition (see Rosenberg 2001: 1). Joseph's perspective on American masculinity and his question for the contemporary American male are relevant to a consideration of *The Adventures of Augie March*. For example, Grandma Lausch, the dominant character in Augie's childhood household, tells him that she is trying to make something of him and that she wants him to be a '*mensch*' (Bellow [1953] 1995: 52). This ambition is related to her concern that he is mixing with friends who will lead him on a path to 'lifelong ignorance and degradation' (52), and is expressed subsequently by Augie himself as his search for a 'worthwhile fate'. However, Augie also speculates later in the novel that Simon, his older brother, considers him 'something of a *schlemiel*' (226). The *schlemiel* is an awkward or unlucky comic character who, as a type in European Yiddish literature, has been seen as a means of coping with the intrinsic vulnerability of the Jewish population and developing a sense of strength through humour and self-deprecation. It has been argued by Ruth Wisse in *The Schlemiel as Modern Hero* that the character of the American Jewish *schlemiel* is 'an expression of heart, of intense, passionate feeling, in surroundings that stamp out individuality and equate emotion with unreason. The schlemiel is used as a cultural reaction to the prevailing Anglo-Saxon model of restraint in action, thought, and speech' (Wisse 1971: 82). The American *schlemiel* may therefore be seen as male persona whose primary characteristics are far from the dominant codes of masculinity identified by Joseph above. Clearly, insofar as Augie's character is a *schlemiel*, he therefore reflects a repudiation of Anglo-Saxon restraint in his abundant emotional expressiveness.

Wisse goes on to argue that 'The garrulous monologues of Joseph and other Bellow characters are filled with suggestions of compromise, uncertainty, weakness, and failure, the inevitable consequence of urban, democratic living' (1971: 81). In this Wisse shows how the *schlemiel* may integrate Jewish and American identities while exposing the difficulties and complexities of American life. The innovative style and form of Bellow's novel – the picaresque narrative and the prolix first-person expression of Augie's thoughts and emotions, the humour and the vulnerability – are therefore intrinsic to opening a critical perspective on an American male identity that is rooted in the Anglo-Saxon model.

Such a perspective foregrounds masculinity as a core element of the novel, whereas critical approaches that place *Augie March* in the genre of the *Bildungsroman* tend to universalise the novel and see Augie as an alienated Everyman struggling with modern life. One critic who has focused on gender in Bellow's fiction is Gloria Cronin. In *A Room of His Own* Cronin provides an analysis of Bellow's representation of male and female characters across his novels. Cronin maintains that the principal masculine construct used by Bellow is 'an ironic version of the self-absorbed male romantic individualist'. Through this male protagonist Bellow 'is at pains to demonstrate a variety of culturally differentiated masculinities'. 'As artists, intellectuals, and sometimes hermetical personalities, Bellow's male protagonists are transgressive figures. They demonstrate American masculinities in disarray' (Cronin 2001: 76). She concludes that in Bellow's novels there is a 'steady attempt by the transgressive male to elude, modify, and transcend the masculinities he inherits in his search for a space that does not seem to exist'. Cronin believes that this space is the 'rejected element of the feminine' and her overall argument is that 'Bellow's androcentric texts represent a search for the absent mother, lover, sister, female friend, female psyche, and anima' (2001: 74, 2). She goes on to discuss the representation of women in Bellow's novels: the 'Bellow text tends to include women only to objectify and silence them, causing woman in both of these instances to become the overdetermined site of male fantasy and hostility' (2001: 14). With specific reference to

The Adventures of Augie March, Cronin argues that in the lack of suitability of existing models of masculinity, Augie 'realizes that he is the product of entirely new social forces that have forged a different kind of American masculinity' (2001: 93).

Cronin therefore echoes the view that Bellow seeks to articulate a critical perspective on American masculinity, but argues that he maintains a perspective of women as 'Other', even if the novels do not consistently present the female characters from a hostile perspective. This suggests that Bellow remains largely bound within dominant expectations of American manhood. In considering such issues in what is a long and complex novel, I will concentrate primarily on the representation of Augie March himself and of his brother, Simon. Augie's other brother, Georgie, is a less active character but is significant, with their mother, as signifying an innocence that results from a disengagement from the world. In contrast, Simon personifies the American ideal of self-advancement, while Augie occupies a less defined position in which he observes others, seeking an alternative male identity.

At the opening of the novel Augie and his brothers – and his mother – have been abandoned by their father, and at the age of nine Augie has to learn how to negotiate the hard circumstances of poverty in the Depression.[8] Their familial history is obscure, but they are identified as a 'handful of Jews' living in Chicago among the Poles, who display the signs of their Catholicism on every kitchen wall (15). The household is dominated by their boarder, Grandma Lausch, an immigrant from Odessa whose values were established in Russia, where she was wealthy. Grandma Lausch is a forceful character and she is shown to embody the masculine traits that are expected of the head of household. Augie's mother and Georgie – 'born an idiot' – in their simple-mindedness and innocence are linked together and contrasted with Grandma Lausch, who is described as 'one of those Machiavellis of small street and neighborhood' (6). She therefore stands for a materialistic world view in contrast to the love and humanity engendered in the family relationships around Georgie.

Grandma Lausch believes that Simon and Augie should aspire to being 'gentlemen' (63) and Augie does perceive Simon's attraction to 'English schoolboy notions of honour', although '*Tom Brown's Schooldays* for many years had an influence that we were not in a position to afford' (6). While Simon's idealisation of English notions of honour reflects one aspect of conventional masculinity derided by Joseph in *Dangling Man*, Simon also seeks other forms of male identity that are typically American. For example,

Augie notes that 'opposed to [Simon's] British style was his patriotic anger at George III' (6). Similarly Simon pursues American examples of self-development with his Sandow muscle builder (16) and an engagement with American values in his success at school (see 36 and 38). Once Simon and Augie reach adolescence they are sent out to work, and this leads to a change in Simon and in particular his attitude to money: 'he had no peace or rest if he ever lacked dough' (40). He develops 'different aims from his original ones and new ideas about conduct' (38). Symbolically, this change is marked by a change in his appearance – he returns from summer work 'brawnier and golden-colored but with an upper-front tooth broken, sharp and a little discolored amongst the whole and white ones' (38). The mystery of his broken tooth marks the emergence of a new element in his character – a wheeler-dealer with an aggressive and menacing air – that continues through the novel (38, and see 293).[9]

Simon's first attempt at raising money by getting involved in a betting pool ends with him being cheated and beaten up while also losing his fiancée to his cousin (211). After this setback he tells Augie that he plans to marry into a wealthy family to provide him with the start that he needs. Simon's approach is unromantic and Augie tells him that his attitude is 'cold-blooded' (231). Moreover, when he tells Augie of his intentions, Simon is completely broke, fat through 'not eating right', and unshaven (227). Augie questions what assets Simon can present to this girl and her family that would make them want him. Simon's response is that they are 'handsome men' and that the family will get full value out of him as he is driven to make money. Augie is perturbed by this boast about the men of their family – 'it made us sound like studs' – but Simon's intention to organise Augie's engagement to another young woman of the family reinforces this perception.

In fact, Simon's self-presentation involves the complex construction of a male identity that will fit the family's expectations. For example, Augie has earlier noted that Simon did assimilate Grandma Lausch's conduct lessons and is able to take care of himself in a respectable household. He has also acquired a variety of masculine skills, such as,

> dancing, conversation with women, courtship, gift-giving, romantic letter-writing, the ins and outs of restaurants and night clubs, dance halls, the knotting of four-in-hands and bow ties, what was correct and incorrect in tucking a handkerchief in the breast pocket, how to choose clothes [. . .] [H]ow to put on a hat, smoke a cigarette, fold a pair of gloves and put them in an inner pocket. (129)

These attributes are on display after Simon has successfully negotiated his marriage, when he is described as wearing 'high quality gray flannel, and shoes with new stitching', with a 'new gray Pontiac at the curb' (249–50). Simon goes to the barber to have 'everything lavished on himself' – groomed, shampooed and 'steamed and singed, manicured' (260). What Simon has developed and puts on display through the adornment of his body is a style of masculinity that reflects wealth and power. Augie notes that Simon enjoys the luxury of his circumstances (129), but the performative element of Simon's masculinity is evident when Augie first meets Simon's wife Charlotte and the rest of the Magnus family. The family are large and stout and buy the best of everything, but Simon is their 'prince' and gives them wit and 'dramatic self-presentation' (252). Augie is astonished by his 'metamorphosis' into a boisterous extrovert. Heterosexual masculinity is significant in these interchanges with the family – Uncle Charlie, who has been supervising Simon's introduction into the family coal business, believes that Simon 'can put it down between the sheets' (256) and Augie's attractiveness to Charlie's daughter Lucy is the subject of ribald comment (256–7). A variation of Simon's performance takes places in the masculine world of 'rich businessmen's restaurants and clubs, fancy steakhouses' (259). Augie notes his aggression and quarrelsomeness in these circumstances, while Simon argues that it is important with these people to be seen to spend.

Simon's efforts are successful, and later in novel he tells Augie that he expects to be a millionaire. He has graduated to a Cadillac and has become 'heftier', and his face is 'larger, and rude, autocratic' (486). Augie sees his brother in the car as a 'Prince of Detroit, full of force and darkness' (488) and later in his apartment as taking on 'like a king' and dominating the rooms where all is vast and excessive (488). Simon's masculinity is therefore shown to be expressed through the gargantuan excesses of American materialism – materialism that is indivisible from American masculinity expressed through luxurious treatment of the body and its presentation in the finest clothes. The world is dominated by the rich American male through force of personality and wealth, symbolised by the 'beautiful enamel shell' and internal 'jewelry' of the Cadillac (486). This male persona conforms to other markers of masculinity prevalent in the period. While the descriptions of Simon emphasise his forcefulness and autocratic behaviour, expressed through a powerful body, he is willing also to turn to actual violence when he considers it necessary. Such an occasion occurs at his coal yard in a dispute with a buyer who has dumped a truckload of coal on the weighing scale. Simon seizes the man and hits him several times with a gun (287–8). Accounts of Simon's heterosexual activities recur through the novel. For example, in the period immediately after his marriage he and Augie visit the North Avenue point on the lake, where they go swimming, and Simon would 'make bullish approaches to women and girls, his eyes big and red' (269). These approaches 'created awe and fear', but the 'girls were not always frightened of him; he had a smell of power, he was handsome' (269). Later Simon takes a young woman – Renée – as his mistress.

However, while Simon displays such traits of conventional masculinity, Augie perceives him as troubled. The description of Simon becoming 'violent and lustful' by the lake and the brute sexual exchanges with the 'bims' is juxtaposed with Augie's concern that while in the water Simon felt the appeal of going down and not coming up again (268). Augie's perception of this self-destructive urge in Simon is repeated on several occasions. Nor indeed is his sexual achievement straightforward, as Simon tells Augie that his honeymoon with Charlotte was 'awful' (251), while his liaison with Renée ends disastrously. Simon is seen by Augie as 'tortured by thought of suicide' (251) and this impulse is linked explicitly to the requirement that he succeed in making money. Augie describes Simon's aggressive and risky driving as showing that 'his feelings were suicidal' and concludes, 'The truth back of all this was that he had his pockets full of money as an advance on his promised ability to make a rich man of himself and now had to deliver' (261). It is clear then that Simon has assimilated the ideology of American materialism and success, and in doing so he conforms to expectations of American manhood. However, the novel offers a critique both of this form of masculinity and the materialism of American culture. Simon is damaged by his aspirations and by the male identity that he has adopted.

Finally, however, responsibility for his circumstances is significantly shifted away from Simon. His marriage to Charlotte may be considered in the light of Gloria Cronin's analysis of Bellow's representation of women. Simon, Charlotte and Augie are reunited in Paris after the Second World War. Here Charlotte recounts the story of the end of Simon's affair with Renée, mocking Simon's fear that he had wasted his life and accusing him of having 'an abnormal idea of being happy' (611). Simon is humiliated and 'stony with shame' (612). Augie feels sympathy for Simon and the narrative turns against Charlotte. Earlier their marriage has been characterised as resting on 'what related to the bank, the stock, the taxes' and Charlotte's first aim was 'to make the union serious by constructing a fortune on it'

(271). In referring to Lady Macbeth's plea – 'Unsex me here!' – Augie sees this ambition as making 'the soul neuter'. The representation of Charlotte as unfeminine continues with her lack of serious interest in 'ladies' trimming and gewgawing' or domestic responsibilities (271). Finally, unlike Renée, who became pregnant, Charlotte cannot have children. Augie sees Charlotte as having threatened to turn Simon to stone 'long ago if it hadn't been for these Renées' and that the secrets she has revealed were just about 'his mismanaged effort to live. To live and not to die' (612). In relation to Simon, then, the novel identifies the corrosive and damaging effects of materialist American society and relates these to conventional formations of male identity. Yet, like other representations of gender in the period, such problems may often be embodied by, or projected onto, the female Other, whose unfeminine behaviour may undermine the autonomy and manhood of the male protagonist.

Augie presents Simon as an embodiment of the American ideology of individual success at the same time as the narrative questions the cost of such materialism. Simon's assimilation into American materialist values is inseparable from the acquisition of a conventional masculine identity. Augie claims to have different values from Simon, which raises the question of whether he aspires to a different sort of male identity. Key aspects of Augie's identity may be illuminated through a consideration of his relationship with Thea Fenchel.

Augie's initial contact with the Fenchel family arises from his job in Evanston with the Renlings, who are sporting goods retailers, and Augie works in their saddle shop selling 'dude-ranch stuff' (151). When Augie is appointed, his Jewishness is noted because 'out on the North Shore they don't like Jews', but Renling believes that the customers will 'probably never know' (151). This cool assessment makes Augie feel like 'Prospective house slaves from the shacks [getting] the same kind of going-over' 'or girls brought to an old *cocotte* by their mothers for training' (151). In these similes he associates himself with the feminine, and considers rejecting the job, but is flattered into acceptance. Once he begins work he is dressed in a British style that suits the expectations of the customers. At the same time, he learns the social skills to deal with these customers. In these ways he constructs a new masculine persona that conceals both his poverty and his Jewishness, in a similar way to Simon's reinvention for the Magnuses. Augie becomes a particular project of Mrs Renling, who wants to 'refine and school [him] in every way' (152). This involves Augie accompanying her when she stays in a hotel to take the mineral baths.

At the hotel Augie is attracted to Esther and Thea Fenchel, falling in love with Esther. Again the constructed nature of his masculine persona is emphasised. Although Augie is ostensibly a rich young man able to present himself 'as if God had not left out a single one of His gifts', he is aware that he has 'forged credentials' and is an 'imposter' (161). However, Augie's love and lust for Esther is authentic and when he asks her for a date and she refuses, he faints. Subsequently Thea tells him that his rejection came about because Esther thought he was Mrs Renling's gigolo (169). She also declares her love for him, but the Fenchels depart the following day. It then becomes apparent that Mrs Renling wants to adopt Augie, offering him the opportunity to become in reality the rich young man. The episode with the Renlings again foregrounds the way a male identity may be constructed and that this presentation of the self may be intrinsic to the American ideal of self-development. For both Simon and Augie, advancement is dependent on the performance of a suitable identity, with the significant difference that with the Renlings, Augie's Jewishness would be suppressed as he moved towards an assimilated identity. This suppression would require the repudiation of Augie's family – Mrs Renling refers to Augie's appeal to his 'folks' as 'baloney' (178). In an environment where everyone is expected to be 'self-seeking' (178), Augie's refusal to be suborned by Mrs Renling appears foolish, but Augie has 'family enough to suit me and history to be loyal to' (178). Moreover, Augie sees Mrs Renling's initiative as part of the efforts of a class of people who use their power to vindicate themselves (176–7). So Augie's refusal of the offer is foolish by conventional standards but is consonant with his desire to maintain his autonomy and rebuff attempts to map out his life and work out his own – as yet undefined – fate.

Later in the novel Thea Fenchel seeks out Augie and they begin a passionate affair. He abandons his job as a union organiser as he 'didn't have the calling to be a union man or in politics' (360) in order to accompany her to Mexico.[10] Augie's relationship with Thea is the most extensively represented love affair in the novel and its sexual element is explicit. In this Thea's strong sexuality is presented to the reader:

> With Thea it wasn't at all as it had been with other women, those who gave you their permission, so to speak, to undo one thing at a time and admire it, the next thing guarded again, and the last thing most guarded of all. She didn't delay or seem to hurry either. (361)

The first-person narrative and Augie's expressiveness and attention to visual detail provide depth to his account of many characters in the novel. However, as discussed by Cronin, Bellow's narrative technique still largely excludes other voices. The reader's perception of Thea is therefore acquired via Augie. Thea comes from a wealthy family and is married to a rich man, but one purpose of the trip to Mexico is to secure her divorce. After her divorce she will no longer be wealthy, as her family disapprove of her scandalous behaviour and will cut off her income. Her plan is to train an eagle in Mexico, catch giant iguanas, and make movies of the hunting that will earn an income.

Thea's wealth and her fascination with hunting register her assimilation into American society. Her ambition to train the eagle is seen by Augie as 'making history' (390), in part because this had been done so rarely since the 'Middle Ages' (370) but also because it is unexpected for a woman to do so (see 405). This gender ambiguity in relation to Thea is expressed through her clothes in Mexico – 'The outer were rugged, the inner silky' (404). Thea acquires the young eagle on the way to Mexico and it is named Caligula by Augie. The bird embodies a form of feral masculinity – the 'Black Prince', 'powerfully handsome, with his onward-turned head and buff and white feathers among the darker, his eyes were gruesome jewels and meant nothing in their little lines but cruelty' (386). Training Caligula to hunt requires a mastery that involves Thea in establishing a form of masculine dominance in the relationship.[11] With Augie's involvement, this then becomes a triangular relationship. Thea's Mexican scheme involves Augie adopting an appropriate masculine persona that has echoes of his time with the Renlings. Thea wants him to look like a 'sportsman' (365) and to this end fits Augie out in appropriate clothing. For example, he gets a heavy leather jacket that 'require you to want to kill game or you couldn't wear it' (365). Augie is being steered towards the kind of American identity derided by Joseph in *Dangling Man*. Augie hates the eagle at first, but then has to get along with him. However, he is put out by Thea's obsession with the bird and 'disconcerted [. . .] at love' when the bird is in the room (390).

When Thea and Augie arrive at their destination in the mountains, Acatla, Caligula is partly trained but needs to learn to hunt. In practice Caligula turns out to be timid in the face of the iguanas and Thea calls him a 'stinking coward' and 'chicken' (410, 411). A second attempt is utterly disastrous, with Augie and the horse falling as he attempts to launch Caligula – Augie hits his head, loses a tooth and is concussed, while the horse breaks a leg and is shot by Thea. Both Caligula and Augie have failed in their attempts at demonstrating the aggressive masculine traits associated with hunting. For Caligula this was supposed to be intrinsic to his nature, but his failure undercuts the validity of such expectations and correspondingly emphasises the constructed element of the masculine hunting persona. Caligula is sent away to a zoo and in the sequel of the 'great flop' Augie is low, and he describes himself with a 'turban of bandages', 'eyes deep-circled, cheeks drawn in, gap-toothed'; he thinks he resembles his mother, and at times his brother Georgie (419). With this comic disaster and its after-effects Augie can be seen as a *schlemiel* and this identification pushes him away from the male hunting identity that Thea had fostered, and back towards the weak and ineffectual, but morally good, characteristics that he sees in Georgie and his mother. This allusion to human frailty contrasts with Thea's ideas about purity and perfection – purity in both the eagle and the idealisation of love.[12]

As Augie's relationship with Thea unravels, he retreats temporarily into what can be seen as a dysfunctional variant of conventional masculinity – gambling and drinking with the American expatriate community in Acatla. At the same time, Thea is away in the mountains – sometimes overnight– catching snakes and then milking their venom, another activity both practically and symbolically indicative of her acquisition of masculine traits and what Augie calls her 'peculiarities' (427). The situation reaches a crisis when Stella – another American visiting Acatla – asks Augie to help her get away from her lover, who is about to be arrested (later in the novel Stella and Augie marry). He drives her to the next town to get a bus to Mexico City but the car gets stuck overnight in the mountains and they have sex. Although he denies the liaison to Thea, she repudiates him, saying that she was mistaken about who he was (457).

Augie's relationship with Thea indicates that he is susceptible to the attractions of expressing his masculinity through an intense sexuality and an excessive display of materialism. This materialism is signified on Augie's body through the wearing of expensive clothing suitable for hunting and in the expectation that he adopts the particular masculine persona of a wealthy hunter. Yet his interest in this is superficial and it is Thea who is the true hunter, as well as taking on other masculine traits – initiating their sexual relationship, displaying independence and leadership. In contrast, Augie surrenders his independence to her schemes. Augie's practical failure at hunting marks the beginning of a change in which he begins to resist Thea's view of the world and begins to reassert his independence.

This autonomy is manifested first in his adoption of male behaviour patterns in Acatla and then in his sexual activity with Stella.

Thea can be seen as one of the 'Machiavellis' of the novel, like Grandma Lausch, Einhorn and Mrs Renling, who continually try to steer Augie into some activity or way of being that they think is best for him. Augie resists these pressures to conform and constantly seeks to maintain his individuality and autonomy. With Thea there is the additional element of an intense erotic connection and the novel suggests there are dangers for men in their sexual relationships.[13] It is in this context that Gloria Cronin states that Thea Fenchel is 'the first real mistress and femme fatale in [Bellow's] novels' and that 'She is the first of Bellow's deathly erotics' (2001: 60). While her teaching of Augie to hunt and shoot is a reversal of the stereotype, Cronin concludes that Thea is 'a controlling, sadistic, erotic bitch' and one of the 'most hostile portraits of a woman' by Bellow. While the first-person narrative does occlude Thea's perspective, and the novel represents Thea negatively in certain respects, she is shown more sympathetically than some female characters in subsequent novels of Bellow, such as Madeleine in *Herzog*. Augie's self-reflection registers his own failings in his love for Thea and describes his anguish over the break-up. Their final meeting, at which Augie hopes to persuade Thea to renew their relationship, is marked by sadness rather than anger, and Augie notes twice that the connection between them was lost (471, 472). This is far from an accusation that Thea has been attempting to destroy Augie. Hostility to female characters, or straightforward misogyny, is clearly an aspect of the construction of women as Other and thereby a means of asserting a distinctive and superior masculinity. Yet Augie's account does not see him trying to assert a conventional masculinity nor project hostility back on to Thea. In fact, his reaction is rather to turn to self-reflection.

Augie realises he is 'in a fork about my course of life' (423). Thea's accusation that he is vain and unreliable, always looking at other women, and without a conscience provokes some troubling self-examination (462). He believes he has abandoned 'money or profession or duties' so that he could be 'free, and a sincere follower of love', but he realises that he is not a servant of love at all. Nor is he 'a bit good-hearted or affectionate' (462). So he doubts that he was on 'his mother's side' where love was concerned. This doubt is related to his intention to be a good person, or a *mensch*. However, he realises that social pressure requires one to construct a public persona to protect the self from 'exposure and shame' (463). This is a requirement to 'invent a man' and this persona 'must appear better and stronger than anyone else' (463). Social interaction therefore requires the construction of a strong male identity, but ultimately this 'huge invention' becomes the 'actual world' (463). Augie seems to problematise the consequences of a powerful masculinity, but the ability to exist as oneself, and not as this invented male persona, requires courage and Augie lacks this courage, seeing himself as a 'weak man', and going to 'whoever would give me cover from this mighty free-running terror and wild cold of chaos [. . .] and therefore to temporary embraces' (464). Augie's analysis suggests first that the traditional strong male persona is incompatible with what it means to be a *mensch*, or 'good-hearted and affectionate'. So too he rejects the 'temporary embraces' of sexual relationships and wishes to commit to a relationship.

When Augie returns to Chicago he tells Simon that he wants to have 'a fate good enough' and that he is on a 'pilgrimage' towards 'a "higher" independent fate' (487, 488). Despite these intentions, he is also a comic figure and is teased by an old friend, Clem Tambow: 'How is your campaign after a worthwhile fate, Augie?' (497). Augie sees the irony of his postion: 'I was only trying to do right, and I had broken my dome, lost teeth, got burned in my progress, a mighty slipshod campaigner' (497). Tambow has been reading psychology and diagnoses Augie with anxiety and recommends some of 'Dr Freud's medicine' (499). He believes Augie has 'nobility syndrome' and tells him, 'You want there should be Man, with capital M, with great stature' (500). The gap between Augie's ideals and the reality of his circumstances is the gap between the ideal masculinity of the *mensch* and the everyday comic actions of the *schlemiel*. Yet in a later conversation with Tambow, Augie outlines a way of living that avoids existence being 'mere clownery, hiding tragedy' (522). His vision is of the 'axial lines of life': 'Truth, love, peace, bounty, usefulness, harmony!' (522). These are the measures through which a man will 'live with true joy' (523). However, following this way of living does not require a man 'to show in some way how *he* held the world together' (524). Augie doesn't want to be 'any model of manhood' but to have something of his own (524). Augie's supposedly practical proposal is that he would get a property, marry and bring his mother and brother Georgie to his property, and then set up a school with foster children (524–5). Tambow is both impressed and astonished by this scheme, but he gently mocks Augie for wanting to be a 'king' (525). Clearly Augie is grasping for a role that is beneficial for others, but lurking behind his idea is the risk that he is simply wanting to assert a form of dominant masculinity as the 'king', while within the scheme are the seeds of an absurdity that could lead him towards appearing to be a *schlemiel*.

Any possibility of implementing this plan is immediately scuppered by the entry of the United States into the Second World War. Augie is politically engaged by the cause of the war, arguing that the enemy would create a 'universal ant heap' if they won (526).[14] This ideological position and his desire 'to do right and not lead a disappointed life' (539) prompts him to sign up with the Merchant Marine. During his training he is based in New York, reconnects with Stella and marries before he sets off on his first voyage. The ship is torpedoed and Augie narrowly escapes with his life. With comic inevitability Augie's sole companion on the lifeboat as they drift in the Atlantic is yet another Chicago Jew – Hymie Bateshaw. Bateshaw is the ship's carpenter, but turns out to be a 'psycho-biophysicist' and Augie despairs that he always has to 'fall among theoreticians' (577, 578). The episode is significant because Bateshaw's vision springs from masculine aspiration and is alarming in the context of the war against fascism. Bateshaw claims that 'Everybody wants to be the most desirable kind of man' (578) and that this ambition sprang from his experience of the municipal swimming pool: 'Shivery little rat. Lips blue, blood thin, scared, your little balls tight, your little thing shrivelled' (578). From this springs his desire for 'true manhood' and then his ambition to be 'the world's leading authority' on boredom – in his experiments he claims to have created life (579, 580). Augie's wry reaction is that if Bateshaw is not a genius then he is in the boat with a maniac (580). That Bateshaw's fixation is indeed crazy becomes apparent when he expresses his intention to 'create a serum' to overcome boredom and to turn every man into a poet and every woman into a saint (585). Although Bateshaw's dream is of a world without bloodshed and cruelty, his vision is clearly totalitarian and Augie refuses any intervention that involves 'doing things to the entire human race' (585). Bateshaw attacks Augie to prevent him from trying to attract a potential rescue ship, but his plans collapse as he is seized with a fever and the pair are rescued by a British tanker.

The Bateshaw episode is another example of Augie as *schlemiel* – his high-minded willingness to sign up is mocked by the fact that his sole wartime engagement is in grappling with a proto-totalitarian Jew in the middle of the Atlantic. Although the comic irony is intended to undercut grandiose visions associated with masculinity, there is a question whether Augie has discovered his fate and whether the novel successfully articulates an alternative vision of masculinity. After the war Augie is in Europe and acting for Mintouchian, an

Armenian entrepreneur, in what seem to be dubious activities. It is at this moment that Augie has constructed his retrospective memoir and has come to two conclusions. First, that he is characterised by 'the animal ridens in me, the laughing creature, forever rising up' (615), while he also sees himself as 'a sort of Columbus of those near-at-hand' (616). These perceptions – articulated in the final pages of the novel – have of course been central to his narrative as he looks back on his experiences. It is one reason why the novel is not a *Bildungsroman* and Augie is shown as having refused the heroic. The novel also offers a critique of masculinities associated with the pursuit of American materialism or with the outdoor life of hunting and shooting. However, the novel resists defining an alternative model of masculinity – or perhaps, in Cronin's view, it fails to do so through its repudiation of the feminine. It is notable that although Bellow repudiates the grandiose masculine vision and undercuts male self-importance through the notion of the 'near-at-hand' – that is, the everyday – and through the ironic self-perception of the animal ridens, Augie's masculinity remains secure in its heterosexuality.

Jo Sinclair, *Wasteland*

This chapter concludes with a brief consideration of Jo Sinclair's novel *Wasteland*. Jo Sinclair was the pen name of Ruth Seid (1913–95), the daughter of Russian Jewish immigrants. Sinclair's formal education finished at high school as she needed to work to support her family. However, she pursued her ambition to write and eventually obtained paid work with the WPA writer's project.[15] Sinclair's first published fiction was in short story form, but her unpublished first novel, *Wasteland*, won the Harper prize for new authors in 1945 and was published in the United States by Harpers in 1946. The Harper prize of $10,000 was a significant recognition of her talents and potential. In the 1930s she was involved with the anti-fascist left and in *Wasteland* she writes from a leftist perspective.[16] However, the novel is also significant in its analysis of the problems of Jewish identity in America; in its representation of gender and masculinity in relation to lesbianism; and in its description of the psychoanalytical process. In all these aspects the novel has a markedly different perspective to *The Adventures of Augie March*, in which Augie boldly claims his American identity, eschews psychoanalytic interpretation and lays claim to a vigorous male heterosexuality.

Sinclair's novel may be considered to have two principal and interlinked themes: the problems of Jewish identity and assimilation in the United States, and issues of gender and sexuality in relation to lesbianism. The novel is located in the early 1940s, but is in effect a family history containing substantial retrospective passages going back to Russia in the late nineteenth century and to the America of the 1930s and the effects of the Depression. The narrative is focused through Jake (or John, or Jack) Brown (originally Braunowitz), who is a successful newspaper photographer, but who is unhappy and sees himself and his family as living in a wasteland. The novel opens with him beginning a consultation with a psychiatrist on the recommendation of his sister Deborah (Debby), who has previously undergone a course of treatment with the same psychiatrist. The novel is structured chronologically through the conversations that Jake has with the psychiatrist. These take the form of directly reported dialogues which turn into third-person narrative as Jake and the psychiatrist delve into past episodes of his life and that of other family members. The narrative is punctuated with the doctor's notes as he sums up Jake's progress. The novel moves towards Jake's reconciliation with his past and a resolution of his problems with his family and his identity.

The narrative focuses on the psychiatric process and valorises psychoanalytic treatment by presenting Jake as changing his perspective by talking through past events. Given this emphasis, it is not surprising that Jake's analysis involves a Freudian Oedipal interpretation of his relationships with his family, and in particular his parents. The analyst perceives him as hating his father and having failed to separate from his mother. Jake feels responsibility for his mother's circumstances and is disgusted in imagining her in bed with his father. However, Jake's familial relationships are inseparable from his Jewish identity, and the conversations with the doctor focus in particular on the Passover rituals which coincide annually with Jake's birthday. Jake has internalised anti-Semitic views and the intertwining of these with his troubled family relationships has led to his rejection of his Jewish identity. At work he is known as John Brown and no one knows about his Jewish family background. Jake's public denial of his Jewish identity is intended to enable his assimilation and his identification as a white American male, but he remains psychologically and emotionally bound into the Jewish rituals of his family. While the novel represents Jake's ambiguous relationship with Jewish culture as grounded in his problematic family relationships, the actuality of anti-Semitism is shown in the way his brother loses his job in the Depression simply because he is Jewish.

The novel makes clear both the priority given to sons in Jewish American families and the patriarchal nature of Jewish religious ceremonies. Jake's involvement in Jewish ritual in the family focuses on the Passover celebrations in which he participates as the youngest son, while his father leads the ceremony. However, there is a failure of masculinity in the Brown family. This is most apparent in Jake's father, who has failed to adapt to American society, as is shown by the primacy of Yiddish in his cultural life. Both Jake and Debby perceive his inadequacies as husband, father and breadwinner, but the psychiatrist persuades Jake to see that he too has abdicated his male responsibilities within the family. Moreover, he comes to understand that he cannot substitute for his father in relation to his mother's lack of a satisfactory husband.

Jake's flawed masculinity is shown through Freudian analysis to be rooted in his family circumstances, but these circumstances cannot be separated from his Jewish identity. His adoption of a non-Jewish persona outside the family at work is indicative of the contradictions of assimilation in the period. Jake, who like Debby is fair, can pass straightforwardly as 'white' and prefers to do so because of his self-hatred, prompted by living in an anti-Semitic culture. The ambivalences around assimilation are articulated in a number of oppositions relating to Jake's experiences and these mark his sense of difference. He feels his greatest sense of American identity when he votes, and in this the novel registers the formal recognition of Jewish American citizenship and valorises the democratic ideology of the United States. Voting is seen by Jake as largely a masculine activity, marking 'the names of the guys you wanted in' and feeling that his 'name was as good as the next guy's' (28). Yet this American activity is juxtaposed with the Friday night Jewish family ritual to which he mostly adheres: 'there were two regular things for him. There was Friday nights and there was voting' (28). Friday night supper is about the Jewish and Russian food that brings the family together, but this is contrasted with the 'American food. Roast beef, steak, apple pie, salad' that he eats in downtown restaurants (29). This divided and uneasily assimilated self is also reflected in his photographic work. His job involves producing images for the newspaper – images that will be professionally acceptable. This is, however, a source of anxiety since he is worried not only that his Jewishness will be revealed one day, but also that his Jewishness would 'mark his work' (99). Again his identity is split, as he produces a completely separate series of photos that have a different meaning for him and which he identifies as 'Jewish pictures' (230).

Jake's heterosexuality is similarly confused. He believes himself to be in love with Laura, a columnist at the paper, even though they have no sexual contact, but during analysis comes to see that she is in fact a mother figure. He is conducting a sexual liaison with Kathy, but downplays the significance of this relationship as he believes that the 'real thing' could only be with a Jewish woman; he would only marry a Jewish woman (11, 12). This split in his sexual desire between American and Jewish women is a further manifestation of his troubled assimilation into American culture and identity. The passiveness of his relationship with Kathy is symptomatic of his failure to achieve the untroubled heterosexuality expected of American men.

Although he passes as a white American, Jake's concealed Jewish identity induces a sense that his social integration and his American masculinity can only ever be provisional. His anxiety about being 'found out' as a Jew echoes Gilman's view that the Other can only ever be a 'shoddy counterfeit, an outsider' (1986: 2). Jake's masculinity is further threatened from within his family by a 'queerness' that permeates his life.[17] It is Jake's sister, Debby, who embodies this queerness. In *The Passing Game* Warren Hoffman examines the way in which the novel makes connections between Jake and Debby and thus between queerness and Jewishness as closeted identities that need to be brought into the open, and which can be through the process of psychoanalysis (2009: 93). However, Hoffman also argues that in relation to gender and sexuality the novel is both 'remarkably advanced and hopelessly outdated at the same time' (102).

As Hoffman notes, the novel's outdatedness is manifested in its adherence to the convention that homosexual identity is marked by inversion. Debby's queerness is signalled through her 'masculine' behaviour and appearance from childhood into adulthood. As the position of the family deteriorates in the Depression when both Sig and their father lose employment, it is Debby who begins to take on a male role. She provides additional income through taking on work with the Works Progress Administration (WPA). On the one hand, this should be a male role and be taken on by Sig as the eldest son, but there is shame attached to the WPA that would compromise his masculinity. There is an irony in that Debby as a female takes on the WPA and loses less in terms of status, but in doing so, she again takes on a male role. The novel is radical in giving narrative space to a female who expresses masculine traits while also occupying male roles. However, the novel also reflects contemporary anxieties in presenting Debby's masculine strengths as necessarily diminishing Jake's masculinity.

In *Wasteland* this tension between Jake and Debby is dramatised, as with many other key elements of the narrative, around the Passover Seder. Jake's sense of the family's wasteland has led to his disillusionment with the Passover rituals, and one year he stays in his room rather than reading out the questions as was his role as the younger son. In his absence, Debby takes over his role. Even though Jake has voluntarily relinquished his responsibility, he is furious with Debby for supposedly stealing it. The psychiatrist identifies Jake's anxiety about this given his investment in Debby as 'the good part of the family' and their hope (216). But Jake then frames the issue as relating to his masculinity: 'Jesus, what kind of man am I that a girl can take my place at the Seder!' (217). The psychiatrist then articulates this as his perception that Debby had stolen 'the last remaining bits of maleness from him' (217). Following the dialogue between Jake and the psychiatrist, there is a shift to third-person narrative followed by Jake's interior monologue, which elaborates his perception of his loss of masculinity to Debby.

> Through the years [Debby] had walked with an ever wider stride, she had worn trousers, she had cut her hair short as a man's, she had borne their mother across the swollen rivers of relief and shame, she had stood up to their father, she had dared to aspire to intellectual heights through the writing of stories. And, with each step that she took closer to the powerful male, to the place occupied by men, he had taken a step backwards; as she strode onward, as she gained masculinity and strength, he stepped backwards, he crawled towards weakness. Through the years, then, had she not taken his masculinity from him and used it for her own? (222)

In this passage Sinclair articulates the anxieties expressed in the period, that active, intellectual women were a threat to male identity and to men's social roles. For example, a *Look* publication, *The Decline of the American Male*, exemplifies such concerns in claiming that young boys are damaged by the increase in competition when 'Girls wear blue jeans and short haircuts like boys, play ball with boys, compete with them in science classes and join in bull sessions' (Attwood et al. 1958: 4). The conservatism of Jake's view seems to be echoed in a revised description of Debby as he begins to respond to his treatment and regain some pride in his Jewish identity, and a sense of his masculine worth. His revivified masculinity is specifically demonstrated in his new role as a mentor and nurturer of his nephew, Bernie. So too his decision to enlist marks his confident assertion of a male social role. As he regains his male identity Debby seems to show more conventional feminine traits. For example, before they go to donate blood, Debby is wearing a dress and Jake perceives her as 'very girlish, very sisterly, her hair not like a boy's but just short, free-looking, and her features were soft, her mouth the softest of all' (331). These are examples of an apparent shift in perspective that seem to lead Hoffman to conclude that the novel is 'outdated': 'Though Sinclair creates a positive space for lesbian identity, *Wasteland* is ultimately antifeminist, as it reconstitutes traditional gender roles at the text's end' (2009: 102).

Hoffman's conclusion about *Wasteland* is indicative of the tensions within the text. One question about the novel might be why Sinclair, who can broadly be identified with Debby, chose to write from the perspective of Jake and not from that of Debby. One answer would be that Sinclair wishes to explore two themes – that of the alienation of American Jews and the social perception of a 'lesbian' woman. For the latter perspective, Jake represents conventional views of lesbian women in terms of their inversion and queerness and his feeling of disgust. To Jake's perspective is added that of the psychiatrist who represents contemporary Freudian orthodoxy. It is only the psychiatrist who actually names Debby as 'lesbian' and both Jake and Debby herself use euphemisms – Debby identifies herself with 'All the odd ones, the queer and different ones' (171). Jake refers to Debby's exterior signs – 'your hair? The way you look?' – and Debby responds with 'The way I am inside' (172). Debby's generalisation of her position outside social norms is not specifically articulated as a sexual identity, but as a more general exclusion that can be related to 'Any group of people wounded by the world. Jews, Negroes, cripples of any sort' (171).

The novel therefore explores contemporary perspectives on gender and sexuality and can be seen as radical in its deconstruction of them. Although Jake and the doctor see Debby in terms of inversion theory – that as a lesbian she must be masculine in appearance and behaviour – the novel moderates this perspective in significant ways.[18] It is the doctor who both names Debby as a lesbian and, more significantly, steers Jake towards a sympathetic understanding of her identity. While the narrative is ambiguous about whether Debby is sexually active, in arousing Jake's sympathy, the doctor challenges conventional American Freudian views on vaginal orgasm, heterosexual norms and motherliness (see the discussion in Chapter 3). Yet the doctor is more conventional in tending to reinforce Jake's perspective on gender traits and roles. For example, when Jake complains that Debby has stolen his maleness, the psychiatrist asks him whether he hasn't stolen from Debby over the years – 'her right to be soft and delicate? Who helped steal her right to be a girl, a baby sister, the one to be protected, not to protect?' (224). Although the psychiatrist steers Jake to a greater understanding of his circumstances and helps him to accept his Jewish identity, it is in fact his conversations with Debby that help him develop a far greater understanding of his social circumstances and a sympathy for other marginalised groups.[19] It is within this context, therefore, that the apparent drift back to 'traditional gender roles' must be read. Debby's appearance in a dress – as referred to above – does not mark a diminution of her important role in the family, but rather a shift in Jake's perception of her. No longer does he see her simply as a queer person – 'half like a man, half like a woman' (37), but as a whole person and part of the world. In fact this more measured perception of Debby is noted earlier in the novel, when Jake is having intimate conversations with his sister. For example, talking late at night, he sees her as 'girlish' and notices her 'beautifully shaped, soft woman's mouth', which also has an 'insistence [. . .], a strength' (163). In other words, the novel disconnects the sexed body from stereotypical attributes of gender – Jake is vulnerable and weak, while Debbie is strong and clear-thinking. At the end the novel does not reinstate gender roles in a simplistic way, but narrates an inclusiveness that allows for difference. Jake certainly begins to adopt the role of a father figure to his nephews, and he signs up for the Signals Corps and expects to serve in the war. However, the context in which he does so may be seen as connected with an idealised version of Jewish masculinity, connected to the contemporary American ideal of human universality. In guiding Bernie, Jake gently warns him of racialism towards the African American boxer they are watching, and his desire to sign up does not come from a desire to assert himself violently in the world. His motivation comes from an inclusiveness that is symbolised as Jake and Debby together donate blood as a contribution to the war effort.

The four novels considered in this chapter interrogate the nature and boundaries of contemporary American masculinity from a Jewish American perspective. Although theoretically American Jews were accepted as white citizens by the late 1940s, the male characters in the novels struggle with anti-Semitism and problems of assimilation. This is in part a consequence of the time in which they are set, and the immediate legacy of the Holocaust, but the novels clearly reflect continuing anxieties. In each novel the emphasis on leading male characters foregrounds the issue of Jewish American masculinity and its problematic relationship to the expectations of contemporary men. In *Young Lions* and *Focus* there is a tendency to idealise the Jewish American male, who may offer an alternative vision of manhood, while depending on recognisable aspects of conventional masculinity. So, for example, Finkelstein offers a model based on an assertiveness that counters cultural feminisation, but that also depends on a willingness to be violent.

Bellow has described problems with contemporary expectations of men and in the character of Simon in *The Adventures of Augie March* he offers a critique of American myths of the self-made man and the damage that American materialist culture can do to men. However, in Augie himself the novel struggles with an alternative position. In an echo of Joseph in *Dangling Man*, Augie rejects the manly ideal of the hunting male associated with Ernest Hemingway and will not go along with Simon's pursuit of the American materialist dream. As Gloria Cronin argues, Augie, like other Bellow characters, is 'an ironic version of the self-absorbed male romantic individualist'. So Augie tries out various identities, drawn from American and Jewish culture – the hunter, the *mensch*, the *schlemiel*, the intellectual, the husband – while maintaining an ironic distance from them. He professes a commitment to the everyday and thus to the idea that he is a new American Everyman – an Everyman whose ironic detachment marks the alienation of modern American life. However, in the end it is perhaps Augie's commitment to heterosexuality as an uncontestable marker of his manhood that roots him in conventional masculinity.

Jo Sinclair's *Wasteland* disrupts conventional gender roles through Debby, a lesbian character. Within her family, in her work and in her appearance Debby behaves like a male, spreading a disruptive queerness that unsettles her brother Jake. In associating queerness with excluded groups such as Jews and African Americans, the novel creates a lesbian space that opens to question normal expectations of gender.

Notes

1. For a personal perspective on the New York intellectuals, see Irving Howe 1968.
2. For a discussion of the importance of 'universalism' in the 1940s, see Hutchinson 2018: 4–6.

3. See for example Saul Bellow's father, Abraham, and his enthusiasm for assimilation and the idea of America (Leader 2015: 93–4).
4. *Ulysses* is of course a prominent defence of Jewishness and Irishness in the figure of Bloom.
5. James Atlas says that *Augie March* 'made Bellow famous' (207), and that the novel sold thirty thousand copies despite not making the bestseller lists (2000: 206).
6. For an overview of the reception of the novel, see Leader 2015: 436–40 and 447–53.
7. *The Catcher in the Rye* is not generally considered with other Jewish American novels as its themes and characters are not obviously Jewish, but J. D. Salinger was largely brought up within Jewish traditions and culture.
8. For analysis of the interplay between Bellow's life and his fiction, see Leader 2015.
9. It shouldn't be forgotten that the context for the early years of Augie's life in Chicago were the Depression, Prohibition and gangsterism. Simon is modelled on Bellow's brother Morris, who is described in 'I got a scheme!' as adopting 'the style of a racketeer and put[ting] himself over as a wheeler-dealer' (13). Bellow also refers to his brother as 'aggressive' and as 'entirely American', representing the 'day-to-day genius of the USA' (2005: 11 and 12).
10. Augie's lack of political commitment echoes Bellow's own move away from his Trotskyism by the early 1950s and the beginning of his reactionary journey.
11. In *H Is for Hawk* Helen Macdonald considers the way gender might affect human relationships with hawks. She argues that from a Freudian perspective, nineteenth-century falconers were 'projecting onto their hawks all the male qualities they thought threatened by modern life: wildness, power, virility, independence and strength. By identifying with their hawks as they trained them, they could *introject*, or repossess, those qualities' (Macdonald 2014: 79).
12. See Leader (2015) on Thea, purity and utopias, 228. Leader also discusses more generally the influence of Mexico on Bellow, 226–36.
13. The starkest example of this may be Simon's early obsession with Cissy Flexner, which leads to his involvement in a betting pool to make money quickly and then the loss of all his cash, their mother's homelessness and Simon's imprisonment and contemplation of suicide.
14. The novel alludes to the Holocaust in Augie's perception that 'amidst the new pyramids there wouldn't any new Moses be bred' (526), but the novel does not directly foreground the legacy of the Holocaust in the same way as Bellow's *The Victim*.
15. See the Jewish Women's Archive Encyclopedia for further biographical and bibliographical information.
16. See Alan Wald's *Trinity of Passion* for discussion of the connections between her political activities and her writing (2007: 236–42).

17. From the 1920s the word queer was commonly used to refer to homosexuals, although it retained the meaning of 'odd' (see Chapter 3). Sinclair exploits this double meaning, for example in Jake's reference to his 'Jewish' photographs as also 'queer' (230). Monica Bachman in 'Someone like Debby' notes the ambiguity about sexual relations between women both in the novel and in letters women wrote to Sinclair in response to the novel. She uses the term 'lesbian-like' to describe 'women whose practices manifest affinities with those of present-day lesbians' (2000: 385).
18. The discussion of *The City and the Pillar* in Chapter 3 shows how Vidal also resisted the stereotyping of inversion.
19. Gay Wilentz argues in 'Healing the "sick Jewish soul"' that Debby has a similar role in 'bringing the necessary cultural markers to Jake's dialogue with the doctor' and compensating for the doctor's lack of knowledge of Jewish culture and religion (2001: 81).

Chapter 5

African American Identity and Masculinity

This chapter explores the relationship between dominant modes of masculinity and the position of African American men, as represented in the novels of several key writers of the period – James Baldwin, Ralph Ellison, Chester Himes and Ann Petry. The chapter relates to Chapter 4, where I discussed 'whiteness' and the way in which it had been both a defining category of American citizenship but also a category subject to redefinition in twentieth-century America. While Jewish Americans had become categorised as 'white' by mid-century, African Americans remained beyond 'whiteness', while the legacy of slavery, the segregationist Jim Crow social and legal structures of the South and institutional racism in the North served to maintain their marginalisation and oppression. The artificial nature of this divide is highlighted by 'passing' and is made vividly by Margo Jefferson in her memoir *Negroland*. Her great uncle Lucious spent his life passing as white, but then 'resumed his life as a Negro': 'We have friends who look as white as Uncle Lucious. But I had always known them as Negroes. [. . .] Who and what are "we Negroes", when so many of us could be white people? [. . .] Suddenly the fact of racial slippage overwhelmed me' (2016: 109–10).

The explanatory academic discourses that focused on the state of American society and culture in this period, and which I briefly surveyed in the Introduction, included the position of African Americans. Such analysis encompassed books by African American journalists and academics such as Roi Ottley, E. Franklin Frazier, Horace R. Cayton, St Clair Drake, John Hope Franklin and a variety of authors in the journal *Phylon*, published from 1940.[1] The Second World War had a significant effect on the state of the debate for both practical and ideological reasons. In practice the United States government had to harness the skills and labour of the African American population in order to fight the war effectively. Segregation in the military and in the workforce strongly militated against this (see for example Franklin (1947) on the military, 559ff). Their exclusion from the opportunities offered in the defence industries was strongly felt by African Americans and in 1941 a planned mass march led to an executive order from Roosevelt designed to end such discrimination (see Ottley 1949: 283ff). Moreover, the ideology articulated in the war against fascism, with its emphasis on democracy and freedom, pointed up the gap between rhetoric and reality, and the seething disillusionment felt by many African Americans was expressed in the riots in Detroit and New York of 1943. This gap between American democratic ideology and the actual circumstances of African American existence was one of the principal arguments made in Gunner Myrdal's *An American Dilemma* (1944).[2] Myrdal's work made clear the oppressive and excluded conditions of African American life. In an unpublished review of *An American Dilemma* written in 1944, Ralph Ellison makes some critical comments, complaining that Myrdal's evaluation, for all its strengths, still views African Americans through a white lens and denies them agency (Ellison 1944: 328–40). For Ellison, African Americans need to take their culture and 'create of it "the uncreated consciousness of their race"' (340). Ellison makes the further point that the American social sciences have contributed to the moral problem that Myrdal defines as the 'American Dilemma'. In particular he cites Robert E. Park, co-founder of the University of Chicago School of Sociology, as describing the Negro as 'primarily an artist, loving life for its own sake. His *métier* is expression rather than action. He is so to speak, the lady among the races' (332). The quotation from Park demonstrates how African American men are feminised in racist American culture. In the South, the diminutive appellation 'boy' infantilised them.

It is not surprising, therefore, that in the face of such attitudes African American men responded by asserting a male identity that was consonant with dominant expectations of masculinity. For example, in 'Mannish Boy' (1955), Muddy Waters (McKinley Morganfield) sings:

Now when I was a young boy, at the age of five
My mother said I was gonna be the greatest man alive
But now I'm a man, I made 21
I want you to believe me honey,
We are having lots of fun

> I'm a man
> I spell M, A, chile, N
> That represents man
> No B, O, chile, Y.

The singer strongly rejects the appellation 'boy', staking a claim for manhood on the basis of his heterosexual performance, simultaneously reinforcing his claim by dismissing the female addressee as 'chile'. The singer thus seeks to associate himself with core masculine traits, while speaking from a subordinate cultural position.

James Baldwin's experience of exclusion in the North, described in 'Notes of a native son', sets an important context for a consideration of African American literature of this period. The narrative framework for 'Notes of a native son', first published in 1955, was the death of Baldwin's father and its conjunction with race riots in Detroit and Harlem (1955: 85).[3] Baldwin considered that his father 'lived and died in an intolerable bitterness of spirit' and he connects this bitterness with the riot, but also recognises that 'this bitterness was now mine' (88). This bitterness was induced in Baldwin during the year he spent working in New Jersey in 1942–3, when he experienced racism because he did not behave in the way expected of Negroes. The culmination of this occurred during his last night in New Jersey, when he was told in the 'American Diner', 'We don't serve Negroes here' (95). Baldwin then describes his nightmarish experience after going back out onto the street:

> People were moving in every direction but it seemed to me, in that instant, that all of the people I could see, and many more than that, were moving toward me, against me, and that everyone was white. I remember how their faces gleamed. [. . .] I wanted to do something to crush these white faces, which were crushing me. (95–6)

He then goes into 'an enormous, glittering, and fashionable restaurant, in which I knew that not even the intercession of the Virgin would cause me to be served' (96). Again he is told that they 'don't serve Negroes' and in response hurls a glass of water at the waitress and shatters a mirror. He escapes the 'violent whipping' (95) that would have ensued had he been caught but perceives that his '*real* life, was in danger, and not from anything other people might do but from the hatred that I carried in my own heart' (98).

In retrospect, Baldwin regards himself in this period as having 'contracted some dread chronic disease, the unfailing symptom of which is a kind of blind fever, a pounding in the skull and fire in the bowels' (94). But this is not an individual affliction: 'There is not a Negro alive who does not have this rage in his blood.' The choice, for Baldwin, is between 'living with it consciously, or surrendering to it' (94). Baldwin's story and his conclusions draw out key elements relevant to an analysis of representations of African American masculinity in this period: the constrained spaces for the expression of male identity; the related dominance of whiteness as an oppressive ideological, physical and cultural constant; and the anger integral to the lives of most African American men, who may often respond with spontaneous violence. Baldwin's conclusion also has significant implications for how writers might approach the representation of black American experience.

Baldwin's account is representative of one aspect of African American literary writing of this period insofar as it is a record of the experience of oppression in a racist society. In comparing Baldwin's account with the example of Muddy Waters' song, different ways of responding to these circumstances are apparent. Baldwin himself acknowledges the attractions of rage and violence as an appropriate reaction, but problematises such a response. 'Mannish Boy' claims a heterosexual hypermasculinity as a means of asserting a resistant identity. Early in his career Richard Wright advocated collective action as a means of radical change (see for example, 'Fire and cloud', a short story published in his first book, *Uncle Tom's Children* (1938, 157–220).[4]

The context of a racist society and culture in America in the mid-twentieth century was problematic for African American writers. For example, in 1992 Toni Morrison explored the notion of whiteness in relation to literature in *Playing in the Dark*. Her starting point was the assumption of literary historians and critics that 'traditional, canonical American literature is free of, uninformed, and unshaped by the four-hundred year presence of, first, Africans and then African Americans in the United States' (1992: 4–5). In challenging that perspective, she developed an argument, which corresponds with that of Valerie Babb, in claiming that literature had a particular role to play in defining American identity as white. Moreover, this cultural identity is gendered: 'the American [is] new, white, and male' (43). Europe was not the sole reference point for this difference: 'Writers were able to celebrate or deplore an identity [. . .] elaborated through racial difference.' She argues that 'The ways in which artists – and the society that bred them – transferred internal conflicts to a "blank darkness", to conveniently bound and violently silenced black bodies, is a major theme in American literature' (38). Morrison names this process in American culture as Africanism – 'a fabricated brew of darkness, otherness, alarm and desire that is uniquely American' (38). The Africanist persona produced from this 'brew' performs 'duties of exorcism and reification and mirroring' (39).

Morrison's analysis exemplifies the way in which racialising discourses are intricately entangled with those of gender, and how the construction of white or Western masculinity is dependent on an Othering that involves both gender and race. Such approaches are pertinent to analysis of American literature of this period. The implications of this American literary tradition are considerable for the African American writers considered in this chapter. Such writers, who themselves are already marginalised in contemporary discourses, face significant obstacles in achieving both an authoritative literary voice and black characters whose agency is convincing.[5]

The question of an appropriate form and approach to writing fiction was the subject of considerable debate amongst African American writers in the period. Richard Wright's 'Blueprint for negro writing' (1937) sparked the debate, while his novel *Native Son* (1940) was highly influential in setting a model for the realist 'protest novel'. Speaking in 1948 at the University of Chicago on 'The dilemma of the negro novelist in America', Himes argues that fear shapes Negro life and that it is necessary to 'know the truth and what it does to us'.

> If this plumbing for the truth reveals within the Negro personality homicidal mania, lust for white women, a pathetic sense of inferiority, paradoxical anti-Semitism, arrogance, Uncle Tomism, hate and fear and self-hate, this then is the effect of oppression on the human personality. These are the daily horrors, the daily realities, the daily experiences of an oppressed minority. (quoted by Sallis 2000: 112)

The writer's role is to 'plumb for the truth' of the 'Negro personality', but it is notable that for Himes this person is inevitably a heterosexual male. Chester Himes's early writing and Anne Petry's *The Street* reflect the influence of Wright's mode of realist writing on other African American authors.

In 1949 James Baldwin published 'Everybody's protest novel', an essay that mounted a strong critical attack on *Native Son*. Baldwin's critique paired Wright's novel with Harriet Beecher Stowe's *Uncle Tom's Cabin* (1852), characterising them both as 'protest novels' and arguing that as such they were more concerned with 'Society' than the true subject for a novelist, the individual: 'The failure of the protest novel lies in its rejection of life, the human being, the denial of his beauty, dread, power [. . .]' (23) Baldwin's characterisation of Bigger Thomas (the principal character in *Native Son*) reflects his analysis of Uncle Tom's Cabin – that Uncle Tom is redeemed only through Stowe's religious transformation of him into a black man 'robbed of his humanity and divested of his sex' (18). For Baldwin, Bigger Thomas's character has 'accepted a theology that denies him life, that he admits the possibility of his being sub-human and feels constrained, therefore, to battle for his humanity according to those brutal criteria bequeathed to him at his birth' (23). Ralph Ellison took a similar position to Baldwin, attacking the 'narrow naturalism' which leads to despair in 'much of our current fiction' and aspiring to a fiction which, 'leaving sociology to the scientists, can arrive at the truth about the human condition' (Ellison 1953: 153).

In 1950 *Phylon* published an issue devoted to the 'Negro in literature', which included an essay by William Gardner Smith titled 'The negro writer: pitfalls and compensations'. The debate centred on the issue of representation, often articulated around the division between the narrow restriction to Negro themes or the need to address 'universal' themes. As William Gardner Smith puts it, the Negro writer is 'invariably bitter' and this means that 'He is driven often to write a tract, rather than a work of art' (298). Such debates are inflected by broader political divisions, driven in particular by the reversal of the American Communist Party's position once the Soviet Union joined the Second World War and by the Cold War. Thomas Schaub's *American Fiction in the Cold War* places the terms of the debate about the protest novel in relation to the emergence of a conservative liberal narrative in American culture. The 'new' liberals were disillusioned with the left and the Soviet Union, and castigated themselves for their facile ideas of progress and the seductions of social realism and proletarian fiction (Schaub 1991: 5, 7).[6]

While Wright's realist form provided an exemplar for other African American writers, his representation of African American masculinity was also influential. Sherley Anne Williams saw a change in the representation of the black male character that was marked by the publication of *Native Son*. She argues:

> *Native Son* began a period in which the black heroic quest was increasingly externalized. A perceptive, though not necessarily articulate or educated, protagonist seeks recognition from the white power structure and in the process comes to recognize – and realize – himself. (S. Williams [1986] 2000: 221)

Subsequent African American critics have echoed this concern about the way dominant forms of masculinity have served as a model for black American masculinity. For example, Devon Carbado argues that gender and sexuality have been marginalised in antiracist discourse (1999: 3). There is a focus on men rather than women, with the consequence that 'Heterosexual Black men occupy a privileged victim status in antiracist discourse' (4). Black men 'are perceived to be *significantly* more vulnerable and *significantly* more "endangered" than Black women. They become the quintessential example of the effects of racial subordination' (4). Carbado maintains that this emphasis constitutes a 'myth of racial authenticity' around the black heterosexual male body, which excludes other bodies and identities (4). Such a view is echoed by bell hooks:

> The discourse of black resistance has almost always equated freedom with manhood, the economic and material domination of black men with castration, emasculation. Accepting these sexual metaphors forged a bond between oppressed black men and their white male oppressors. (1990: 58)

Many African American men therefore identify with and make claim to the attributes of dominance associated with hegemonic masculinity (see Mutua 2006: 12–21). Patricia Hill Collins argues that both the underlying vision of masculinity as dominance and the acceptance of traditional gender roles have hindered antiracist scholarship and social policy (2006: 75–6).[7] As African American men internalise the notion of masculinity as dominance, so they are likely to 'embrace unrealistic strategies for dealing with relations of dominance' (75). Collins provides a number of examples of these 'unrealistic' strategies, including aggressiveness and violence, sexual assertiveness and illegal economic activities (86–90). The juxtaposition of Himes's agenda for the Negro novelist with later, feminist analyses of African American masculinity suggests some continuity of the issues facing black American males. I will begin with a discussion of such issues in Chester Himes's novel.

Chester Himes, *If He Hollers Let Him Go*

Chester Himes is well known as the writer of a series of genre crime novels set in Harlem. In contrast, his early writing career involved the publication of two realist novels set in Los Angeles in the

Second World War: *If He Hollers Let Him Go* (1945) and *The Lonely Crusade* (1947).[8]

If He Hollers Let Him Go is the account of Bob Jones, written as a first-person narrative. Through his experiences, Himes analyses the effects of the pervasive fear that he identified in the quotation about the role of the novelist printed above. Jones continually oscillates between what Baldwin refers to as 'living with it [rage] consciously, or surrendering to it'. On one side is the example of his girlfriend, Alice Harrison – a member of the black bourgeoisie in Los Angeles, with a prominent doctor father – who encourages him to compromise in order to survive. On the other is his own sense of manhood, which he experiences as a constant pressure to resist white America and assert himself. Jones is a worker in the Los Angeles shipyards and his treatment by the management is part of what fuels his anger, together with his perception of the general oppression of African Americans by 'whites'. The novel opens with a dream that symbolises Jones's conflicts in life. Part of the dream anticipates Jones's conflict at work; he is asking two white men for work, but they don't want to give it to him and laugh at him because he doesn't have any tools. Jones describes himself as feeling 'small and humiliated and desperate, looking at the two big white men laughing at me' (2). Jones wakes from this dream feeling 'scared' and speculates whether this anxiety had started when he arrived in Los Angeles and was being rejected from jobs, or whether it coincided with the bombing of Pearl Harbor, which triggered a 'crazy, wild-eyed, unleashed hatred' in white people's faces (4).[9] This fear is emasculating as Jones no longer feels 'like fighting any more' (5), a stance which he was accustomed to draw on (3). He does, however, overcome these feelings, and getting dressed for work restores his sense of masculine confidence:

> Something about my working clothes made me feel rugged, bigger than the average citizen, stronger than a white-collar worker – stronger even than an executive. Important too. It put me on my muscle. I felt a swagger in my stance [. . .] (10)

As can be seen from this quotation, the combination of the narrative perspective and the muscular writing style, echoing the approach exemplified by Dashiell Hammett and Raymond Chandler, serves to emphasise a particular notion of masculinity. Such a masculinity is represented in Jones's delight in his car – 'My car was proof of something to me, a symbol' (37) – in his job, and in his belief in the efficacy of violence: 'I wanted to kill the son of a bitch and keep on living myself' (43). Here the novel shows how violence may be a route to masculine identity for subordinated men. It is apparent, moreover, that such a model of masculinity is racially inflected:

> All the tightness that had been in my body, making my motions jerky, keeping my muscles taut, left me and I felt relaxed, confident, strong. I felt just like I thought a white boy oughta feel; I had never felt so strong in all my life. (45)

What is striking is Jones's aspiration to feel what a 'white boy' feels, and the ultimate impossibility of this aspiration. As a consequence, his occupation of such a male identity is unstable and constantly under threat, provoking a sense of emasculation and anxiety – 'as long as I was black I'd never be anything but half a man at best' (202).

The situation in which Jones finds himself is created by the racism endemic to the economic, political and cultural structures of contemporary America. This is demonstrated not just in the interactions he has with other characters but in his perception of the whiteness of the world and his alienation from it: 'It was the white folks' world and they resented me just standing in it' (96). His reaction to this is a kind of paranoia in that he perceives white people as deliberately targeting him as an individual: 'I knew with the white folks sitting on my brain, controlling my every thought, action, and emotion, making life one crisis after another, day and night, asleep and awake, conscious and unconscious, I couldn't make it' (185). However, it is also possible to see his attempts to occupy the identity of conventional masculinity as an internalisation of the values of the dominant white culture. He recognises this in subscribing to the democratic myth of America: 'All men are created equal' (187). He concludes that, 'I'd settle for a leaderman job at Atlas Shipyard – if I could be a man, defined by Webster as a male human being' (190).

While Jones is constantly aware of the economic and cultural oppression of blacks in America, his sense of constraint and oppression, and resistance, is primarily articulated in the narrative through his relationships with women – with the black bourgeois, Alice, and with a white Texan woman worker at the shipyard, Madge Perkins. In particular, in an echo of Muddy Waters' claims in 'Mannish Boy', Jones's primary measure of his masculinity is his sexuality. Elements of this can be seen in the opening chapter of the novel. For example, Jones's dream, with his lack of 'tools' for the job, has sexual overtones.

The representation of male sexuality here bears similar characteristics to those discussed in Chapter 3, with the foregrounding of heterosexuality as a key element of masculinity, and with underlying anxieties about adequacy. However, any representation of African American heterosexuality is inevitably bound up with wider cultural representations of race. In these the black male rapist is a dominant trope. In *Women, Race & Class*, Angela Davis argues that 'the fraudulent rape charge stands out as one of the most formidable artifices invented by racism' (1982: 173). Whereas Himes personalises circumstances in relation to his fictional character, Davis is interested in the political implications. She quotes Gerda Lerner, who argues that 'The myth of the black rapist of white women is the twin of the myth of the bad black woman – both designed to apologize for and facilitate the continued exploitation of black men and women' (quoted in Davis 1982: 174). In further considering Himes's representation of interracial sexual desire and tension, I want to bring to the fore the way in which it is informed by this myth.

The novel's account of Jones's relationship with Madge explores the understanding of desire and sexuality across the borders of race in America. The divide in the novel is starkly between 'blacks' and 'whites', and although there are some references to Japanese, Jews and Mexicans, there are no such significant characters in the novel. The narrative presents sexual desire between Jones and Madge as inseparable from race. Their first significant encounter is framed by Jones's reflections on the wartime context of the shipyard, which brought together white and black workers, and men and women in unfamiliar circumstances. One aspect of this was that 'the coloured men [. . .] wanted to prove to the white folks that they could work with white women without trying to make them' (22). Madge's response to Jones has been consistent in its performance of a 'scared-to-death act', 'as if she was a naked virgin and I was King Kong' (23). Jones is used to white women trying to 'tease or annoy the coloured men' but this time he feels a 'blinding fury', which seems to give her 'a sexual thrill'. Jones then reacts with lust, which 'poured out of my eyes in a sticky rush and spurted over her from head to foot' (23). Madge blushes and Jones imagines 'it going down over her over-ripe breasts and spreading out over her milk-white stomach' (23). The writing here rehearses clichés of male desire, but it is arguable that this is significant in positioning black male heterosexual desire in conformity with dominant representations of male sexuality. While this encounter sets the tone for Jones's interactions with Madge, the turning point comes when a white leaderman – Don – agrees that

Madge can help out Jones's work team. She simply responds, 'I ain't gonna work with no nigger!', to which Jones responds, 'Screw you then, you cracker bitch!' (33). The consequence is that Jones is disciplined and demoted from his supervisory role, which is a protected job, and he therefore becomes vulnerable to being drafted (36).

As the novel develops, there are further incidents between Madge and Jones. Jones's self-esteem rests on sexual achievement and he decides: 'I was going to have to have [Madge]' (152). Late in the evening he arrives at her room when she is in bed and reluctantly she lets him in. They struggle but reach an impasse, but then Madge opens her robe, showing her naked body: '"Ain't I beautiful?" she said. "Pure white." [. . .] "This'll get you lynched in Texas."' (181) Further struggling ensues and then Jones 'slowly broke her down to the floor, and she looked me in the eyes, hers buck-wild. "All right, rape me then, nigger!" Her voice was excited [. . .]' (182) The word 'rape' startles Jones, and he runs out of the room but waits in his car when she asks him to. However, when she comes down he rejects her, calling her 'a big beat bitch with big dirty feet' (183).

The final incident involving Jones and Madge takes place within the confines of a ship being repaired in the shipyard. By chance, Jones discovers her asleep and unambiguously rejects her advances. When a naval inspector arrives, Madge attacks Jones and starts calling for help from a 'white man' (222), claiming she is being raped. The accusation triggers a claustrophobic sense of being trapped in Jones, who feels 'stripped of my manhood, and black against the whole white world' (224). Jones is beaten up, arrested and charged, and at that point his perception of his situation changes. Whereas in the heat of the moment he was 'instinctively scared of being caught with a white woman screaming, "Rape"', he becomes frightened instead of 'America, of American justice' (231). He considers that 'American tradition had convicted me a hundred years before' (232). In this perception, the narrative moves out beyond the immediate circumstances of an individual to dramatise the way in which the black rapist myth functions as an oppressive means of controlling and marginalising African American males. Ultimately, the charges against Jones are dropped on condition that he signs up for the army.

The plot involving Madge is paralleled in the account of Jones's involvement with Alice. While Madge personifies the racist, sexualised gaze of white America, Alice is representative of the ambitious, integrationist black middle class. On the one hand, Jones's frustrations in relation to the hostile attitude of white America constantly threaten to spill over into violence. On the other, he resists the compromises to his masculinity involved in the relationship with Alice. Although Jones's circumstances are specific to racial identity and the oppression of African Americans in American culture, his grasping for a secure male identity can be situated in relation to wider anxieties about masculinity. Alice's appearance can provoke Jones's lust – he 'caught an edge like a rash from head to foot, blinding and stinging' (64). However, she responds dismissively in 'her best social worker's voice' (64). Alice's response is unmanning and Jones's experience echoes the abundant anxieties around masculine identity discussed in the Introduction and Chapter 1. Alice is better educated than Jones and her middle-class employment as a social worker is symptomatic of the supposed feminisation of society. While Jones is uncertain about his masculinity in relation to Alice, he is also struggling to assert his authority at work.

Yet, if Jones is ambivalent about the compromises required by the aspirational dreams of the Harrisons, his sexual relationship with Alice is inextricably tangled with the cultural politics of race. While Jones resents and resists the racism of American society, the novel suggests that part of the attraction of Alice is her pale skin, which she inherits from her mother, who is a 'very light-complexioned woman with sharp Caucasian features and glinting grey eyes' (59). When Alice dresses up for a date with Jones, he compares her with Bette Davis, with her low-cut dress showing 'the tops of her creamy-white breasts with the darker disturbing seam down between' (64). As was noted earlier, Himes's descriptions of women's bodies are banally conventional in their objectification, but Jones's perception of the darkness of Alice's skin in relation to her otherwise creaminess as 'disturbing' is indicative of the inescapable structuring of human value through racial appearance and skin colour in America. Alice's whiteness is also disturbing for Jones because he suspects that not only does it open the possibility for friendships with white people, but also the opportunity to 'pass' as white in social situations. There is a sexual dimension to this in Alice's friendship with her colleague Tom Leighton. Jones's perspective is that 'many light-complexioned Negro women [are] absolutely pure nuts about white men' (106). Later, after Jones has turned down the opportunity to go out with Alice, she accompanies Leighton to a lecture. Jones sees them together as they are leaving and considers her skin as looking 'too white, as if she had powdered it with chalk' (175). In reflecting on this date, he asserts that he 'wouldn't have minded so much if he had been the sharpest, richest, most important colored guy in the world [. . .] But a white guy had his color – I couldn't compete with that' (176).

The issues of whiteness, passing and social exclusion are narrated in an episode that echoes Baldwin's description of being excluded from restaurants in New Jersey. Jones has booked a table at the best hotel, and he knows that such an act is deliberately provocative and exposes Alice to humiliation. The hotel is full of 'solid white America' and Jones notes that this whiteness is circumscribed: 'I didn't see but one Jew I recognized as a Jew, and nobody of any other race at all' (68). They are given a table by the pantry door, thus dramatising the spatial marginalisation of the African American community, showing how for African American men social spaces in which normative heterosexual masculinity can be expressed are simply not available. However, Himes adds a complexity to this in Alice's comment to Jones that if she had come with white friends she could have passed as white herself. The episode can be read in a number of ways. The narrative explains the way in which in Los Angeles there are certain manoeuvres that create a segregated world without necessarily involving crude exclusions. Indeed, Jones's ploy gets him a table even if his bill comes with a note warning him that he will not be welcome in the future. Alice's potential for passing emphasises the artificial and constructed nature of racial identity, which is dependent on the one hand on simple visual recognition by skin colour, but supposedly marks deep differences in character and worth. In this respect passing might be seen as a subversion of the artificial spatial boundaries policed in a racist culture, but Jones sees Alice's friendship with whites and her ability to pass as white as a form of betrayal of his blackness. In this difference between them lies a threat to his masculine identification, which requires him to assert himself.

Jones's masculinity is also threatened by Alice's flirtation with lesbianism (see 79–83). Alice takes Jones to visit some friends who are represented as two lesbians and a gay man, Chuck. One of the girls, Stella, flirts with Alice, while the other, Dimples, looks on with 'sullen envy' (82). Jones's response is to get drunk, and he then 'slaps' Alice and punches Chuck to the ground (83). The violence and homophobia described in this passage are not articulated with any critical distance. One reading of these passages is that Jones is represented as faced with an insoluble dilemma – that his choice is between resistance to daily racist oppression, leading to violent repression, or compliance, which is in effect acceptance of the status quo. However, it is also possible to read the representation of Jones's behaviour as complicit with normative expectations of masculinity – that homophobia and violence are symptomatic of a striving towards a normative masculinity, even if the route to that identity is blocked for African American men. Himes's novel may then be positioned as exemplary of an emphasis on the problems of African American males, which has been subject to recent criticism by critics such as Collins, Carbado and Mutua. In relation to Williams's identification of the black male 'heroic quest' in *Native Son*, it is possible to argue that in some respects the narrative of *If He Hollers Let Him Go* conforms to such a trajectory. However, Bob Jones's defeat and conscription into a segregated army, with the risk of losing his life in the violence of war, positions him as a victim in line with Carbado's analysis.

Ann Petry, *The Street*

Himes's novel shows how the resistance of an African American male to the strictures of racist America can take angry and violent forms that assert masculine identity against women. A novel that offers a critique of these forms of masculinity is Ann Petry's *The Street*, first published in 1946. *The Street*, Petry's first novel, was a commercial and literary success. Barbara Smith describes the novel as 'one of the best delineations in literature of how sex, race and class interact to oppress Black women' (B. Smith [1977] 2000: 134). The novel is set in Harlem in the Second World War; its protagonist is Lutie Johnson, whose values and aspirations are ground down as she struggles with poverty and single motherhood. *The Street* dramatises the poverty and social deprivation that are the outcomes of racism and a segregationist reality. 'The Street' of the title is a 'bad street' but it is symbolic of all the streets 'where people were packed together like sardines in a can'. The city is symbolic of all the cities where white and black are separated and 'black folks were crammed together on top of each other – jammed and packed and forced into the smallest possible space until they were completely cut off from light and air' (Petry [1946] 1991: 206).[10] The novel demonstrates the racist oppression of the marginalised African American community, but Petry also satirises the hypocrisy relating to American narratives of freedom and equality. Lutie Johnson's ambitions were stimulated during the period she worked as a maid for the Chandlers, a wealthy white family in Connecticut, and she believes that with hard work and determination she can succeed. Johnson's ambitions are thwarted, however determined she is, by her disadvantaged position as a black woman, and the novel registers that the Chandlers are wealthy and successful simply because they are white, and despite alcoholism and suicide in the family. American foundational myths are parodied in the character of Junto, whose name alludes ironically to Benjamin Franklin's group the Junto.[11] In the novel Junto is a white man operating bars, dance halls, brothels and apartment buildings in Harlem, exploiting the black inhabitants.

The novel represents the general exploitation and marginalisation of the African American population by the white majority, but gender is central to Petry's critique and has two elements: one is about the general exploitation of women by men, and the other is about male sexuality.

Johnson is married with a young son, but when she is living in the Street in Harlem she is single. When she was away working for the Chandlers, her husband had moved another woman into their house and she had consequently left him. Her reflection on the situation of other women in the Street summarises the novel's general critique:

> [. . .] here on this street the women trudged along overburdened, overworked, their own homes neglected while they looked after someone else's while the men on the street swung along empty-handed, well dressed, and carefree. Or they lounged against the sides of the buildings, their hands in their pockets while they stared at the women who walked past, probably deciding which woman they should select to replace the wife who was out working that day. (65)

Although she acknowledges that there is a lack of employment for these men, this doesn't alter the representation here of the double oppression of women that has been described and analysed by African American feminists. This is the general context in which Johnson tries to build a better life for herself and her son, but her personal experience of men focuses on male sexual desire.

Johnson is represented throughout the novel as a physically attractive woman, although this is a perspective that comes from others and is not how she thinks of herself. Her perspective on her sexuality is connected with her marriage before it ended and on her sense of loneliness as she struggles to keep her life afloat in the environment of the street. For others her body is either something to be traded for advantage, probably financial, or an object of desire. When she is working for the Chandlers, she is continually aware that white people consider black women easy and available:

> Apparently it was an automatic reaction of white people – if a girl was colored and fairly young, why, it stood to reason she had to be a prostitute. If not that – at least sleeping with her would be just a simple matter [. . .] In fact, white men wouldn't even have to do the asking because the girl would ask them on sight. (45)

A similar view is echoed by Mrs Hedges, a black woman who runs a brothel where Johnson lives. However, Hedges believes that Johnson's financial vulnerability will motivate her to sleep with 'a nice white gentleman' (84). This obsession with her body and her sexual availability is as much an obstacle to her progress as the range of other hurdles put in the way of all black people that the novel describes. Indeed, the plot hinges on the sexual desire for her of three men – first the supervisor of her apartment building, William Jones, and then in her entanglement with Boots Smith – a black musician and bandleader – and Junto – the 'nice white gentleman'.

Jones makes Johnson uncomfortable when she is deciding whether to move into an apartment on the Street. She sees in his eyes 'a hunger so urgent that she was instantly afraid of him' (10). And as she walks up the stairs with him behind her, she is aware of him 'staring at her back, her legs, her thighs' (13). Johnson's perception is shown to be justified when the episode is focalised through Jones and he is described as 'wanting her so badly it was like a pain in his chest' as he watched her walking up the stairs (99). Jones imagines forcing himself on Johnson while his love-making with other women is violent (99, 87). Jones becomes sexually obsessed with Johnson, trying to ingratiate himself with her son, Bub, in order to win her approval. Jones begins stalking Johnson, continually watching her and using Bub to let him into the apartment when Johnson is absent. While there he fingers her blouses and in the bathroom imagines her in the shower and bathtub (108–9). Finally, this obsession leads him to attack her late at night in the hall of the apartment block. He attempts to drag her into the basement but she is rescued by the physical intervention of Mrs Hedges, who threatens to have Jones locked up (234–8). Hedges tells Jones that he has 'lived in basements so long you ain't human no more' (237), and his history of working and living in isolation in ships and basements is presented as distorting his character and sexuality. After this episode Jones vows to strike back at Johnson, and does so by engineering the arrest of her son for stealing letters from apartment buildings. Jones's attack on Johnson shows the way in which male desire can be transformed through fantasy and unreal expectations into a dangerous, violent assault. In comparison, Boots Smith and Junto Johnson echo Mrs Hedges in seeing female bodies as having exchange value in a masculine sexual economy – an attitude that leads to violence when thwarted.

Smith has been a Pullman porter, and the novel describes his humiliating experiences at the hands of white people in that role. His current success and wealth is dependent not simply on his musical talent but also on the patronage of Junto. He operates on the borderlines of legality and exudes a threatening masculinity. When Johnson first meets him, he is described as having a face that is

> tough, hard-boiled, unscrupulous. There was a long, thin scar on his left cheek. It was a dark line that stood out sharply against the dark brown of his skin. [. . .] There was no expression in his eyes, no softness, nothing, to indicate that he would ever bother to lift a finger to help anyone but himself. (152)

Smith hears Johnson singing casually along to a record in the bar and invites her for an audition with his band. She is successful and while her sexual allure is part of this, it is also apparent that she has singing talent, which is recognised by the band and the audience. On this basis, Johnson begins to dream of earning enough money to change her life significantly. However, at this point Junto intervenes with Smith – he is determined to sleep with Johnson and willing to reward her compliance. The relationship between Smith and Junto exemplifies a homosocial connection that is aimed at achieving the sexual outcome, although the transaction is unequal because Junto has the power to destroy Smith's living as a musician. There is an agreement that Smith will seek to deliver Johnson, and Junto instructs Smith not to pay her for singing with the band but to give her presents; he also tells Smith to 'leave her alone. I want her myself' (274).

Johnson is of course ignorant of this arrangement and rejects the offer of 'employment' as a singer when she hears that she will not be paid. Later, however, she does get back in touch with Smith after Jones gets her son arrested and she believes falsely that she needs $200 for a lawyer to represent him in a Children's Court. She arranges to go to Smith's apartment for the money but when she arrives she finds that Junto is also there. Throughout the novel there is a constant emphasis on the way in which Johnson perceives herself in a confined space both physically and metaphorically. The Street is a focus for this, as is shown in the quotation above, but when Smith tries to persuade her to be 'nice' to Junto, she reacts strongly, thinking, 'Junto has a brick in his hand. Just one brick. The final one needed to complete the wall that had been building up around her for years, and when that one last brick was shoved in place, she would be completely walled in' (423). Junto leaves, but on the understanding that he will be back and that by then Smith will have persuaded Johnson to comply.

Smith decides that in the meantime he will have sex with Johnson and starts to kiss her, groping for her breast (427). Johnson reacts angrily, calling him a 'no good bastard' and he hits her twice, saying, 'I don't take that kind of talk from dames. [. . .] Maybe after I beat the hell out of you a coupla times, you'll begin to like the idea of sleeping with me and with Junto' (429). The sequence of events thus moves from an expectation about the right of men to have sex with a woman – an expectation largely based on the situation where women cannot establish viable financial independence – to the extension of that right to rape where the woman is not compliant with the men's wishes. The strength of Petry's narrative lies in the way it both contextualises the specific racial oppression experienced by Johnson, but also, through the shared expectations of the two men, white and black, demonstrates the congruencies of masculine identifications across race. The denouement is violent, with Johnson battering Smith to death with an iron candlestick. Johnson's act destroys all her dreams and disconnects her from her son as she flees from New York to Chicago to seek anonymity.

Himes's and Petry's novels are associated with the realist protest fiction whose primary example was Wright's *Native Son*. The remainder of this chapter considers novels by Ralph Ellison and James Baldwin, who consciously distanced themselves from Wright's approach.

Ralph Ellison, *Invisible Man*

I discussed above the debate about African American fiction and James Baldwin's attack on *Native Son*. Elements of this debate were rehearsed again in an exchange between the critic Irving Howe and Ellison in the early 1960s. Howe's essay 'Black boys and native sons' (1963) was primarily an advocacy for Richard Wright and a critique of James Baldwin, but also made some negative comments about Ellison and *Invisible Man*. Ellison responded vigorously and extensively in two essays brought together as 'The world and the jug' in his collection *Shadow and Act*.[12] Ellison reiterates and elaborates views that he had expressed in other essays. He rejects an essentialist view of race and criticises Howe for making of '"Negroness" a metaphysical condition, one that is a state of irremediable agony which all but engulfs the mind' (Ellison 1963 and 1964: 177). He goes on to argue that 'It is not skin color which makes a Negro American but cultural heritage as shaped by the American experience [. . .] through which it has come to constitute a subdivision of the larger American culture' (177). He references Du Bois's notion of double consciousness in claiming that Negro experience 'imposes the uneasy burden and occasional joy of a complex double vision, a fluid, ambivalent response to men and events which represents, at its finest, a profoundly civilized adjustment to the cost of being human in this modern world' (178). Clearly Ellison has an integrationist perspective and he also makes clear that this is an individualist view. He maintains that 'protest' should not be seen narrowly and that it may take the form of a 'technical assault' against previous styles – the work of art can be 'social action in itself' (183). Ellison particularly repudiates Howe's argument that as a writer he merely followed in Wright's footsteps. In doing so he distinguishes between the relatives and the ancestors of a writer. Writers can choose their ancestors but not their relatives, so Wright and Langston Hughes were Ellison's 'relatives'; Hemingway, Eliot, Malraux, Dostoevsky and Faulkner were his chosen 'ancestors' (185). Furthermore, the writer must 'pit his talents against the standards set by the best practitioners of the craft, both past and present' (184).[13]

Ellison therefore repudiates any obligation to write realist 'protest' fiction, although he points out that 'protest' can be expressed through innovative formal technique. His emphasis is on 'culture' as the particular expression of African American experience. Writing in 1970, Larry Neal points out that Ellison 'almost overwhelmingly locates his cultural, philosophical, and literary sensibility in the West' ([1970] 1987: 121), but the form of the novel embeds African American culture within that context. Neal argues that *Invisible Man* 'attempts to construct its own universe, based on its own imperatives, the central ones being the shaping of a personal vision, as in the blues, and the celebration of a collective vision as is represented by the living culture' (115). For Neal, then, the form of the novel represents a unique aesthetic – an aesthetic derived from an intertwining of black American culture with Western high culture. However, Ellison's vision of culture was clearly gendered. First, in his identification of the literary 'ancestors', he lays claim to a place in a tradition of male authors, and in the novel, as I discuss below, the carriers of an authentic and vibrant African American culture are male. Moreover, these men represent an individualism or non-conformity – a resistance to subordination to institutional structures – that are markers of masculinity in the post-war period. In his association of African American culture with the masculine, Ellison clearly repudiates Park's feminisation of the 'Negro' as the 'lady among the races'.

Invisible Man is the story of the unnamed narrator's attempt as a young African American man to find a place and a male identity in mid-century American society. The narrator's quest is of course specifically for an African American identity and Ellison's novel represents the circumstances and culture of the African American population at mid-century. The idea of invisibleness reflects the way in which the African American population were all too visible as a group (for example, as the 'Negro problem' of the post-war period) but invisible as individuals. Ellison's point is metaphorical but intended to show that African Americans were not seen as autonomous human individuals with their own particular way of being in the world. The narrator's awareness of his invisibility is a step towards his own recognition of his individual humanity, a status that has been denied him. Yet the novel is marked by a dearth of black female characters, and can therefore be seen as articulating the problem of African American identity as an issue of black male identity. The problem of the narrator's lack of humanity is therefore signalled as emasculation in two visions, at the beginning and end of the novel. In the first he dreams of finding in his prize briefcase an 'engraved document' with the following message in letters of gold: 'Keep this Nigger-Boy running' (33). At the end, as the narrator retreats underground, he has a vision of the men who have indeed kept him running, holding him prisoner and castrating him: 'Jack and old Emerson and Bledsoe and Norton and Ras [. . .], all of whom had run me' (569).

The narrator had sought to gain favour with each of these older and more experienced men (apart from Ras), who seem to offer him a path towards satisfying his ambitions, but in fact block his adult manliness by keeping the 'boy running'. All these men also require conformity from the narrator to a set of beliefs. His ambition is for an ideal black male identity, which involves a notion of 'leadership', but he comes to realise that he has been misled by his ambitions and that the leaders whom he has admired have exploited him. For the reader, Ellison constantly signals the narrator's naivety and gullibility, but includes for each episode in which the narrator is kept 'running' an alternative perspective built around the invisible man's encounters with men whose insights derive from their participation in African American culture and history.

This alternative perspective is signalled at the beginning of the novel with his grandfather's paradoxical advice to 'keep up the good fight' but to 'overcome 'em with yeses, undermine 'em with grins, agree 'em to death and destruction, let 'em swoller you till they vomit or bust wide open' (16). Other African American men who offer their experience to the narrator, in words or by example, even if he is unable to understand its relevance to him, are the ex-serviceman doctor, whom he meets in the Golden Day, Jim Trueblood, Lucius Brockway, the seller of yams, Peter Wheatstraw, Brother Tarp and Tod Clifton. It is not feasible to analyse all these encounters, so I will concentrate on his attendance at college and his relationship with the Brotherhood, before moving on to consider how issues of sexuality and violence in relation to masculinity are represented in Ellison's novel.

The narrator's aspiration to leadership is initially modelled on Booker T. Washington, whom he quotes in his graduation day speech, later delivered again in humiliating circumstances after the Battle Royal in chapter 1. The quotations are from Washington's 'Atlanta compromise' speech of 1895, in which he advocated compromise with the South and gradualism rather than an assertion of the rights of African Americans.[14] Washington advocated making friends across racial divisions in a 'manly way', but the weakness of his argument and the actual 'unmanly' situation of the invisible man in following Washington is revealed during the events at the smoker and afterwards, which is when he dreams of the message: 'Keep this Nigger-Boy running' (33).

The narrator's prize is a scholarship to a Negro college, and in its similarities to Tuskegee, founded by Booker T. Washington, the novel exposes the consequences for African American leadership of Washington's politics. It is at the college that the narrator encounters Dr Bledsoe, its president, whose leadership the novel exposes as corrupt and self-serving, although for the narrator,

> [Bledsoe] was the example of everything I hoped to be: Influential with wealthy men all over the country; consulted in matters concerning the race; a leader of his people; the possessor of not one but *two* Cadillacs, a salary and a soft, good-looking and creamy-complexioned wife. [. . .] H]e had achieved power and authority. (101)[15]

Bledsoe's imbrication in the networks of white power is made apparent to the reader, while the narrator is blind to reality. The invisible man is asked to look after Mr Norton, one of the white, Northern philanthropist millionaires who support the college. In driving Norton on a brief tour of the environs of the college, the invisible man exposes him both to Jim Trueblood's tale of incest and to the anarchic behaviour of the injured veterans at the Golden Day bar and brothel. The mishandling of Norton's visit results in the expulsion of the invisible man from the college.

Norton has been a Trustee of the college since its foundation and is the embodiment of originary, white, male American citizenship. However, his patronising sang-froid is disturbed by events at the Golden Day, which is a bar and a brothel. On that day, the Golden Day is occupied by African American war veterans from the local 'semi-madhouse' (90), who are an anarchic force. Norton receives medical treatment from one of the vets, a former doctor. The doctor tells Norton that for some of the veterans in the Golden Day he is 'the great white father' but for others 'the lyncher of souls' (93). He explains how he developed high levels of medical skill during the war and afterwards in France, but that in returning to America he had forgotten the 'fundamentals', by which he means the segregationist ideology that led to a situation in which 'Ten men in masks drove me from the city at midnight and beat me with whips for saving a human life' (93). Instead of 'lovingly' using a scalpel, he yearns 'to caress a trigger' (93). The doctor's ambiguous attitude to violence also echoes that of the invisible man's grandfather, who gave up his gun after Reconstruction (16). He recounts this in order to teach the invisible man something about his circumstances. He describes how the apparatus of the college and its white benefactors, like Norton – the 'lyncher of souls' – destroys the invisible man's humanity and potential for manliness, rendering him invisible (94). The invisible man is blind to the ideology of whiteness and in this lack of understanding is complicit in his failure to see his own humanity.[16] The doctor is a non-conformist – categorised as a 'nut' (155) – but his independent thinking is contrasted with Bledsoe, whose institution is committed to instilling a blindly conventional and passive conformity in its students.

The narrator leaves the college for New York and finds a possible alternative means of achieving his ambitions with the Brotherhood.[17] Brother Jack is the dominant figure in the Brotherhood and represents another leader who seeks to 'Keep this Nigger-Boy running'. Significantly, the Brotherhood's model of black leadership is again Booker T. Washington (305), a choice that foreshadows their willingness to sacrifice the black population of Harlem for their own longer-term aims.

It is in the narrator's relationship with the Brotherhood that Ellison draws most sharply on that distinction between the individual and conformist organisations that was such a predominant theme in the period. The subordination of the narrator in his relationship with the Brotherhood is symbolised in his being given a new name and a new identity (309). The narrator is willingly complicit in this, hoping that he would be 'on the road to something big' (335). In fact becoming 'someone else' involves the suppression of the individual to the demands of the organisation. The novel's representation of the Brotherhood is of an organisation whose active members are male – all the female characters involved with the Brotherhood are white and sexualised – so when the narrator is removed from his Harlem role and told to lecture downtown on 'the Woman Question', this is simultaneously a demotion and a symbolic association with the feminine. The narrator, however, is blind to the realities of his circumstances and in persuading himself that his new assignment was in fact 'proof of the committee's goodwill' (408) fails to understand that submitting himself to the Brotherhood has emasculated him.

However, within the Brotherhood offices in Harlem is Tarp, one of the men who offer alternative models of African American culture and manhood. Tarp offers Frederick Douglass as a positive example of African American leadership by hanging up his image in the narrator's office. Moreover, Tarp represents a deep connection with African American history, momentarily appearing to be the invisible man's grandfather and offering a corresponding example of African American male individualism, rooted in forms of resistance to white power. Tarp had been on a chain gang for nineteen years before he came north, locked up for defending his property (387). Tarp had finally broken a link on the chain that held him and escaped. As a gesture he presents the narrator with the broken link – 'a thick dark, oily piece of filed steel [. . . that] bore the marks of haste and violence'. The link is compared with one from the days of slavery kept by Bledsoe in his office. The smoothness of Bledsoe's example echoes the lack of authenticity and integrity in his model of black leadership. The narrator takes up Tarp's link, slips it over his knuckles and strikes it against the desk (389), indicating its potential as a weapon. This gesture reiterates the signs of violence on the metal itself and suggests the need for forms of resistance to the oppression of African Americans. Tarp's personal history and his gifts of the chain link and the image of Douglass signify his resistance to assimilation into the Brotherhood and the maintenance of his individuality. However, although Tarp's gestures tug at the invisible man's sensibility, ultimately he decides 'There was no time for memory, for all its images were of time past' (390).

After his orchestration of Tod Clifton's funeral, the narrator comes to a final showdown with Jack and the committee of the Brotherhood, during which Jack tells the narrator that he was 'not hired to think', signifying a racism that is 'naked and old and rotten' (469). The narrator again grips Tarp's chain link around his knuckles

(473) as he challenges Jack's dismissal of the importance of the black people of Harlem. He questions whether Jack's assertion of leadership wouldn't be better described as the 'great white father' (473), echoing the description of Norton. In the confrontation, Jack loses his glass eye, symbolising his failure of vision. The narrator becomes aware that he is invisible to Jack – 'He doesn't even see me' (475). In submitting to the discipline of the Brotherhood, the narrator had again become invisible and lost his male identity.

The narrator's experience of Bledsoe and the college and with the Brotherhood exemplify the ways in which American educational and political culture in both the South and the North serve to block his acquisition of a black masculine identity. Both the traditional structures of white authority personified by Norton – supported by collaborationist black leaders like Bledsoe – and supposedly oppositionist white organisations like the Brotherhood equally maintain and enforce a racist society through the suppression of the individual and the imposition of forms of conformity.

In this book I have argued that two key elements of masculinity as represented in mid-century novels are heterosexuality and aggression. Both *If He Hollers Let Him Go* and *The Street* problematise interracial sexuality, with Himes's novel foregrounding the legacy of lynching and the rape myth, which casts a morbid shadow over black male sexuality. The subject is also significant in *Invisible Man*. Although there is a passing reference to the narrator visiting the Golden Day as a customer (73), his sexual experiences relate only to white women, whom he meets through the Brotherhood. From Ras's nationalist perspective, Tod Clifton and the narrator are betraying 'the black people' for 'A pat on the back and a piece of cunt without no passion' (373).

The narrator's sexual experiences in the novel begin when he is directed by the Brotherhood to speak about 'the woman question' and it turns out that the class struggle has turned into the 'ass struggle' (418). On the first occasion the narrator is approached by a woman after his talk and she invites him home, supposedly so he can clarify some ideological issues. In the intimacy of her apartment, she believes she is flattering him by saying that his speaking is 'so powerful, so – so primitive' and that she hears 'tom-toms beating' in his voice (413). Although the narrator is taken aback by this racism, he is sexually attracted to the woman and goes to bed with her. The woman's racialised objectification of the narrator reinforces his emasculation by the Brotherhood. In the subsequent sexual episode with Sybil, the novel explicitly engages with the rape myth.

The narrator has decided to act against the Brotherhood and his approach is to try to find out what the Brotherhood plans by establishing a sexual relationship with a woman inside the hierarchy. He therefore initiates contact with Sybil – 'one of the big shot's wives' (516). The evening begins with Sybil manifesting similar racist fantasies as the other woman; the narrator is cast as 'Brother Taboo-with-whom-all-things-are-possible' (517). But the 'starch' is taken out of the narrator when Sybil confesses that her over-riding fantasy is that he rape her (518). The narrator's response is again ambivalent. While he considers that the situation is the consequence of his 'obscene scheme of the evening' (517), a 'trap' he has set for himself (521), he can neither 'deliver' nor be 'angry' (520). He reflects on the culture that produces this desire and how African Americans are expected to be entertainers (521). In the end Sybil becomes so drunk that she passes out and he writes 'Sybil, you were raped by Santa Claus, Surprise' on her belly with lipstick. But he rubs this off and pretends that he has carried through her wishes. Through all this his emotions range from amusement, to pity, to desire, to self-disgust and to suppressed anger – he is 'determined not to let her provoke me to violence' (518). This tale of sexual confusion is not set up to assert the narrator's masculinity through the expression of his sexual virility, but as evidence of the troubles around sexuality and race. Although the narrator believes he is in control, even the drunken Sybil, through her articulation of the deeply embedded racism of American culture and its obsession with black men's sexuality, undermines his humanity and pulls him into a vortex of conflicting emotions. The dark humour of the message from Santa Claus – representing a supposedly kindly white paternalism – reflects the absurdity of the situation. However, the erasure of the message is substituted with a darker pretence – that the rape has actually been carried out. However, Ellison seeks to subvert the rape myth for the reader by counteracting the racist fantasies of Sybil with the restrained, sympathetic and human response of the narrator. His behaviour expresses a different masculinity from the racist clichés.

However, it is also possible to argue that the representation of the invisible man's sexuality and masculinity comes with the kinds of closure generally associated with male sexuality in the period. The narrator's sexuality is unambiguously heterosexual and the representation of the one gay character in the novel – Emerson's son – is dismissive. He is represented as frustrated and neurotic (185ff) and as both racist and predatory in suggesting the invisible man comes to a party as his valet (192).[18] Manliness and sexuality are also represented at the price of any more sympathetic rendering of female characters. The racist view of African American men's unbridled sexuality is displaced onto Sybil and she becomes a drunken caricature. The lack in the novel of rounded female characters is a mark of the way in which the problem of racism for African Americans is transposed into a problem of black masculinity and identity. The one sympathetic female character with any significance is Mary Rambo, but she is limited to a motherly role and she also expects the narrator as a male to perform 'some act of leadership, some newsworthy achievement' (258), which reinforces the emphasis on the primacy of masculinity in African American identity.

The relationship between black masculinity and sexuality is foregrounded in the Jim Trueblood epiosode. Trueblood's tale of incest and the impregnation of both his wife and daughter is analysed by Houston Baker in 'To move without moving' (1983). Baker sees the black phallus as a major symbol in Ellison's novel, arguing that it is 'a symbol of unconstrained force that white men contradictorily envy and seek to destroy', as in the Battle Royal episode at the beginning of the novel (1983: 833). He goes on to maintain that in the Trueblood episode the phallus is 'symbolic of a type of royal paternity, an aristocratic procreativity turned inward to ensure the royalty (the truth, legitimacy, or authenticity) of an enduring black line of descent' (834). Trueblood is, moreover, the 'quintessential' trickster figure, who successfully evades 'ordinary codes of restraint' in his incestuous coupling (834). He is also a carrier of African American culture expressed in the arts of story-telling and singing – the latter a skill that was exploited by Bledsoe's college for 'special white guests' (47). He can be seen as following the same line as the invisible man's grandfather in that he tells white audiences what they want to hear but manipulates them to his own financial advantage. Trueblood can therefore be seen as the embodiment of African American cultural values expressed through masculine virility. Yet Ellison also seeks to turn back on itself the reaction of the local whites and Norton to Trueblood's story, showing how the myth of black sexuality is shown to act as a displacement for the white population through which it can negate and deny its own sense of sexual guilt. Moreover, Trueblood's reflective moral and spiritual journey after his incest reveals his humanity. As John S. Wright puts it, 'Trueblood gives eloquent testimony to his own tragic sense of life and to that need for transcendence he finally satisfies in the resolving poetry of the blues' (2004: 241).

If Trueblood is one of the male African Americans who provide lessons for the invisible man about the significance of black culture, he also shows how through his mastery as a narrator he can control his own narrative and is confident in his individuality and his humanity. However, his narrative mastery comes at the expense of Kate, his wife, and Matty Lou, his daughter. Although Baker argues that Trueblood's wife Kate is 'a figure of moral outrage, she is a fertile woman who, like her husband, provides "cultural gifts" in the form of new life' (836), neither her perspective nor Matty Lou's is represented, except through Jim Trueblood's words. Moreover, after his period of withdrawal from the family, he returns and asserts his patriarchal right to control their bodies, even threatening to kill the midwife who might abort Mary Lou's foetus (67). Trueblood then is an ambiguous icon of black masculinity – while embodying the values of African American oral and blues culture, he can also be seen to display characteristics of that macho identity rooted in the misogyny of American masculinity that Sherley Anne Williams identifies in *Native Son*.

Trueblood's threat to the midwife draws attention to the theme of violence in the novel and the question of whether its representation of masculinity and violence echoes other novels of the period in which bodily strength, aggression and physical violence – or the threat of violence – can be seen as inherent to conventional expectations of masculinity. The invisible man's grandfather appears to repudiate violence in giving up his gun in the Reconstruction (although it's possible that he regrets doing so) (16). Similarly, Jack tells the narrator and Tod Clifton that the Brotherhood is 'against all forms of violence' (366). Yet the novel is permeated with violence, in the assaults on the boys at the smoker to the Harlem riots, in the shooting of Tod Clifton and in the medical 'treatment' of the narrator after the paint explosion. The events at the smoker and the paint factory hospital, with the mirroring of electrical torture in both episodes, foreground the violence endemic to American racism. The black male body is subject to constraint through a violence that objectifies and dehumanises the individual. This is the violence that leads to the finality of Clifton's death. If there is no doubt that American racism is grounded in the violence of transportation and slavery, what is the appropriate response? And how far is the invisible man's growth towards an adult male identity built on the expression of violence?

One response to racist oppression might be the anarchic chaos created by the vets at the Golden Day and their vicious retributive attack on Supercargo, to which the narrator responds with 'such an excitement that I wanted to join in' (84). This 'excitement' seems to represent not just the susceptibility of the individual to the power of the mob, but violence again as an expression of the bitterness described by James Baldwin. The rioters in Harlem might be seen as a reacting in a similar way to the vets. The narrator's reaction to the potential of the riots to expose the population of Harlem to physical harm is one of anger and despair. There is no suggestion that the violent assertion of the self is an admirable attribute of male identity. There is instead the realistic observation that where power and the ability to exert social violence are unbalanced, attempts to resist through counter-violence are doomed. Violent oppression creates anger and a desire to strike back, but this is not a successful strategy for the longer term. This perspective suggests that the odds are too unfavourably stacked for African Americans to change society through violence and this may be one reason why the narrator's grandfather returned his gun.

Yet there are occasions in which personal acts of violence may be tied to an expression of male identity. For the narrator these are episodes connected with resistance to Ras, the Brotherhood and the death of Tod Clifton. In contrast with the older African American men who act as exemplars and guides for the narrator, even if he fails to recognise the value of their experience, Tod Clifton is more like an alter ego. The description of Clifton's first appearance at a committee meeting emphasises his physical attractiveness. The narrator notes 'a woman's pleasurable sigh' as he enters, and goes on to list admiringly his physical attributes – 'very black and very handsome' – with an emphasis on his masculinity: 'tall and relaxed', 'the broad, taut span of his knuckles', 'the muscular, sweatered arms, the curving line of the chest rising to the easy pulsing of his throat, to the square, smooth chin' (363).[19] However, Clifton's cheek is marked by a plaster protecting a wound received fighting Ras. Ras himself reinforces this portrait of Clifton: 'You black and beautiful' and 'In Africa this mahn be a chief, a black king!' (373, 372). Clifton therefore embodies an idealised black masculinity and his bravery and willingness to fight is integral to this, drawing on conventional expectations of manliness. The narrator and Clifton subsequently form a brotherhood, forged in a street fight against Ras and his followers. They fight first with their fists and the narrator disarms Ras after he pulls a knife on Clifton. Yet Clifton's death undercuts what appears at first an endorsement of his aptitude for street fighting. As with the rioting, violent resistance by an unarmed man against the gun-carrying policeman can only result in his death.

Maggie McKinley has argued in *Masculinity and the Paradox of Violence in American Fiction* that despite the ambiguous attitude to violence in the novel, the narrator's existential sense of his masculine identity rests on moments of violence. So, in his final confrontation with Ras during the riots, the narrator first avoids being killed when Ras throws a spear at him and then hurls the same spear back at Ras, locking his jaws together and thus silencing him. McKinley argues that this act 'serves as another significant rebirth' with the narrator only beginning to live again 'when he finally retaliates with violence' (2015: 36). This violence becomes the 'necessary final step in the individualist ethic' (36). However, there are significant aspects of these events that serve to maintain the ambiguity in the novel about violence. The violence here is between African Americans and the narrator is fiercely opposed to Ras's black nationalist ideology and in contrast supports an integrationist stance. He therefore first tries to deflect Ras and his men by arguing that they are being manipulated by the white men of the Brotherhood. This point is repeated after the narrator has thrown the spear at Ras when he is chased by Ras's men and he wants to say to them, 'we're all black folks together' (560). So the novel repeats the point that violence serves the interests of the white not the black population. Furthermore, Ellison's representation of Ras during the riots is intended to undermine the black nationalism that he pursues. Ras is described as 'dressed in the costume of an Abyssinian chieftain' and as a 'figure more out of a dream than out of Harlem' (556). In general, the events in Harlem that night juxtapose the surreal, the absurd and, indeed, the comic, with the fear and anger of the population. That the fight between the narrator and this African 'chieftain' is with a spear adds a surreal, comic-book element to the violence, and so the fastening of Ras's jaws becomes a symbolic gesture with no description of an actual wound. The narrator's throwing of the spear at Ras is an action of self-defence that marks his choosing life and a refusal to die for Ras or Jack and a desire to 'live out one's own absurdity' (559). While this is an assertion of his individual identity, it does not seem to be a male identity constructed from violence. Indeed, the immediate ensuing action is that the narrator has to run away from Ras's men. Then, in an example of Ellison's recurrent use of the metaphor of sight, his continuing lack of true understanding is demonstrated to the reader when the police horse's tail lashes his face and he flounders blindly into the full force of the spray of a burst water main (560–1).

The Prologue opens with an episode in which violence and its effects are described in a much more explicit way. The narrator has explained why he describes himself as invisible and how that invisibility leads to 'constantly being bumped against by those of poor vision' and to doubts about whether 'you really exist' (4). In reaction, he says, 'you strike out with your fists', although this is 'seldom successful'. The text then proceeds with an example of this striking out when the narrator accidentally bumps into another man, who then insults him. The narrator responds with considerable physical violence, head-butting the man and then kicking him repeatedly, and only draws back from slitting the man's throat at the last moment (4). But then he considers that his victim might in fact not have seen him, and he feels 'disgusted and ashamed' (5). The narrator returns to the issue at the end of the Prologue, maintaining that the man had bumped and insulted him and was therefore responsible for the 'near murder' (14). He then argues ironically that the responsible action would have been to have used his knife to 'protect the higher interests of society', but he was a 'coward'. The events described here occur after the narrator has gone underground and can be seen as the fruit of his experience. McKinley therefore argues that the narrator has completed a journey toward the 'intersection of masculine power, liberation, and violence' (22). However, the novel constantly refuses a model of masculinity that depends on violence as a liberating force. The narrator is ashamed of his attack and when he considers that he should have used his knife he 'shirks that responsibility' because he is too 'snarled in the incompatible notions that buzzed within my brain. I was a coward . . .' (14).

It seems that rather than drawing on violence as a constituting element of his masculinity, the narrator faces a dilemma in a racist society whose foundations lie in the violence of slavery and the dissolution of hopes of equality in the post-Reconstruction United States. This is the conundrum of his grandfather's advice, and the narrator returns to it in the Epilogue. His grandfather seemed to have set him a model of behaving as a man in a divided world, but the narrator has struggled with what the advice means from the earliest events that he has recounted. He wonders whether what his grandfather meant was an affirmation of 'the principle on which the country was built' and whether the African American population had a particular responsibility for upholding the principles of democracy and freedom (574). The narrator 'can't figure it out', but he does ask 'Weren't we *part of them* as well as apart from them' (575). However, the narrator concludes that his world is 'one of infinite possibilities' (576) and moves towards an individualistic perspective: 'I know men are different and that all life is divided and that only in division is there true health'

(576). This individuality is set against conformity – 'Whence all this passion towards conformity anyway?' (577).

The question of individuality is related to 'history'. The older African American men in the novel draw their experience from their historical circumstances, but Clifton 'plunges outside of history' in abandoning the Brotherhood, selling the paper dolls and being shot (438). The narrator's initial perception of history is therefore derived from the determinist view of the Brotherhood, where supporters must lose their individuality in service of historical inevitability, and he is bemused at Clifton's decision to 'leave the only organisation offering him a chance to "define" himself' (438). Clifton, however, is described earlier as looking 'somehow like a hipster, a zoot suiter' (366) and later, after Clifton's death, the narrator sees three African American youths in the subway dressed in zoot suits. These are 'men out of time' (441) according to the Brotherhood's analysis, but the narrator wonders if they are not 'the saviors, the true leaders, the bearers of something precious'. From this perspective, 'history' is not 'a reasonable citizen' but 'a gambler'.

However, the novel poses a further question about history and who records it – where were the historians to witness Clifton's shooting? (439) Such a question is relevant to Ellison's purpose and ambitions. In *From Behind the Veil*, Robert B. Stepto places *Invisible Man* within a tradition of African American narratives, beginning with the 'slave narratives' of the mid-nineteenth century. For Stepto, these narratives draw on a primary myth of African American culture that he characterises as 'the quest for freedom and literacy' (1979: ix). In African American narratives, the successful outcome of this quest is registered in the written expression of the authentic individual voice. So, for example, Frederick Douglass in his *Narrative* (1845) identifies literacy as the pathway from slavery to freedom at the moment he is stopped by his master from learning the alphabet (see Stepto 1979: 21). So too the protagonist of *Invisible Man* registers his progress from ignorance and naivety to a state of greater knowledge and insight through writing a narrative of his experience. Similarly, the example of Jim Trueblood valorises narrative mastery.

Two specific examples from *Invisible Man* can serve to show how Ellison made explicit connections to earlier writers. First is his reference to the trope of the 'veil', which is a central image in W. E. B. Du Bois's *The Souls of Black Folk* and related to his notion of double consciousness. In *Invisible Man* the narrator, looking back from his subterranean perspective, remembers the statue of the college Founder, a statue that shows the Founder lifting a veil from the eyes of a kneeling slave. The motionless statue is, however, ambiguous in its meaning: is the veil 'really being lifted, or lowered more firmly in place'? (36). Then a flock of starlings covers the statue with excrement and the invisible man ponders why the statue then seems more 'commanding' – an ironic authorial signal to the reader. As the narrative proceeds, it becomes clear to the reader, and, eventually, the invisible man, that the college under its leader Dr Bledsoe is indeed dedicated to keeping the veil in place. In contrast, Tarp, with his personal history, makes a connection for the narrator back to Frederick Douglass, with the references to Du Bois and Douglass acting as alternatives to Washington's approach. Yet these exemplary narratives, discussed by Stepto, are all by male writers. The voice of the invisible man draws on this tradition of a male protagonist finding his black masculine identity in relation to the context of American culture. This identity is not expressed in the same forms as other novels considered in this book where notions of otherness, sexuality and aggression are the primary markers of gender. In *Invisible Man* the mark of adult masculinity can be seen as displayed in the skilful account of the way the protagonist moves through his experiences, from naivety and ignorance to some kind of insight into his predicament, even if he cannot articulate what action he will take now his 'hibernation is over' (580). Of course, for Ellison himself, the novel, in its fusion of African American culture and history with modernist mastery, is a claim for recognition in mid-century America. Moreover, in its individualist ideology and rejection of 'conformity', Ellison's novel is of its time.

James Baldwin, *Giovanni's Room*

Giovanni's Room was James Baldwin's second novel, and followed the publication of his essays in *Notes of a Native Son* (1955). As discussed above, Baldwin's critique of fiction with a sociological approach came with an advocacy for fiction with a humanist emphasis on individual experience. In *Giovanni's Room* Baldwin attempts to put his advocacy into practice through his characterisation of both David and Giovanni as individuals responding to their particular circumstances.

David, the first-person narrator of *Giovanni's Room*, is a white American, with gleaming blond hair, whose 'ancestors conquered a continent, pushing across death-laden plains, until they came to an ocean which faded away from Europe into a darker past' (9). In declaring his occupation of this character's voice on the first page of the novel, Baldwin repudiated the subject matter conventionally expected of a black author.[20] That the story related by the narrator was of his struggle with his homosexual identity was a further distancing of Baldwin from the usual narrative priorities of novelists, black or white. From this distance, Baldwin casts a different light on masculinity, and by implication, through his own identity as an African American author, on black masculinity. David's story of his exile from America serves as a metaphor for his alienation from his homosexual identity. However, this exile also reverberates with Baldwin's own distance from conventional American masculine identity, in its presumed heterosexuality and whiteness. In this way the novel is reflective of African American experience.

In the character of David and his psychological denial of his sexuality, Baldwin echoes Vidal's and Capote's explorations of homosexuality in the period. Baldwin himself wrote about sexuality and gender in an essay called 'Preservation of innocence' published in 1949. Baldwin argues that recognising the complexity of the nature of men and women and their relationship to one another is 'the signal of maturity, it marks the death of the child and the birth of the man' ([1949] 1973: 17–18). He maintains that in America there is a contrary obsession with holding onto innocence and that it is out of this impulse that the 'mindless monster, the tough guy' (19) has emerged. Baldwin argues that the contemporary attitude towards women is 'the wedding of the most abysmal romanticism and the most implacable distrust' (19). The novels therefore dream of a love in which the Boy gets the Girl, but in which relationships between men and women are never represented. Related to this is a concern that the trajectory of Boy gets Girl might be disrupted by the 'invert', who is an ever-present threat to the 'normal man'. Baldwin refers to *Serenade* by James M. Cain, where the invert arrives at a 'sordid and bloody end' to protect an 'immaculate manliness' (20). For Baldwin, like Vidal, the homosexual is not an identity, and a novel should insist on the 'presence and passion of human beings, who cannot ever be labeled' (22).

Baldwin's novel explores these themes in the character of David, who is caught up in American expectations of masculinity and identity, and his sense that homosexuality is inconsistent with manhood is repeated through the novel. This tension between David's expectations and his homosexual impulses are described in his first sexual experience in his late teens with a friend – Joey. This was an intense encounter, but one that David seeks to repudiate and forget. He perceives his friendship with Joey as 'proof of some horrifying taint in me' (J. Baldwin [1956] 2000: 12). One element of this is the threat to his masculinity – he saw Joey's body as 'the black opening of a cavern [. . .], in which I would lose my manhood' (14). However, he recognises retrospectively that his self-perception as a person with a strong will who was master of his destiny was in fact 'self-deception' (24). So his decision to forget Joey was hardly a decision, but more part of 'elaborate systems of evasion, of illusion' (24). He sees that he 'succeeded very well – by not looking at the universe, by not looking at myself, by remaining in effect, in constant motion' (25). This motion prompts an ennui that drives David abroad to France, where he would find the self that 'would turn out to be only the same self from which I had spent so much time in flight' (25). In relation to Baldwin's essay, one can see David as seeking to preserve his 'innocence' in this flight abroad.

In France, David initially continues with the denial of his sexuality and establishes a close relationship with Hella, another American who came to Paris to study art, but he then engages in an intense love affair with Giovanni, an Italian barman. David's social contacts in Paris are mostly of what he refers to as 'le milieu' – the gay community – but he was 'intent on proving, to them and to myself, that I was not of their company' (26). One of these acquaintances is Jacques, a well-off, 'aging, Belgian-born, American businessman' (26). Jacques clearly perceives David as a homosexual even if he presents himself as a heterosexual, and teases him about not risking the 'immaculate manhood which is your pride and joy' (33). Together with David's protection of his masculinity through a heterosexual identity, goes a dismissive attitude towards camp men. For example, in the bar where he goes with Jacques and first meets Giovanni, there are young boys who might be after 'money or blood or love' (30). One with make-up and earrings sometimes also wears a dress, and David describes his uneasiness at this 'utter grotesqueness', which is comparable to 'the sight of monkeys eating their own excrement' (30). If through David the novel is negative about men who are not properly masculine, it is equally conventional in its expectation of women. Giovanni refers to 'absurd women running around today, full of ideas and nonsense, and thinking themselves equal to men – *quelle rigolade!* – they need to be beaten half to death so that they can find out who rules the world' (77). Giovanni is similarly scathing about Hella, who has left Paris to go to Spain to decide whether she wants to commit to her relationship with David, describing her as a 'silly little girl' (77). When Hella returns, she has decided she wants to marry David, but this is in light of her perception that 'I'm not really the emancipated girl I try to be at all. I guess I just want a man to come home to me every night. [. . .] I want to start having babies. In a way, it's really all I'm good for' (117–18).

The novel therefore rehearses conventional attitudes to masculinity, femininity and sexuality in a way that ironises David's self-exile from the normal sexual mores of the United States – he has both internalised those mores and discovers that they remain normative cultural values in France. Insofar as these values constantly lead him to question his own sexual identity and masculinity, he is overwhelmed with self-disgust. David's identity is expressed or constricted in a variety of spaces – at the meta level between America and Europe, and then in the most significant metaphor, in Giovanni's room, where their relationship is focused, beginning and ending there. Life in the room is described as 'occurring underwater' (82), which implies a different world from normality, but also a lack of the oxygen necessary for life. Their relationship proceeds alongside an image painted on the wall of a man and a woman walking together surrounded by roses. The image questions whether their relationship is feasible in its diversion from the norm, but also whether any permanent sexual relationship is viable – the lovers in the image are described as 'trapped' (84). But the room is also a project – Giovanni has always had 'great plans for remodelling this room', but it is never finished, so David and Giovanni live in squalor. It is David's perception, however, that Giovanni's disorganisation is 'not a matter of habit or circumstances or temperament; it was a matter of punishment and grief' (84). He sees that Giovanni expects him to destroy the room and 'give to Giovanni a new and better life' (84).

In order to do so, David has to commit to the relationship with Giovanni and respond to his love. However, his ambivalence, rooted in his desire to protect his 'immaculate manhood', prevents him from doing so. As the story unfolds, it is therefore possible to discern two perspectives on David. On the one hand, perhaps, there is sympathy for him and identification with his dilemma as he struggles with his internalisation of values that condemn him to exile. On the other, there is a critical perspective on his behaviour in which he becomes a more typical representative of white American masculinity. This critical perspective is seen through the eyes of the Europeans who observe the behaviour of white American tourists or expatriates like David. Giovanni, for example, describes how if he had stayed, David might have been like the other Americans: 'coming through our village in the ugly, fat American motor car [. . .] looking at me and looking at all of us and tasting our wine and shitting on us with those empty smiles Americans wear everywhere' (131). Earlier he tells David that he sees Americans as 'another species' (36), who do not believe in 'pain and death and love' (37). Perhaps the most damning episode is David's encounter with Sue, another American expatriate living in Paris. The circumstances are that he has just heard from Hella, who is returning to Paris from Spain and clearly wants to commit to a relationship with David. This is a decisive moment for David, as he will have to break with Giovanni if he is to take up again with Hella. What it provokes in him is a 'real fear' that drives him to find 'any girl at all' (91) – the implication being that this fear is about whether the experience with Giovanni has resulted in a 'sea change' in his sexuality, and by implication his manhood (82). Sue is clearly lonely and vulnerable, and when David starts to flirt with her he acknowledges that he was 'doing something very cruel' (93). He describes feeling 'a hardness and a constriction in her, created already by too many men like me [. . .] What we were about to do would not be pretty' (95). In relation to conventional morality he considers that what he did with Giovanni could not be 'more immoral than what I was about to do with Sue' (95). The effect of this on Sue was 'the strangest smile [. . .] It was pained and vindictive and humiliated' (98).

The cruelty, exploitation and emotional dishonesty of this episode casts a similar light on David's relationships both with Giovanni and Hella. When David breaks off with Giovanni, the flaws in David's character are excoriatingly described by Giovanni. He accuses him of never loving anyone: 'You love your purity, you love your mirror. [. . .] You want to be clean. [Y]ou are immoral' (133–4). This is behaviour that relates to Giovanni's assessment of Americans and locates David's values as those of a white, middle-class American male. In a response that emphasises David's view that manhood and homosexuality are incompatible, he argues that Giovanni has wanted to turn him into his 'little *girl*' (135). This is followed by his assertion, 'I'm a man [. . .], a man' – the repetition of the claim underlining the insecurity of his own masculinity, and an ironic echo of Muddy Waters' boasting.

The consequence of David's dismissal of Giovanni is disastrous. In the first place, Giovanni's life falls apart as he is dismissed from his job, and he loses his self-esteem as he becomes involved in male prostitution. He ends up murdering his employer and under sentence of execution by the guillotine. David escapes with Hella to a 'great house in the south of France' (9) – a move to a space that is supposed to anticipate their construction of a heterosexual home. However, in the face of Giovanni's death sentence and his own divided self, David abandons Hella for a fling with a sailor in Nice, where she finds him. The discovery leads her to return to America, declaring that 'to be a woman doesn't simply mean humiliation' (154). For David, the novel ends with him longing to become a 'man', to move from the innocence that for Baldwin seems inherent to contemporary American identity (158).

The approach in this chapter has foregrounded the notion that there is no single masculine identity, but a range of masculinities. From this perspective there is no single black masculinity, as is evident from the different sexual identities of the characters in the novels. And yet, the argument can be made, on the evidence of these novels, that there are some powerful core elements to the ideologies of gender and sexuality that function as irresistible aspirations for most men. This is not to underestimate the power of racism in American society in the middle of the twentieth century, but it is notable that the African American men represented in these novels strive for a masculinity largely defined by dominant cultural forces. By contrast, in *Giovanni's Room* Baldwin, through the characterisation of David, seeks to deconstruct the conventional expectations of masculinity and sexuality that appear to be required of American male identity.

Notes

1. The journal was subtitled *The Atlanta University Review of Race and Culture*, and the editor-in-chief in 1940 was W. E. B. Du Bois.
2. In *Cold War Civil Rights* (2000), Mary Dudziak considers the continuing tensions between ideology and civil rights in relation to American foreign policy during the Cold War.
3. Baldwin's title references Richard Wright's *Native Son*, published in 1940. The Harlem riot is also represented in Ralph Ellison's *Invisible Man*.
4. In this period Wright had come to 'the view that Communism was the most effective path to solidarity between workers of all races' (Rowley 2001: 80). However, in 1944 Wright publicly cut his ties with the Communist Party (see Rowley 2001). Wright was not alone amongst African Americans in doubting the Communist Party's commitment to African American interests; see for example Ralph Ellison's representation of the main protagonist's experiences in *Invisible Man*.
5. The obstacles involved in establishing a legitimate voice and a sense of security for both African American literary authors and jazz musicians in the period after World War II are perhaps exemplified in the number of individuals who emigrated to Europe or spent long periods of

African American Identity and Masculinity 233

time there. Writers include Richard Wright, Chester Himes and James Baldwin; jazz musicians include Dexter Gordon, Bud Powell and the Art Ensemble of Chicago.

6. Schaub's argument relates to the New York Jewish intellectuals' post-war shift to anti-communism (see 163–4 above).
7. Collins makes the point that the reaction of African American men to black feminist analyses of masculinity in the 1970s and 1980s was profoundly negative, with accusations that feminists were 'colluding with the white supremacist emasculation of black males' (2006: 77).
8. For an account of Himes's career, see Margolies and Fabre 1997.
9. For the complexity of African Americans' identifications in the immediate period after America's entry into World War II, see Myrdal 1944: vol. 2, 1006. For example, Japan was a 'colored' nation, and some African Americans identified with the Japanese.
10. Petry's representation of the pressure-cooker environment created in Harlem by extreme poverty, deprivation, racism and exclusion links with Baldwin's and Ellison's representations of the Harlem riots.
11. Johnson's ambition is explicitly linked with Benjamin Franklin, see 63–4.
12. The two parts of 'The world and the jug' were first published in December 1963 and February 1964. Although the exchange with Howe occurred more than ten years after the publication of *Invisible Man*, Ellison provides an informative commentary on his approach in the novel.
13. In *Black Male Fiction and the Legacy of Caliban*, James Coleman argues that Ellison's self-positioning in relation to the 'white male masters' is indicative of the constriction of African American writers within the confines of Calibanic discourse, which associates the black male body with 'criminality, danger, and inferiority' (133, 3).
14. In its critique of Washington the novel echoes and endorses Du Bois's *The Souls of Black Folk*, which, while recognising Washington's prominence and influence, contains a strong critique of his approach. Du Bois criticises Washington's abandonment of claims for civil and political equality, for practically accepting the 'alleged inferiority of the Negro races', and advocates a doctrine of 'manly self-respect' (37, 43–4).
15. The issue of black leadership was important to Ellison, who perceived that in the 1940s 'Negro leaders did not represent the Negro community' (1961: 77).
16. The doctor's diagnosis echoes psychoanalytical approaches of postcolonial theory, which explore the internalisation of negative attributes by the colonised subject, as well as desire between the coloniser and colonised. See for example, Frantz Fanon, *Black Skin White Masks*, Edward Said, *Orientalism*, Mary Louise Pratt, *Imperial Eyes*, and Homi K. Bhabha, *The Location of Culture*.

17. The Brotherhood is generally regarded as a satire on the Communist Party of the United States, although Ellison subsequently maintained that it was meant to stand for political organisations in general.
18. For a wider discussion of homophobia in *Invisible Man*, see Kim 1997.
19. The narrator's lack of engagement with young adult black female characters can be contrasted with his relationship with Tod Clifton, which has unacknowledged homoerotic elements.
20. Mae G. Henderson describes the focus of the novel as enabling Baldwin to 'explore the complex personal, social, sexual and cultural dimensions of identity uncomplicated by the extra-literary preoccupation with the "Negro problem"' (2000: 313).

Afterword

In these final paragraphs I briefly discuss some conclusions to be taken from this study and then reflect on current circumstances in the United States.

Although the novels of the Forties and Fifties represented masculinity as diverse, contradictory, conflicted and contested, they also frequently manifest a concept of gender identity that is deeply rooted in biological difference. R. W. Connell's theorisation of hegemonic masculinity and its derivation from Gramsci's ideas remind us of the ideological nature of such formulations, and of the way they are constructed in culture and then internalised as 'common sense'. This essentialist notion of gender identity articulated a core set of attributes and behavioural codes to which men and women were expected to conform and which shaped the dominant form of masculinity. Even in novels where contestation, anxiety and complexity are evident, there is frequently a striving for a masculine identity shaped by such cultural expectations. The strength of these expectations may be seen in the way that novels such as Vidal's *The City and the Pillar*, Jones's *From Here to Eternity* and Himes's *If He Hollers Let Him Go* continue to valorise, recirculate and identify with dominant forms of masculinity despite the fact that these forms marginalise and oppress their characters.

Related to this essentialist notion of gender is the problem of articulating alternative ways of being a man. Salinger's *The Catcher in the Rye*, Bellow's *The Adventures of Augie March* and Ellison's *Invisible Man*, from their different perspectives, certainly represent the unsatisfactory aspects of contemporary models of manhood, but none of their novels have leading characters who are comfortable with their male identity in the context of post-war America.

Following the period covered by this book, second-wave feminism developed an extensive and sophisticated analysis of gender, emphasising in particular the constructed nature of identity and challenging biological determinism. Black feminist writers then challenged the singular perspective of some second-wave feminists and established the need to consider race and class in analysis of gender inequalities. Such developments in academic writing, in journalism and in cultural forms combined forces with political campaigning to make progress in removing inequalities.

However, there have been significant limits to such change and, as mentioned in the Introduction, divisions around gender identity and equality have become sharper in recent years. After Obama's term in office, the presidency now grants greater latitude to the 'alt-right' and fosters hostility towards women, immigrants, African Americans and Latinos. With conservative appointments to the Supreme Court and attacks on abortion rights in a number of states, many women perceive an attempt to push back in areas where women's rights have advanced. The popularity of the television adaptation of Margaret Atwood's *The Handmaid's Tale* (1985) reflects concerns about the threats to women's rights and freedom. Moreover, violent attacks by men – most recently in 2018 in Toronto – reflect the discourse of hostility to women generated in online social groups such as the 'incels' (involuntary celibates). The murderous attack in 2016 on Pulse, a gay nightclub in Orlando, is a reminder of the linkages in extreme right discourses between misogyny, racism and hostility to the LGBT+ community. It is notable that young black American men remain intensely vulnerable to violent police action, echoing the anxieties of Lutie Johnson about her son in *The Street* and the death of Tod Clifton in *Invisible Man*. Jordan Peterson's view that feminism is 'a murderous equity doctrine' was quoted in the Introduction (page 18), but may seem relatively mild compared to the quotations advocating rape and violence against women from the advocates for white male supremacy quoted on the Southern Poverty Law Center (SPLC) website (see Elam for an example of male supremacist attitudes). The SPLC website argues that there is an explicit connection between male supremacy and the development of the racist 'alt-right'. There is here a hateful discourse based in misogyny and racism.

The manifestation of extreme misogyny is related to a more widespread view that feminism has gone too far in challenging masculine privilege and in denigrating admirable masculine characteristics, while supposedly neutering men and confusing boys in the process. Such views can be seen to reflect the tenacity of ideas about gender rooted in biological essentialism. The present anxieties about threats to masculinity can be seen in relation to Judith Gardiner's observation from 2002 that masculinity is a 'nostalgic formation, always missing, lost, or about to be lost, its ideal form located in a past that advances with each generation in order to recede just beyond its grasp' (Gardiner 2002: 10). In another pertinent analysis, Sally Robinson in *Marked Men* (2000) shows how white men were represented as victims by male novelists of the Sixties (see Introduction, pages 18 and 25). In *Angry White Men* (2013, 2017) the sociologist Michael Kimmel develops an analysis of the current attitude of many white men in America in relation to nostalgia and victimhood. He argues that they are struggling with social change and look back to a time of an idealised masculinity in which they could have expected to assume a rewarding place on the 'economic ladder simply by working hard and applying themselves' (Kimmel 2013, 2017: 18). Kimmel calls this a sense of entitlement and regards some white men as angry and aggrieved because their expectations are no longer being met. In seeking an outlet for their anger, they blame women and feminists, immigrants and minority groups. It is the sense of loss and the ensuing anger that create the linkages that fuel misogyny and racism amongst some white men in America.

In fact Kimmel has some sympathy with the alienation of ordinary white men, and argues that their legitimate concerns have been exploited and their anger turned to the wrong targets – aimed at those below them economically rather than at the very wealthy (see Kimmel 2013, 2017: ch. 1, 'Manufacturing rage'). These men have reason to be angry, as American culture taught them that their expectations were reasonable provided they adhered to the ideology of American masculinity – the self-made man – and the American Dream. Yet the realities of the economy – particularly since the crash of 2008 – have disrupted such expectations, and anger comes from what Kimmel calls aggrieved entitlement, coupled with a sense of humiliation that these men have failed to achieve what they expected of themselves.

Yet Kimmel argues that these angry white men 'are on the losing side of history' (280). Similarly, Connell maintains that although the institutional structures of patriarchy have not crumbled away, there has been a significant cultural shift in favour of equality for women, and therefore the renewed hostility to women in the United States may be seen as an extreme and hysterical response to a battle that has in essence been lost (Connell 1995: 226). Evidence for change can be seen in the extension of women's rights, the introduction of gay marriage and the growing push for trans rights. There is of course strong resistance to misogyny and racism, for example in the #MeToo and Black Lives Matter movements.

These observations raise important questions for masculinity studies as a critical and ethical practice with an aspiration to effect political change. Are men locked into a view of women's rights as a zero-sum game, or are they willing to change? And are there viable alternative models of masculinity that were not available to writers in the Forties and Fifties? In *Recreating Men* Bob Pease considers the argument that it is not in men's interests to change in order to achieve gender equality: men benefit from patriarchy, and while some men will identify with the idea of gender equality on ethical grounds, their numbers are not sufficient to support a mass movement (Pease 2000: 128–9). However, he believes that men can 'feel empathy for different positions and loosen their connection to heterosexual dominance and patriarchy' (142). Kimmel maintains that 'we [need to] empower men to embrace a new definition of masculinity, decoupled from that false sense of entitlement, so that white men may move confidently into the more egalitarian future that is inevitable' (Kimmel 2013/2017: 284).

Connell advocates new levels of sophistication in the analysis of hegemonic masculinity as one means of effecting change (Connell 1995: 242), and I hope this book makes such a contribution. Kimmel's book is certainly an example. His complex account of the relationship between white American men and their notions of masculinity are evidence of the importance of sociological analysis of masculinity in contributing to an understanding of how notions of gender have an impact on behaviour and on the experience of men and women. The methodologies of sociologists such as Kimmel, Pease and Connell engage largely with lived experience in the here and now, but contributions to understanding how the ideology of masculinity shapes gender relations can also be made from a historical perspective. Moreover, fictional works of art have a unique role in the imagining of human experience and subjectivity. As I have argued, attending to the representation of men from a variety of perspectives and in relation to other discourses shows both the diversity of male identities and the residual power of traditional masculinity. Such analysis shows how dominant forms of masculinity are riven with contradictions but continue to work powerfully in men's imaginations. Two elements of reading fiction in context can particularly contribute to a cultural deconstruction of hegemonic masculinity. The first is that the women novelists considered in this book are consistently more alert to the oppressive nature of traditional masculinity, so it is important to pay great attention to women writers' representations of masculinity. Second, is the ability of fiction to create an empathetic response in readers to the life and circumstances of the Other. Enhancing readers' responses in such a way should be a political, educational and ethical priority.

Works Cited and Consulted

Abelove, Henry ([1986]), 'Freud, male homosexuality and the Americans', in Henry Abelove, Michèle Aina Barale and David M. Halperin (eds) (1993), *The Lesbian and Gay Studies Reader*, New York: Routledge, 381–93.
Adams, Laura (1976), *Existential Battles: The growth of Norman Mailer*, Athens: Ohio University Press.
Aldridge, John W. (1951), *After the Lost Generation: A critical study of the writers of two wars*, New York: McGraw-Hill.
Aldridge, John W. [1956] (1967), *In Search of Heresy: American literature in an age of conformity*, New York: Kennikat Press.
Alexander, Franz (1941), 'The psychiatric aspects of war and peace', *American Journal of Sociology*, 46, 504–20.
Allen, Jennifer, and Iris Marion Young (eds) (1989), *The Thinking Muse: Feminism and modern French philosophy*, Bloomington and Indianapolis: Indiana University Press.
Alter, Judy (1980), 'Introduction', in Kantor, *Gentle Annie*, v–ix.
Amburn, Ellis (1998), *Subterranean Kerouac: The hidden life of Jack Kerouac*, New York: St Martin's Press.
American Social Hygiene Association (1948), *Problems of Sexual Behavior: Proceedings of a symposium on the first published report of a series of studies of sex phenomena by Professor Alfred C. Kinsey, Wardell B. Pomeroy, and Clyde E. Martin*, New York: American Social Hygiene Association.
Atlas, James (2000), *Saul Bellow: A biography*, London: Faber.
Attaway, William [1941] (2005), *Blood on the Forge*, New York: New York Review of Books.
Attwood, William, George B. Leonard, Jr, and J. Robert Moskin (Editors of *Look*) (1958), *The Decline of the American Male*, New York: Random House.
Awkward, Michael [1995] (2000), 'A black man's place in black feminist criticism', in Napier, *African American Literary Theory*, 540–56.
Babb, Valerie (1998), *Whiteness Visible: The meaning of whiteness in American literature and culture*, New York: New York University Press.

Bachman, Monica (2000), '"Someone like Debby": (De)Constructing a lesbian community of readers', *GLQ*, 6: 3, 377–88.
Baker, Houston A., Jr (1983), 'To move without moving: an analysis of creativity and commerce in Ralph Ellison's Trueblood episode', *PMLA*, 98: 5, 828–45, <http://www.jstor.org/stable/462262> (last accessed 6 December 2016).
Baker, Houston A., Jr (1984), *Blues, Ideology, and Afro-American Literature: A vernacular theory*, Chicago: University of Chicago Press.
Baker, Houston A., Jr (2001), *Critical Memory: Public spheres, African American writing, and black fathers and sons in America*, Athens: University of Georgia Press.
Baldwin, Clive (2007), '"Digressing from the point": Holden Caulfield's women', in Graham, *J. D. Salinger's* The Catcher in the Rye, 110–18.
Baldwin, Clive (2009), '"The orgasm of a frigidaire": male sexuality and the female other in post-World War II American fiction', in Ellis and Meyer, *Masculinity and the Other*, 138–60.
Baldwin, James [1949], 'Everybody's protest novel', in Baldwin, *Notes of a Native Son*, 13–23.
Baldwin, James [1949] (1973), 'Preservation of innocence', in *Zero, Vols 1–4, 1949–50*, Nendeln, Liechtenstein: Krauss Reprint.
Baldwin, James [1954] (2001), *Go Tell It on the Mountain*, London: Penguin.
Baldwin, James (1955a), 'Notes of a native son', in Baldwin, *Notes of a Native Son*, 85–114.
Baldwin, James (1955b), *Notes of a Native Son*, Boston: Beacon Press.
Baldwin, James [1956] (2000), *Giovanni's Room*, London: Penguin.
Baldwin, James [1961] (1964), 'The black boy looks at the white boy', in James Baldwin, *Nobody Knows My Name: More Notes of a Native Son*, London: Michael Joseph, 177–96.
Barber, Fionna (2004), 'Abstract expressionism and masculinity', in Paul Wood (ed.), *Varieties of Modernism*, Milton Keynes: The Open University, and London: Yale University Press, 147–86.
Bayer, Ronald (1981), *Homosexuality and American Psychiatry: The politics of diagnosis*, New York: Basic Books.
Beasley, Christine (2008), 'Rethinking hegemonic masculinity in a globalizing world', *Men and Masculinities*, 11: 86–103.
Bell, Kevin (2007), *Ashes Taken for Fire: Aesthetic modernism and the critique of identity*, Minneapolis: University of Minnesota Press.
Bellow, Saul [1944] (2007), *Dangling Man*, London: Penguin.
Bellow, Saul [1947] (1996), *The Victim*, London: Penguin.
Bellow, Saul [1953] (1995), *The Adventures of Augie March*, London: Everyman's Library.
Bellow, Saul (2005), 'I got a scheme!', *The New Yorker*, 81: 10, 72–85.
Benston, Kimberley W. (ed.) (1987), *Speaking for You: The vision of Ralph Ellison*, Washington, DC: Howard University Press.
Bergler, Edmund (1956), *Homosexuality: Disease or way of life?*, New York: Hill and Wang.

Bergler, Edmund, and William S. Kroger (1954), *Kinsey's Myth of Female Sexuality: The medical facts*, New York: Grune and Stratton.
Bérubé, Allan (1990), *Coming Out under Fire: The history of gay men and women in World War Two*, New York: Free Press.
Bhabha, Homi K. (1994), *The Location of Culture*, London: Routledge.
Bigsby, Christopher (2005), *Arthur Miller: A critical study*, Cambridge: Cambridge University Press.
Bloom, Alexander (1986), *Prodigal Sons: The New York intellectuals and their world*, New York: Oxford University Press.
Bloom, Harold (1987), *J. D. Salinger*, New York: Chelsea House.
Bloom, Harold (ed.) (2009), *Ralph Ellison's* Invisible Man, New York: Bloom's Literary Criticism/Infobase Publishing.
Bolton, Isabel [1946, 1949, 1952] (1998), *Do I Wake or Sleep?*; *The Christmas Tree*; *Many Mansions*, in *New York Mosaic: Three novels by Isabel Bolton*, London: Virago.
Bone, Robert [1958] (1965), *The Negro Novel in America*, New Haven: Yale University Press.
Botting, Fred (1996), *Gothic*, London: Routledge.
Bourke, Joanna (1999), *An Intimate History of Killing: Face-to-face killing in twentieth-century warfare*, London: Granta.
Bowles, Nellie (2018), 'Jordan Peterson, custodian of the patriarchy', *New York Times*, 18 May 2018, <https://www.nytimes.com/2018/05/18/style/jordan-peterson-12-rules-for-life.html> (last accessed 21 June 2018).
Brady, Sean (2010), Rev. of *Masculinity in the Modern West: Gender, civilization and the body* by Christopher E. Forth, *Social History of Medicine*, 23, 203–4.
Breit, Harvey [1953] (1957), 'Saul Bellow', in Harvey Breit, *The Writer Observed*, London: Alvin Redman, 271–4.
Brod, Harry (1995), 'Of mice and supermen: images of Jewish masculinity', in T. M. Rudavsky (ed.), *Gender and Judaism: The transformation of tradition*, New York and London: New York University Press, 279–93.
Brodkin, Karen (1998), *How Jews Became White Folks: And what that says about race in America*, New Brunswick, NJ: Rutgers University Press.
Brookeman, Christopher (1984), *American Culture and Society since the 1930s*, London: Macmillan.
Brookeman, Christopher (1991), 'Pencey Preppy: cultural codes in *The Catcher in the Rye*', in Salzman, *New Essays on* The Catcher in the Rye, 57–76.
Brooks, Gwendolyn [1953] (1993), *Maud Martha*, Chicago: Third World Press.
Buhle, Mari Jo (1998), *Feminism and its Discontents: A century of struggle with psychoanalysis*, Cambridge, MA: Harvard University Press.
Burke, Kenneth (1987), 'Ralph Ellison's Trueblooded bildungsroman', in Benston, *Speaking for You*, 349–59.
Burns, John Horne [1947] (2004), *The Gallery*, New York: New York Review of Books.

Butler, Judith (1990), *Gender Trouble*, London: Routledge.
Butler, Judith (1993), *Bodies that Matter: On the discursive limits of 'sex'*, New York: Routledge.
Butler, Robert J. (ed.) (2000), *The Critical Response to Ralph Ellison*, Westport, CT: Greenwood Press.
Callahan, John F. (2004), *Ralph Ellison's* Invisible Man*: A casebook*, New York: Oxford University Press.
Campbell, Anne (1993), *Men, Women, and Aggression*, New York: Basic Books.
Campbell, James (2002), *Talking at the Gates: A life of James Baldwin*, Berkeley and Los Angeles: University of California Press.
Capote, Truman [1948] (1994), *Other Voices, Other Rooms*, New York: Vintage.
Carbado, Devon W. (ed.) (1999), *Black Men on Race, Gender, and Sexuality: A critical reader*, New York: New York University Press.
Carby, Hazel [1998] (2000), 'Introduction to *Race Men*', in Napier, *African American Literary Theory*, 660–4.
Cayton, Horace R., and St Clair Drake (1946), *Black Metropolis*, London: Jonathan Cape.
Charters, Ann (1991), Introduction, in Kerouac [1957] (2000), *On the Road*, vii–xxix.
Chavkin, Allan (ed.) (2012), *Critical Insights: Saul Bellow*, Pasadena, CA: Salem Press.
Clark, Dorothy G. (2009), 'Being's wound: (un)explaining evil in Jim Thompson's *The Killer Inside Me*', *The Journal of Popular Culture*, 42, 49–66.
Clark, Keith (2002), *Black Manhood in James Baldwin, Ernest J. Gaines, and August Wilson*, Urbana and Chicago: University of Illinois Press.
Cohen, Josh (1998), *Spectacular Allegories: Postmodern American writing and the politics of seeing*, London: Pluto Press.
Coleman, James W. (2001), *Black Male Fiction and the Legacy of Caliban*, Lexington: University Press of Kentucky.
Coles, Robert (2000), 'Anna Freud and J. D. Salinger's Holden Caulfield', *Virginia Quarterly Review*, 76, 214–15.
Collins, Patricia Hill (2006), 'A telling difference: dominance, strength, and black masculinities', in Athena D. Mutua (ed.), *Progressive Black Masculinities*, New York: Routledge, 73–97.
Connell, R. W. (1987), *Gender and Power: Society, the person and sexual politics*, Cambridge: Polity Press.
Connell, R. W. (1995), *Masculinities*, Cambridge: Polity Press.
Connell, R. W., and James W. Messerschmidt (2005), 'Hegemonic masculinity: rethinking the concept', *Gender and Society*, 19: 6, 829–59.
Connor, Steven (2000), 'The shame of being a man', <http://www.stevenconnor.com/shame/> (last accessed 20 July 2018).
Corber, Robert J. (1993), *In the Name of National Security: Hitchcock, homophobia, and the political construction of gender in postwar America*, Durham, NC: Duke University Press.

Corber, Robert J. (1997), *Homosexuality in Cold War America: Resistance and the crisis of masculinity*, Durham, NC: Duke University Press.
Cory, Donald Webster [Edward Sagarin] (1951), *The Homosexual in America: A subjective approach*, New York: Greenberg.
Cowley, Malcolm (1954), *The Literary Situation*, New York: The Viking Press.
Cronin, Gloria L. (2001), *A Room of His Own: In search of the feminine in the novels of Saul Bellow*, Syracuse: Syracuse University Press.
Cuordileone, K. A. (2005), *Manhood and American Political Culture in the Cold War*, New Abingdon: Routledge.
D'Emilio, John (1983), *Sexual Politics, Sexual Communities: The making of a homosexual minority in the United States 1940–1970*, Chicago: University of Chicago Press.
Davenport, Stephen (2002), 'Road work: rereading Kerouac's mid-century melodrama of beset sonhood', in Milette Shamir and Jennifer Travis (eds), *Boys Don't Cry? Rethinking narratives of masculinity and emotion in the US*, New York: Columbia University Press, 167–84.
Davidson, David (1947), *The Steeper Cliff*, New York: Random House.
Davidson, David (1949), *The Hour of Truth*, London: The Falcon Press.
Davies, Robert Gorham (1953), 'Augie just wouldn't settle down', *The New York Times*, 20 September, <http://www.nytimes.com/books/97/05/25/reviews/bellow-march.html> (last accessed 23 October 2017).
Davis, Angela (1982), *Women Race and Class*, London: Women's Press.
Davison, Neil R. (2010), *Jewishness and Masculinity from the Modern to the Postmodern*, New York and London: Routledge.
Demetriou, Demetrakis Z. (2001), 'Connell's concept of hegemonic masculinity: a critique', *Theory and Society*, 30, 337–61.
Dempsey, David (1948), 'The dusty answer of modern war', Rev. of *The Naked and the Dead* by Norman Mailer, *New York Times*, 9 May 1948, np, <http://movies2.nytimes.com/books/97/05/04/reviews/mailer-dead.html> (last accessed 21 June 2019).
Dempsey, David (1951), 'Tough and tormented, this was the Army to Mr Jones', Rev. of *From Here to Eternity* by James Jones, *New York Times Book Review*, 25 February, 4–5.
Dickens, Charles [1850] (nd), *David Copperfield*, London: Collins.
Dinnerstein, Leonard (1994), *Antisemitism in America*, New York: Oxford University Press.
Dittman, Michael J. (2004), *Jack Kerouac: A biography*, Westport, CT: Greenwood Press.
Doane, Ashley 'Woody', and Eduardo Bonilla-Silva (eds) (2003), *White Out: the continuing significance of racism*, New York: Routledge.
Douglas, George H. (1991), *The Smart Magazines: 50 years of literary revelry and high jinks at Vanity Fair, The New Yorker, Life, Esquire, and The Smart Set*, Hamden, CT: Archon Books.
Doyle, Laura (1994), *Bordering on the Body: The racial matrix of modern fiction and culture*, New York: Oxford University Press.

Du Bois, W. E. B. [1903] (1996), *The Souls of Black Folk*, Harmondsworth: Penguin.

Du Bois, W. E. B. (1996), *The Oxford W. E. B. Du Bois Reader*, ed. Eric J. Sundquist, New York: Oxford University Press.

Dudziak, Mary L. (2000), *Cold War Civil Rights: Race and the image of American democracy*, Princeton: Princeton University Press.

Eadie, Jo (2001), 'Masculinity, terminable and interminable', *Sexualities*, 4, 237–45.

Eagleton, Terry (1983), *Literary Theory: An introduction*, Oxford: Blackwell.

Ehrenreich, Barbara (1983), *The Hearts of Men: American dreams and the flight from commitment*, London: Pluto Press.

Elam, Paul (2017), 'An ear for men', *Sex Robots: Part 3 – Disempowering Pussy*, quoted on SPLC Southern Law Poverty Center, 'Male supremacy', np, <https://www.splcenter.org/fighting-hate/extremist-files/ideology/male-supremacy> (last accessed 10 July 2019).

Elkin, Henry (1946), 'Aggressive and erotic tendencies in army life', *The American Journal of Sociology*, 51, 408–13.

Ellis, Heather, and Jessica Meyer (eds) (2009), *Masculinity and the Other: Historical perspectives*, Newcastle-upon-Tyne: Cambridge Scholars.

Ellison, Ralph (1940), 'The birthmark', *New Masses*, 36, 16–17.

Ellison, Ralph [1944, unpublished], 'An American dilemma: a review', in Ellison, *Collected Essays*, 328–40.

Ellison, Ralph [1952] (2001), *Invisible Man*, Harmondsworth: Penguin.

Ellison, Ralph [1953], 'Brave words for a startling occasion', in Ellison, *Collected Essays*, 151–4.

Ellison, Ralph [1961], 'That same pain, that same pleasure: an interview', in Ellison, *Collected Essays*, 63–80.

Ellison, Ralph [1963 and 1964], 'The world and the jug', in Ellison, *Collected Essays*, 155–88.

Ellison, Ralph (2003), *The Collected Essays of Ralph Ellison*, ed. John F. Callahan, New York: The Modern Library.

Ellison, Ralph (2016), *Flying Home and Other Stories*, London: Penguin/Random House UK.

Fairchild, Johnson E. (ed.) (1952), *Women: Society and sex*, New York: Sheridan House.

Fanon, Frantz [1952] (1970), *Black Skin White Masks*, trans. Charles Lam Markmann, London: Paladin.

Farnham, Marynia (1952), 'The lost sex', in Fairchild, *Women*, 33–52.

Ferber, Edna [1952] (2000), *Giant*, New York: Harper Collins.

Ferrebe. Alice (2005), *Masculinity in Male-Authored Fiction, 1950–2000: Keeping it up*, Basingstoke: Palgrave Macmillan.

'Fiction in the US: we need a novelist to re-create American values instead of wallowing in the literary slums', Editorial, *Life*, 16 August 1948, 24.

Fiedler, Leslie [1948] (1952), 'Come back to the raft ag'in, Huck honey!', in Leslie Fiedler, *An End to Innocence: Essays on culture and politics*, Boston: Beacon Press, 142–51.
Fiedler, Leslie (1951), 'James Jones' dead-end Young Werther', *Commentary: A Jewish review*, 12, 252–5.
Firestone, Shulamith (1971), *The Dialectic of Sex: The case for feminist revolution*, London: Jonathan Cape.
Fleissner, Robert F. (2001), 'Salinger's Caulfield: A refraction of Copperfield and his caul', in Robert F. Fleissner, *Names, Titles, and Characters by Literary Writers: Shakespeare, 19th- and 20th-century authors, Studies in Onomastics*, 2, 177–80, New York: Edwin Mellen Press.
Foley, Barbara (2010), *Wrestling with the Left: The making of Ralph Ellison's Invisible Man*, Durham, NC: Duke University Press.
Foley, Neil (1997), *The White Scourge: Mexicans, blacks and poor whites in Texas cotton culture*, Berkeley: University of California Press.
Forth, Christopher E. (2008), *Masculinity in the Modern West: Gender, civilization and the body*, Basingstoke, Hampshire: Palgrave Macmillan.
Foucault, Michel [1976] (1998), *The Will to Knowledge: The history of sexuality Volume 1*, trans. Robert Hurley, Harmondsworth: Penguin.
Frank, Arthur W. (1991), 'For a sociology of the body: an analytical review', in Mike Featherstone, Mike Hepworth and Bryan S. Turner (eds), *The Body: Social process and cultural theory*, London: Sage, 36–102.
Franklin, John Hope (1947), *From Slavery to Freedom: A history of American Negroes*, New York: Alfred A. Knopf.
Frazier, E. Franklin (1939), *The Negro Family in the United States*, Chicago: University of Chicago Press.
Frazier, E. Franklin [1949] (1957, rev. edn), *The Negro in the United States*, New York: Macmillan.
Freedman, Estelle B. (1987), '"Uncontrolled desires": The response to the sexual psychopath, 1920–1960', *The Journal of American History*, 74, 83–106.
Freud, Sigmund [1905] (1977), *Three Essays on the Theory of Sexuality*, trans. James Strachey, in Sigmund Freud, *On Sexuality: Three Essays on the Theory of Sexuality and Other Works*, comp. and ed. Angela Richards, The Penguin Freud Library, vol. 7, Harmondsworth: Penguin.
Friedan, Betty [1963] (1971), *The Feminine Mystique*, London: Gollancz.
'From here to obscenity', Editorial, *Life*, 16 April 1951, 40.
Frosh, Stephen (1994), *Sexual Difference: Masculinity and psychoanalysis*, London: Routledge.
Fuchs, Daniel (1984), *Saul Bellow: vision and revision*, Durham, NC: Duke University Press.
Fussell, Paul (2004), 'Introduction', in Burns, *The Gallery*, vii–xi.
Gardiner, Judith Kegan (ed.) (2002), *Masculinity Studies and Feminist Theory: New directions*, New York: Columbia University Press.
Garner, Steve (2007), *Whiteness: an introduction*, London: Routledge.

Garrett, Leah (2015), *Young Lions: How Jewish authors reinvented the American war novel*, Evanston, IL: Northwestern University Press.
Garson, Helen S. (1980), *Truman Capote*, New York: Frederick Ungar.
Gates, Henry Louis, Jr (1984), 'The blackness of blackness: a critique of the sign and the Signifying Monkey', in Henry Louis Gates, Jr (ed.), *Black Literature and Literary Theory*, New York and London: Methuen, 285–321.
Gates, Henry Louis, Jr (1988), *The Signifying Monkey: A theory of Afro-American literary criticism*, New York: Oxford University Press.
Gathorne-Hardy, Jonathan (1998), *Sex the Measure of All Things: A life of Alfred C. Kinsey*, London: Chatto and Windus.
Gayle, Addison, Jr (1975), *The Way of the New World: The Black novel in America*, New York: Anchor Press.
Geddes, Donald Porter (ed.) (1954), *An Analysis of the Kinsey Reports on Sexual Behaviour in the Human Male and Female*, London: Muller.
Geddes, Donald Porter, and Enid Curie (eds) (1948), *New Light on Sexual Knowledge: About the Kinsey Report: Observations by 11 experts on 'Sexual Behavior in the Human Male'*, New York: New American Library of World Literature, Signet Special Book.
Gerhard, Jane (2001), *Desiring Revolution: Second-wave feminism and the rewriting of American sexual thought 1920 to 1982*, New York: Columbia University Press.
Gilbert, James (2005), *Men in the Middle: Searching for masculinity in the 1950s*, Chicago: University of Chicago Press.
Gillespie, Diane F. (1990), 'Dorothy Richardson (1873–1957)', in Bonnie Kime Scott (ed.), *The Gender of Modernism: A critical anthology*, Bloomington: Indiana University Press.
Gilman, Sander L. (1986), *Jewish Self-Hatred: Anti-semitism and the hidden language of the Jews*, Baltimore: Johns Hopkins University Press.
Gilmore, David D. (1990), *Manhood in the Making: Cultural concepts of manhood*, New Haven: Yale University Press.
Ginsberg, Allen (1956), *Howl and Other Poems*, San Francisco: City Lights.
Ginzberg, Eli, John L. Herma and Sol W. Ginzberg (1953), *Psychiatry and Military Manpower Policy: A reappraisal of the experience in World War II*, New York: King's Crown Press, Columbia University.
Glover, David, and Cora Kaplan (2000), *Genders*, London: Routledge.
Goldstein, Eric L. (2006), *The Price of Whiteness: Jews, race and American identity*, Princeton: Princeton University Press.
Gómez, Laura E. (2007), *Manifest Destinies: The making of the Mexican American race*, New York: New York University Press.
Gorer, Geoffrey (1948), *The American People: A study in national character*, New York: W.W. Norton.
Graham, Maryemma (ed.) (2004), *The Cambridge Companion to the African American Novel*, Cambridge: Cambridge University Press.
Graham, Sarah (2007), *J. D. Salinger's* The Catcher in the Rye, London: Routledge.

Grimshaw, Jean (1999), 'Working out with Merleau-Ponty', in Jane Arthurs and Jean Grimshaw (eds), *Women's Bodies: Discipline and transgression*, London: Cassell, 91–116.
Grosz, Elizabeth (1990), 'The body of signification', in John Fletcher and Andrew Benjamin (eds), *Abjection, Melancholia and Love: The work of Julia Kristeva*, London: Routledge, 80–103.
Grosz, Elizabeth (1994), *Volatile Bodies: Toward a corporeal feminism*, Bloomington: Indiana University Press.
Grunwald, Henry Anatole (ed.) (1964), *Salinger: A critical and personal portrait*, London: Peter Owen.
Gussow, Adam (1984), 'Bohemia revisited: Malcolm Cowley, Jack Kerouac, and *On the Road*', *Georgia Review*, 38, 291–311.
Halberstam, Jack (Judith) (1998), *Female Masculinity*, Durham, NC: Duke University Press.
Hale, Nathan G. (1995), *The Rise and Crisis of Psychoanalysis in the United States: Freud and the Americans 1917–1985*, New York: Oxford University Press.
Hall, Stuart (2000), 'Who needs "identity"?', in Paul du Gay, Jessica Evans and Peter Redman (eds), *Identity: A reader*, London: Sage, 15–30.
Halliwell, Martin (2007), *American Culture in the 1950s*, Edinburgh: Edinburgh University Press.
Halliwell, Martin (2013), *Therapeutic Revolutions: Medicine, psychiatry and American culture, 1945–1970*, New Brunswick, NJ: Rutgers University Press.
Hamilton, Ian (1988), *In Search of J. D. Salinger: A biography*, New York: Random House.
Hamilton, Peter (1983), *Talcott Parsons*, Chichester: Ellis Horwood.
Harper, Phillip Brian (1996), *Are We Not Men? Masculine anxiety and the problem of African American identity*, Oxford: Oxford University Press.
Harrison, Russell (1997), *Patricia Highsmith*, New York: Twayne.
Hassan, Ihab (1961), *Radical Innocence: Studies in the contemporary American novel*, Princeton: Princeton University Press.
Heath, Clark W., W. L. Woods, L. Brouha, C. C. Seltzer and A. V. Brock (1943), 'Personnel selection: a short method for selection of combat officers', *Annals of Internal Medicine*, 19, 415–26.
Heath, Clark W., in collaboration with Lucien Brouha, Lewise W. Gregory, Carl C. Seltzer, Frederic L. Wells and William L. Woods (1946), *What People Are: A study of normal young men* (The Grant Study, Department of Hygiene, Harvard University), Cambridge, MA: Harvard University Press.
Hebert, Laura A. (2007), 'Taking difference seriously: Feminisms and the "man question"', *Journal of Gender Studies*, 16, no. 1, 31–45.
Heggarty, George (2006), *Queer Gothic*, Urbana: University of Illinois Press.

Helton, Roy (1940), 'The inner threat: our own softness', *Harpers Magazine*, September, 181, 337–43, <https://search-proquest-com.libezproxy.open.ac.uk/docview/1301527061/fulltextPDF/3BF53B75456F4908PQ/2?accountid=14697> (last accessed 23 June 2018).

Henderson, Mae G. (2000), 'James Baldwin: expatriation, homosexual panic, and man's estate', *Calaloo* 23, 313–27, <http://www.jstor.org/stable/3299564> (last accessed 8 July 2009).

Hersey, John (1944), 'Joe is home now', *Life*, 3 July, 68–80.

Higgins, Charlotte (2018), 'Patriarchy: How feminism's big idea came back to life', *Guardian*, 22 June, 9–11.

Highsmith, Patricia [1950] (1999), *Strangers on a Train*, London, Vintage.

Highsmith, Patricia [1952] (2015), *The Price of Salt*, New York: Dover Publications (originally published under the pseudonym Claire Morgan by Coward-McCann, New York).

Highsmith, Patricia [1955] (1999), *The Talented Mr Ripley*, London: Vintage.

Hilfer, Anthony Channell (1984), '"Not really such a monster": Highsmith's Ripley as thriller protagonist and protean man', *The Midwest Quarterly: A journal of contemporary thought*, Pittsburgh: University of Pittsburgh Press, xxv: 4, 361–74.

Himes, Chester [1945] (1999), *If He Hollers Let Him Go*, London: Serpent's Tail.

Himes, Chester [1947] (1997), *Lonely Crusade*, Edinburgh: Payback Press.

Hoffman, Warren (2009), *The Passing Game: Queering Jewish American culture*, Syracuse: Syracuse University Press.

Holmes, John Clellon [1952] (1967), 'This is the Beat Generation', in John Clellon Holmes, *Nothing More to Declare*, New York: Dutton, 109–15.

Holmes, John Clellon [1952] (1997), *Go*, New York: Thunder's Mouth Press.

hooks, bell (Gloria Watkins) (1990), *Yearning: Race, gender, and cultural politics*, Boston, MA: South End Press.

hooks, bell (Gloria Watkins) (2004), *We Real Cool: Black men and masculinity*, New York: Routledge.

Horlacher, Stefan, and Kevin Floyd (eds) (2013), *Post-World War II Masculinities in British and American Literature and Culture: Towards comparative masculinity studies*, Farnham and Burlington: Ashgate.

Horney, Karen (1967), *Feminine Psychology*, ed. and intro. Harold Kelman, New York and London: W. W. Norton & Company.

Howe, Irving (1963), 'Black boys and native sons', *Dissent*, Autumn, 353–68.

Howe, Irving (1968), 'The New York intellectuals: A chronicle and a critique', *Commentary*, 46: 4, 29–51.

Hutchinson, George (2018), *Facing the Abyss: American literature and culture in the 1940s*, New York: Columbia University Press.

Jackson, Lawrence P. (1999), 'Ralph Ellison, Sharpies, Rinehart, and Politics in *Invisible Man*', *The Massachusetts Review*, 40: 1, 71–95, <http://www.jstor.org/stable/25091503> (last accessed 1 December 2016).

Jacobson, Matthew Frye (1998), *Whiteness of a Different Color: European immigrants and the alchemy of race*, Cambridge, MA: Harvard University Press.
Jefferson, Margo (2016), *Negroland: A memoir*, London: Granta.
Jewish Women's Archive/Encyclopedia; 'Jo Sinclair', <https://jwa.org/encyclopedia/article/sinclair-jo> (last accessed 15 February 2018).
Johns, Gillian (2007), 'Jim Trueblood and his critic-readers: Ralph Ellison's rhetoric of dramatic irony and tall humor in the mid-century American literary public sphere', *Texas Studies in Literature and Language*, 49: 3, 230–64.
Jones, James [1951] (1952), *From Here to Eternity*, New York: Charles Scribner's Sons.
Jones, James (1975), *WWII: A chronicle of soldiering*, London: Leo Cooper.
Jones, James H. (1997), *Alfred C. Kinsey: A public/private life*, New York: W.W. Norton.
Jones, Peter G. (1976), *War and the Novelist: Appraising the American war novel*, Columbia: University of Missouri Press.
Jurca, Catherine (1999), 'The sanctimonious suburbanite: Sloan Wilson's *The Man in the Gray Flannel Suit*', *American Literary History*, 11, 82–106.
Kantor, MacKinlay [1942] (1980), *Gentle Annie*, Boston: Gregg Press.
Kantor, MacKinlay (1945), *Glory for Me*, New York: Coward-McCann.
Kaplan, Fred (1999), *Gore Vidal: A biography*, London: Bloomsbury.
Kaufman, Michael (ed.) (1987), *Beyond Patriarchy: Essays by men on pleasure, power, and change*, Toronto: Oxford University Press.
Kazin, Alfred (1942), *On Native Grounds: An interpretation of modern American prose literature*, New York: Reynal and Hitchcock.
Kent, George E. (1987), 'Ralph Ellison and Afro-American folk and cultural tradition', in Benston, *Speaking for You*, 95–104.
Kerouac, Jack [1957] (2000), *On the Road*, London: Penguin.
Kerouac, Jack (2007), *On the Road: The original scroll*, London: Penguin.
Kim, Daniel Y. (1997), 'Invisible desires: homoerotic racism and its homophobic critique in Ralph Ellison's *Invisible Man*', *Novel: A Forum on Fiction*, 30: 3, 309–28.
Kimmel, Michael (2002), 'Foreword', in Gardiner, *Masculinity Studies and Feminist Theory*, ix–xi.
Kimmel, Michael (2006, 2nd edn), *Manhood in America: A cultural history*, New York: Oxford University Press.
Kimmel, Michael (2013, 2017), *Angry White Men: American masculinity at the end of an era*, New York: Bold Type Books.
Kinsey, Alfred C., Wardell B. Pomeroy and Clyde E. Martin [1948] (1968), *Sexual Behavior in the Human Male*, Philadelphia: W. B. Saunders.
Kinsey, Alfred C., Wardell B. Pomeroy, Clyde E. Martin and Paul H. Gebhard (1953), *Sexual Behavior in the Human Female*, Philadelphia: W.B. Saunders.

Knights, Ben (1999), *Writing Masculinities: Male narratives in twentieth-century fiction*, London: Palgrave.
Kristeva, Julia [1979] (1986), 'Women's time', in Toril Moi (ed.), *The Kristeva Reader*, Oxford: Blackwell, 187–213.
Kristeva, Julia (1982), *Powers of Horror: An essay on abjection*, trans. Leon S. Roudiez, New York: Columbia University Press.
Krutnik, Frank (1991), *In a Lonely Street: Film noir, genre, masculinity*, London: Routledge.
Lacan, Jacques (2002), 'The signification of the phallus', in Jacques Lacan, *Écrits: A selection*, trans. Bruce Fink, New York: W. W. Norton, 271–80.
Leader, Zachary (2015), *The Life of Saul Bellow: To fame and fortune, 1915–1964*, London: Jonathan Cape.
Levinson, Julian (2008), *Exiles on Main Street: Jewish American writers and American literary culture*, Bloomington and Indianapolis: Indiana University Press.
Lieberman, Jennifer L. (2015), 'Ralph Ellison's technological humanism', *Melus*, 40: 4, 8–27.
Lott, Eric (1997), 'All the king's men: Elvis impersonators and white working-class masculinity', in Harry Stecopoulos and Michael Uebel (eds), *Race and the Subject of Masculinities*, Durham, NC: Duke University Press.
Lundberg, Ferdinand, and Marynia F. Farnham (1947), *Modern Woman: The lost sex*, New York: Harper & Brothers.
Macauley, Robie (1951), 'Private Jones's revenge', *Kenyon Review*, 13, 526–9.
Macauley, Robie (1952), *The Disguises of Love*, New York: Random House.
Macauley, Robie (1958), *The End of Pity and Other Stories*, London: George Harrap.
McCarthy, Barry (1994), 'Warrior values: a socio-historical survey', in John Archer (ed.), *Male Violence*, London: Routledge, 105–20.
McCarthy, Mary [1954] (1991), *The Group*, San Diego: Harvest.
McCarthy, Mary (1970), 'J. D. Salinger's closed circuit', in Mary McCarthy, *The Writing on the Wall and Other Literary Essays*, London: Weidenfeld and Nicolson, 35–41.
Macdonald, Helen (2014), *H Is for Hawk*, London: Vintage Books.
MacInnes, John (1998), *The End of Masculinity*, Buckingham: The Open University Press.
McKinley, Maggie (2015), *Masculinity and the Paradox of Violence in American Fiction, 1950–75*, New York and London: Bloomsbury Academic.
McKinley, Maggie (2017), *Understanding Norman Mailer*, Columbia: University of South Carolina Press.
McLaren, Angus (1999), *Twentieth-Century Sexuality: A history*, Oxford: Blackwells.
MacShane, Frank (1985), *Into Eternity: The life of James Jones, American writer*, Boston: Houghton Mifflin.

Mailer, Norman [1948] (1993), *The Naked and the Dead*, London: Flamingo.
Mailer, Norman [1959] (1961), 'The white negro: superficial reflections on the hipster', in Norman Mailer, *Advertisements for Myself*, London: Andre Deutsch, 281–302.
Malcolm, Douglas (1999), '"Jazz America": Jazz and African American culture in Jack Kerouac's *On the Road*', *Contemporary Literature*, 40, 85–110.
Malinowski, Bronislaw (1941), 'An anthropological analysis of war', *The American Journal of Sociology*, 46, 521–50.
Marcuse, Herbert [1956] (1998), *Eros and Civilisation: A philosophical enquiry into Freud*, London: Routledge.
Margolies, Edward, and Michael Fabre (1997), *The Several Lives of Chester Himes*, Jackson: University Press of Mississippi.
Marshall, S. L. A. (1947), *Men against Fire: The problem of battle command in future war*, Washington, DC: The Infantry Journal and New York: William Morrow.
Martinez, Manuel Luis (2003), *Countering the Counterculture: Rereading postwar American dissent from Jack Kerouac to Tomás Rivera*, Madison: University of Wisconsin Press.
May, Elaine Tyler [1988] (1999, 2nd edn), *Homeward Bound: American families in the Cold War era*, New York: Basic Books.
Mead, Margaret (1948), 'An anthropologist looks at the report', in American Social Hygiene Association, *Problems of Sexual Behavior*, 58–69.
Mead, Margaret (1949), *Male and Female: A study of the sexes in a changing world*, London: Victor Gollancz.
Mesher, David R. (1980), 'Arthur Miller's *Focus*: The first American novel of the Holocaust?', *Judaism: A Quarterly Journal of Jewish Life and Thought*, 29: 4, 469–78.
Miller, Arthur [1940] (2000), *Death of a Salesman*, London: Penguin.
Miller, Arthur [1945] (2009), *Focus*, London: Penguin.
Miller, Neil (1995), *Out of the Past: Gay and lesbian history from 1869 to the present*, London: Vintage.
Mills, C. Wright (1953), *White Collar: The American middle classes*, New York: Oxford University Press.
Mitchell, Juliet, and Jacqueline Rose (eds) (1982), *Feminine Sexuality: Jacques Lacan and the école freudienne*, trans. Jacqueline Rose, Basingstoke: Macmillan.
Mitchell-Peters, B. (2000), 'Camping the gothic: que(e)ring sexuality in Truman Capote's *Other Voices, Other Rooms*', *Journal of Homosexuality*, 39, 107–38.
Moi, Toril (2002, 2nd edn), *Sexual/Textual Politics: Feminist literary theory*, London: Routledge.
Moller, Michael (2007), 'Exploiting patterns: a critique of hegemonic masculinity', *Journal of Gender Studies*, 16, 263–76.

Moore-Gilbert, Bart (1997), *Postcolonial Theory: Contexts, Practices, Politics*, London: Verso.
Morrison, Toni (1992), *Playing in the Dark: Whiteness in the literary imagination*, New York: Vintage.
Mumford, Lewis (1961), *The City in History: Its origins, its transformations, and its prospects*, London: Secker and Warburg.
Mutua, Athena D. (2006), 'Theorizing progressive Black masculinities', in Athena D. Mutua (ed.), *Progressive Black Masculinities*, New York: Routledge, 3–42.
Myrdal, Gunnar, with the assistance of Richard Sterner and Arnold Rose (1944), *An American Dilemma: The Negro problem and American democracy*, 2 vols, New York: Harper.
Nadel, Alan (1988), *Invisible Criticism: Ralph Ellison and the American Canon*, Iowa City: University of Iowa Press.
Napier, Winston (ed.) (2000), *African American Literary Theory: A reader*, New York: New York University Press.
Neal, Larry [1970] (1987), 'Ellison's zoot suit', in Benston, *Speaking for You*, 105–24.
Needles, William (1946), 'The regression of psychiatry in the Army', *Psychiatry: Journal of the Biology and the Pathology of Interpersonal Relations*, 9, 167–85.
New York City Guide (1939), New York: Random House.
Niebuhr, Reinhold (1954), 'Kinsey and the moral problem of man's sexual life', in Geddes, *An Analysis of the Kinsey Reports*, 61–9.
Niederland, William G. (1952), 'Some psychological disorders of femininity and masculinity', in Fairchild, *Women*, 117–29.
Nietzsche, Friedrich (1883–91), *Thus Spake Zarathustra: A book for all and none*, trans. Thomas Common, Project Gutenberg, <http://www.gutenberg.org/files/1998/1998-h/1998-h.htm#2H_4_0004> (last accessed 13 October 2010).
Noble-Goodman, Stuart (1998), 'Mythic guilt and the burden of sin in Ellison's *Invisible Man*', *Midwest Quarterly* 39: 4, 409–31, <http://web.b.ebscohost.com.libezproxy.open.ac.uk/ehost/pdfviewer/pdfviewer?vid=2&sid=f3472a81-d237-46dd-891d-611d3d9e82e0%40sessionmgr104> (last accessed 24 February 2017).
Noonan, Peggy (2001), 'Welcome back, Duke', *The Wall Street Journal*, 12 October, <https://www.wsj.com/articles/SB122451174798650085> (last accessed 19 June 2018).
O'Meally, Robert (ed.) (1988), *New Essays on* Invisible Man, New York: Cambridge University Press.
Olderman, Raymond M. (1966), 'Ralph Ellison's blues and *Invisible Man*', *Wisconsin Studies in Contemporary Literature*, 7: 2, 142–59; <http://www.jstor.org/stable/1207243> (last accessed 24 February 2017).
Orleck, Annelise (2013), *The Problem of Citizenship in American History*, <http://www.flowofhistory.org/the-problem-of-citizenship-in-american-history-2/> (last accessed 25 July 2018).

Osgerby, Bill (2001), *Playboys in Paradise: Masculinity, youth and leisure-style in modern America*, Oxford: Berg.
Osgerby, Bill (2009), 'Two-fisted tales of brutality and belligerence: masculinity and meaning in the American "true adventure" pulps of the 1950s and 1960s', in Ellis and Meyer, *Masculinity and the Other*, 163–89.
Ottley, Roi (1943), *'New World A-Coming': Inside Black America*, Boston: Houghton Mifflin.
Ottley, Roi (1949), *Black Odyssey: The story of the Negro in America*, London: John Murray.
Pareda, Prudencio de (1948), *All the Girls We Loved*, New York: Signet.
Parsons, Talcott, and Robert F. Bales, in collaboration with James Olds, Morris Zelditch, Jr, and Philip E. Slater (1956), *Family: socialization and interaction process*, London: Routledge and Kegan Paul.
Patterson, James T. (1997), *Grand Expectations: The United States, 1945–1974*, New York, Oxford University Press.
Payne, Kenneth (2002), 'The killers inside them: the schizophrenic protagonist in John Franklin Bardin's "Devil Take the Blue-Tail Fly" and Jim Thompson's "The Killer Inside Me"', *The Journal of Popular Culture*, 36, 250–63.
Pease, Bob (2000), *Recreating Men: Postmodern masculinity politics*, London: Sage.
Peters, Fiona (2011), *Anxiety and Evil in the Writings of Patricia Highsmith*, Farnham: Ashgate.
Peterson, Jordan (2018a), *12 Rules for Life: An antidote to chaos*, London: Allen Lane.
Peterson, Jordan (2018b), <https://twitter.com/jordanbpeterson/status/955440524575391744?lang=en> (last accessed 21 June 2018).
Peterson, Jordan (2018c), 'Jordan Peterson: Masculinity is not fundamentally toxic' (Parts 1 and 2), Interview with Rebel Wisdom, <https://www.youtube.com/watch?v=iNlQVMCG-eo> (last accessed 21 June 2018).
Petry, Ann [1946] (nd), *The Street*, New York: Houghton Mifflin.
Pifer, Ellen (1990), *Saul Bellow: Against the grain*, Philadelphia: University of Pennsylvania Press.
Pinsker, Sanford, and Ann Pinsker (1999), *Understanding The Catcher in the Rye: a student casebook to issues, sources and historical documents*, Westport, CT: Greenwood Press.
Pleck, Joseph (1981), *The Myth of Masculinity*, Cambridge, MA: MIT Press.
Polito, Robert (1997), *Savage Art: A biography of Jim Thompson*, London: Serpent's Tail.
Pratt, Mary Louise (1992), *Imperial Eyes: Travel writing and transculturation*, London: Routledge.
Pugh, W. W. T. (1998), 'Boundless hearts in a nightmare world: queer sentimentalism and southern gothicism in Truman Capote's *Other Voices, Other Rooms*', *The Mississippi Quarterly*, 51, 663–82.

Rampersad, Arnold (2007), *Ralph Ellison: A biography*, New York: Alfred A. Knopf.

Ramsey, Priscilla R. (2006), 'Racial myths and masculinity in African American literature', *The Journal of African American History*, 91, 3: 352.

Reisman, Judith (nd), 'The Kinsey Coverup', <http://www.drjudithreisman.com/the_kinsey_coverup.html> (last accessed 11 July 2018).

Reumann, Miriam G. (2005), *American Sexual Character: Sex, gender, and national identity in the Kinsey Reports*, Berkeley: University of California Press.

Rideout, Walter B. (1956), *The Radical Novel in the United States 1900–1954: Some interrelations of literature and society*, Cambridge, MA: Harvard University Press.

Riesman, David, in collaboration with Reuel Denney and Nathan Glazer (1950), *The Lonely Crowd: A study of the changing American character*, New Haven: Yale University Press.

Riesman, David (1952), Rev. of C. Wright Mills, *White Collar: The American Middle Classes*, *The American Journal of Sociology*, 57, 513–15.

Robinson, Paul [1967] (1989, 2nd edn), *The Modernization of Sex: Havelock Ellis, Alfred Kinsey, William Masters and Virginia Johnson*, New York: Cornell University Press.

Robinson, Sally (2000), *Marked Men: White masculinity in crisis*, New York: Columbia University Press.

Robinson, Sally (2007), 'Masculine protest in *The Catcher in the Rye*', in Graham, *J. D. Salinger's* The Catcher in the Rye, 69–76.

Rolo, Charles J. (1948), Rev. of *The City and the Pillar* by Gore Vidal, *The Atlantic*, February, 110.

Rolo, Charles J. (1948), Rev. of *Other Voices, Other Rooms* by Truman Capote, *The Atlantic*, March, 109.

Rolo, Charles J. (1951), 'This man's army', Reader's Choice, *The Atlantic*, March, 83–4.

Rose, Jacqueline (1982), 'Introduction – II', in Mitchell and Rose, *Feminine Sexuality*, 27–57.

Rosen, Steven J. (1999), 'African American anti-Semitism and Himes's *Lonely Crusade*', in Charles L. P. Silet (ed.), *The Critical Response to Chester Himes*, Westport, CT: Greenwood Press.

Rosenberg, Warren (2001), *Legacy of Rage: Jewish masculinity, violence, and culture*, Amherst: University of Massachusetts Press.

Rosenthal, Raymond, 'Underside of the War', Rev. of *The Naked and the Dead* by Norman Mailer, *Commentary*, July 1948, vol. 6, 91–3, <https://search-proquest-com.libezproxy.open.ac.uk/docview/1290077347/fulltext/BE829862BDF4897PQ/15?accountid=14697> (last accessed 21 June 2019).

Rowley, Hazel (2001), *Richard Wright: The life and times*, New York: Henry Holt.

Saad, Gad (2018), 'Is toxic masculinity a valid concept?', *Psychology Today*, 8 March, <https://www.psychologytoday.com/gb/blog/

homo-consumericus/201803/is-toxic-masculinity-valid-concept> (last accessed 19 June 2018).
Said, Edward [1978] (1985), *Orientalism*, London: Penguin.
Salinger, J. D. (1946), 'Slight rebellion off Madison', *The New Yorker*, 21 December, 76–9.
Salinger, J. D. [1952] (1994), *The Catcher in the Rye*, London: Penguin.
Sallis, James (2000), *Chester Himes: A life*, Edinburgh: Payback Press.
Salzman, Jack (ed.) (1991), *New Essays on* The Catcher in the Rye, Cambridge: Cambridge University Press.
Saunders, Frances Stonor (1999), *The Cultural Cold War: The CIA and the world of arts and letters*, New York: The New Press.
Savran, David (1998), *Taking It like a Man: White masculinity, masochism, and contemporary American culture*, Princeton: Princeton University Press.
Schaub, Thomas (1991), *American Fiction in the Cold War*, London: University of Wisconsin Press.
Schenkar, Joan (2009), *The Talented Miss Highsmith: The secret life and serious art of Patricia Highsmith*, New York: St Martin's Press.
Schlesinger, Arthur M., Jr [1949] (1998), *The Vital Center: The politics of freedom*, New Brunswick, NJ: Transaction Publishers.
Schlesinger, Arthur M. [1958] (1964), 'The crisis of American masculinity', in Arthur M. Schlesinger, *The Politics of Hope*, London: Eyre and Spottiswoode, 237–46.
Schoene-Harwood, Berthold (2000), *Writing Men: Literary masculinities from* Frankenstein *to the New Man*, Edinburgh: Edinburgh University Press.
Schoenvogel, Robert (nd), 'Mailer, Norman: *The Naked and the Dead*', *20th Century American Bestsellers*, <http://bestsellers.lib.virginia.edu/submissions/40> (last accessed 9 July 2018).
Sedgwick, Eve Kosofsky (1985), *Between Men: English literature and male homosocial desire*, New York: Columbia University Press.
Sedgwick, Eve Kosofsky (1995), 'Gosh, Boy George, you must be awfully secure in your masculinity', in Maurice Berger, Brian Wallis and Simon Watson (eds), *Constructing Masculinity*, London: Routledge, 11–20.
Segal, Lynne (1994), *Straight Sex: The politics of pleasure*, London: Virago.
Segal, Lynne (1997, 2nd edn), *Slow Motion: Changing masculinities, changing men*, London: Virago.
Segal, Lynne (1999), *Why Feminism? Gender, psychology, politics*, New York: Columbia University Press.
Self, Will, and David Gamble (2000), *Perfidious Man*, Harmondsworth: Viking.
Seltzer, Carl C. (1949), 'The relationship between the masculine component and personality', Clyde Kluckhohn and Henry A. Murray (eds), *Personality in Nature, Society, and Culture*, London: Jonathan Cape, 84–96.
Shannon, Edward A. (2004), '"Where was the sex?" Fetishism and dirty minds in Patricia Highsmith's *The Talented Mr Ripley*', *Modern Language Studies*, 34: 1 and 2, 16–27.

Shapiro, Edward S. (1992), *A Time for Healing: American Jewry since World War II*, Baltimore: Johns Hopkins University Press.
Shaw, Irwin [1948] (2000), *The Young Lions*, Chicago: University of Chicago Press.
Sinclair, Jo (1948), *Wasteland*, London: Macmillan.
Smethurst, James (2004), '"Something warmly, infuriatingly feminine": gender, sexuality, and the work of Ralph Ellison', in Steven C. Tracy (ed.), *A Historical Guide to Ralph Ellison*, Oxford: Oxford University Press, 115–42.
Smith, Barbara [1977] (2000), 'Towards a Black feminist criticism', in Napier, *African American Literary Theory*, 132–46.
Smith, Harrison (1951), 'Manhattan Ulysses, Junior', *Saturday Review of Literature*, 14 July, <http:/nths.newtrier.k12.il.us/academics/english/catcher/SatReview.html> (last accessed 15 April 2002).
Smith, Valerie (2004), 'The meaning of narration in *Invisible Man*', in Callahan, *Ralph Ellison's* Invisible Man, 189–220.
Smith, William Gardner [1948] (1949), *Last of the Conquerors*, London: Victor Gollancz.
Smith, William Gardner (1950), 'The Negro writer: pitfalls and compensations', *Phylon*, 11, 297–306.
Smyth, J. E. (2010), *Edna Ferber's Hollywood: American fictions of gender, race, and history*, Austin: University of Texas Press.
Stead, Christina [1940] (1970), *The Man Who Loved Children*, Harmondsworth: Penguin.
Stepto, Robert B. (1979), *From behind the Veil: A study of Afro-American Narrative*, Urbana: University of Illinois Press.
Strecker, Edward A. (1946), *Their Mothers' Sons: The psychiatrist examines an American problem*, Philadelphia: J. B. Lippincott.
Strecker, Edward A., and Kenneth E. Appel (1945), *Psychiatry in Modern Warfare*, New York: Macmillan.
Summers, Claude J. (1990), *Gay Fictions: Wilde to Stonewall: Studies in a male homosexual literary tradition*, New York: Continuum.
Summers, Claude J. (1992), '*The City and the Pillar* as gay fiction', in Jay Parini (ed.), *Gore Vidal: Writer against the grain*, New York: Columbia University Press, 56–75.
Tanner, Tony [1971] (1976), *City of Words: A study of American fiction in the mid-twentieth century*, London: Jonathan Cape.
Tate, Claudia (1987), 'Notes on the invisible women in Ralph Ellison's *Invisible Man*', in Benston, *Speaking for You*, 163–72.
Thompson, Graham (2003), *Male Sexuality under Surveillance: The office in American literature*, Iowa City: University of Iowa Press.
Thompson, Jim [1952] (2006), *The Killer Inside Me*, London: Orion.
Thompson, Jim [1954] (2014), *A Hell of a Woman*, New York: Mulholland Books.
Tosh, John (1999), *A Man's Place: Masculinity and the middle-class home in Victorian England*, New Haven: Yale University Press.
Trilling, Diana (1950), 'Men, women and sex', *Partisan Review*, 17, 365–78.

Trilling, Diana (1978), *Reviewing the Forties*, New York: Harcourt Brace Jovanovich.
Trilling, Lionel [1940] (1951), 'Freud and literature', in Lionel Trilling, *The Liberal Imagination*, London: Secker and Warburg, 34–57.
Trilling, Lionel (1948), 'Sex and science: The Kinsey Report', *Partisan Review*, 15, 184–200.
Trilling, Lionel [1953] (2001), 'A triumph of the comic view', in Arthur Krystal (ed.), *A Company of Readers*, New York: The Free Press, 100–6.
Tuttle, William M. (1993), *'Daddy's Gone to War': The Second World War in the lives of America's children*, New York: Oxford University Press.
Valente, Joseph (2013), 'Other possibilities, other drives: queer, counterfactual "life" in Truman Capote's *Other Voices, Other Rooms*', *Modern Fiction Studies*, 59: 3, 526–46.
Van Leer, David (1991), 'Society and identity', in Emory Elliott (ed.), *The Columbia History of the American Novel*, New York: Columbia University Press, 485–509.
Vidal, Gore [1946] (2003), *Williwaw*, London, Abacus.
Vidal, Gore (1948), *The City and the Pillar*, New York: Grosset & Dunlap.
Vidal, Gore [1948] (1965, rev. edn), 'Afterword', in Gore Vidal, *The City and the Pillar*, London: Heinemann.
Vidal, Gore [1948] (1997), *The City and the Pillar*, London: Abacus.
Vidal, Gore (1949), *The City and the Pillar*, London: John Lehmann.
Vidal, Gore (1995), *Palimpsest: A Memoir*, London: André Deutsch.
Wagner, Philip S. (1946), 'Psychiatric activities during the Normandy offensive, June 20–August 20, 1944: An experience with 5,203 neuropsychiatric casualties', *Psychiatry: Journal of the Biology and the Pathology of Interpersonal Relations*, 9, 341–64.
Wald, Alan M. (1987), *The New York Intellectuals: The rise and decline of the anti-Stalinist left from the 1930s to the 1980s*, Chapel Hill: University of North Carolina Press.
Wald, Alan M. (2007), *Trinity of Passion: The literary left and the antifascist crusade*, Chapel Hill: University of North Carolina Press.
Waldmeir, Joseph J., and John C. Waldmeir (1999), *The Critical Response to Truman Capote*, Westport, CT: Greenwood Press.
Wallace, Maurice O. (2002), *Constructing the Black Masculine: Identity and ideality in African American men's literature and culture, 1775–1995*, Durham, NC: Duke University Press.
Warnes, Andrew (ed.) (2007), *Richard Wright's* Native Son, Abingdon: Routledge.
Warren, Robert Penn [1946] (2007), *All the King's Men*, London: Penguin.
Warren, Robert Penn (1953), 'The man with no commitments: the comic and heroic philosophy of *The Adventures of Augie March*', *New Republic*, 2 November, <https://newrepublic.com/article/122717/man-no-commitments> (last accessed 1 November 2017).
Washington, Booker T. (1895), 'Cast down your bucket where you are' (The Atlanta compromise speech), <http://historymatters.gmu.edu/d/88> (last accessed 7 March 2017).

Watts, Jerry Gafio (1994), *Heroism and the Black Intellectual: Ralph Ellison, politics, and Afro-American intellectual life*, Chapel Hill: University of North Carolina Press.

Wedgwood, Nikki (2009), 'Connell's theory of masculinity – its origins and influences on the study of gender', *Journal of Gender Studies*, 18, 329–39.

Weeks, Jeffrey (2003, 2nd edn), *Sexuality*, London: Routledge.

Wenke, Joseph (1987), *Mailer's America*, Hanover: University Press of New England.

Wetherell, Margaret, and Nigel Edley (1999), 'Negotiating hegemonic masculinity: imaginary positions and psycho-discursive practices', *Feminism and Psychology*, 9, 335–56.

Wheeler, Elizabeth A. (2001), *Uncontained: urban fiction in postwar America*, New Brunswick, NJ: Rutgers University Press.

Whitehead, Stephen M., and Frank J. Barrett (2001), *The Masculinities Reader*, Cambridge: Polity Press.

Whiting, Gilman W., and Thabiti Lewis (2008), 'On manliness: black masculinity revisited', *On Manliness: Black American Masculinities, Ameriquests*, 6: 1–9, <http://ejournals.library.vanderbilt.edu/ameriquests/viewissue.php?id=12> (last accessed 16 November 2010).

Whyte, William H. [1956] (nd), *The Organization Man*, New York: Doubleday Anchor.

Wickware, Francis Sill (1948), 'Report on Kinsey: Indiana expert on the private lives of gall wasps and American men has stirred up the greatest biological commotion in the US since Darwin', *Life*, 2 August, 87–98.

Wiegman, Robyn (1995), *American Anatomies: Theorizing race and gender*, Durham, NC: Duke University Press.

Wiegman, Robyn (2002), 'Unmaking: men and masculinity in feminist theory', in Gardiner, *Masculinity Studies and Feminist Theory*, 31–59.

Wilentz, Gay (2001), 'Healing the "sick Jewish soul": psychoanalytic discourse and Jo Sinclair (Ruth Seid)'s *Wasteland*', *Literature and Psychology*, 47: 1–2, 68–93.

Williams, Sherley Anne [1986] (2000), 'Some implications of womanist theory', in Napier, *African American Literary Theory*, 218–23.

Williams, Simon J., and Gillian Bendelow (1998), *The Lived Body: Sociological themes, embodied issues*, London: Routledge.

Wilson, Andrew (2010), *Beautiful Shadow: A life of Patricia Highsmith*, London: Bloomsbury.

Wilson, Sloan [1955] (1983), *The Man in the Gray Flannel Suit*, New York: Four Walls Eight Windows.

Winnicott, D. W. [1960] (1979), 'The theory of the parent-infant relationship', in D. W. Winnicott, *The Maturational Processes and the Facilitating Environment: Studies in the theory of emotional development*, London: Hogarth Press, 37–55.

Wirth-Nesher, H., and M. Kramer (eds) (2003), *The Cambridge Companion to Jewish American Literature*, Cambridge: Cambridge University Press, <https://doi.org/10.1017/CCOL0521792932> (last accessed 25 July 2018).

Wisse, Ruth R. (1971), *The Schlemiel as Modern Hero*, Chicago: University of Chicago Press.

Wisse, Ruth R. (2003), 'Jewish American renaissance', in Wirth-Nesher and Kramer, *Cambridge Companion to Jewish American Literature*, 190–211.

Wright, John S. (2004), 'The conscious hero and the rites of man: Ellison's war', in Callahan, *Ralph Ellison's* Invisible Man, 221–52.

Wright, Richard [1937] (2004), 'Blueprint for Negro writing', in Henry Louis Gates, Jr, and Nellie Y. McKay (eds), *The Norton Anthology of African American Literature* (2nd edn), New York: Norton, 1403–10.

Wright, Richard [1940] (2000), *Native Son*, London: Vintage.

Wright, Richard [1940] (2008), *Uncle Tom's Children: Five long stories*, New York: Harper.

Wright, Richard [1945] (1947), *Black Boy: A record of childhood and youth*, London: Readers Union; Victor Gollancz.

Wright, Richard (1946), 'Introduction' in Cayton and Drake, *Black Metropolis*, ix–xxxii.

Wylie, Philip (1942), *Generation of Vipers*, New York: Farrar and Rinehart.

Zaretsky, Eli (2004), *Secrets of the Soul: A Social and Cultural History of Psychoanalysis*, New York: Knopf.

Zelditch, M. (1956), 'Role differentiation in the nuclear family', in Parsons and Bales, *Family*, 307–52.

Zimmerman, Carle C. (1948), 'A sociologist looks at the report', in American Social Hygiene Association, *Problems of Sexual Behavior*, 82–105.

Žižek, Slavoj (nd), 'When straight means weird and psychosis is normal', <http://www.lacan.com/ripley.html> (last accessed 7 April 2015).

Index

Adventures of Augie March, The
   (Bellow), 27, 160, 171–86,
   193, 235
African Americans, 45, 196
   culture, 45, 221–2
   and double consciousness, 214, 226
   'Negro problem', 162, 215
   and passing, 196, 207–8
   and segregation, 196–7
'Aggressive and erotic tendencies in
   army life' (Elkin), 149–50
Aldridge, John, 140, 151
Alexander, Franz, 8, 79–80
All the Girls We Loved (Pareda),
   150–1
American Dilemma, An (Myrdal), 197
American Fiction in the Cold War
   (Schaub), 201
American People, The (Gorer), 39, 54
American Sexual Character
   (Reumann), 111–12
anti-Semitism, 162–3, 192
Antisemitism in America (Dinnerstein),
   162
Atlas, James, 171
Atwood, Margaret, 236

Babb, Valerie, 161, 199
Baldwin, James, 1–3, 28, 45, 196,
   198–9, 200–1, 203, 208, 213,
   223, 227–32
behaviourism, 115, 116, 120
Bellow, Saul, 27, 160, 163, 171–86,
   193, 235
Bergler, Edmund, 114
Between Men (Sedgewick), 42, 147
Bhabha, Homi, 154

Bigsby, Christopher, 166
Bildungsroman, 171–3, 174, 186
bisexuality, 14, 134
'Black boy looks at the white boy, The'
   (Baldwin), 45
'Black boys and native sons'
   (Howe), 213
Bloom, Alexander, 163–4
'Blueprint for negro writing'
   (Wright), 200
Bodies That Matter (Butler), 132
Botting, Fred, 138–9
Bourke, Joanna, 79, 82–3
Brady, Sean, 21
Burns, John Horne, 1–2, 27, 111,
   151–5, 156
Butler, Judith, 105–6, 132

Campbell, Anne, 76
Capote, Truman, 27, 131, 137–41,
   155, 228
Carbado, Devon, 202, 209
Catcher in the Rye, The (Salinger), 2,
   3, 24, 26, 30, 48–62, 68, 172, 235
Cayton, Horace R., 196
Christian Front, 162, 166
CIA, the, 120–1, 164
City and the Pillar, The (Vidal), 27,
   131, 134–7, 140–1, 143, 235
City in History, The (Mumford), 33–4
Cohen, Elliott, 164
Cold War, 6, 12–13, 121, 164, 201
Collins, Patricia Hill, 202, 209
Coming of Age in Somoa (Mead), 6
Commentary, 87, 163–4, 172
communism, 3, 12–13, 34, 112, 121,
   140, 162, 164

Communist Party, American, 13, 163, 201
conformity, 5, 6, 7, 12, 13–14, 27, 31–3, 34, 35, 39, 40, 46, 49, 118, 129, 165–6, 217, 219, 226, 227, 235
  and the Organization, 31–3, 35–7, 39, 41
Congress for Cultural Freedom, 121, 164
Connell, R. W., 19–20, 76, 78, 90, 155, 235, 237, 238
Corber, Robert J., 13, 141
Cory, Donald Webster, 141
Coughlin, Father Charles, 162
Countering the Counterculture (Martinez), 40, 41, 45
Cowley, Malcolm, 40, 151
'Crisis of American masculinity, The' (Schlesinger), 13
Cronin, Gloria, 174–5, 178, 181, 183, 186, 193
Cultural Cold War, The (Saunders), 120–1, 164
Cuordileone, K. A., 13

'Daddy's Gone to War' (Tuttle), 125–6
Dangling Man (Bellow), 171, 173, 175, 181, 193
David Copperfield (Dickens), 60
Davies, Robert, 172
Davis, Angela, 205
de Beauvoir, Simone, 22–3
Decline of the American Male (*Look* magazine), 3, 13–14, 190
Dempsey, David, 87, 98
Desiring Revolution (Gerhard), 113, 122–3
Deutsch, Helen, 114, 116
Dickens, Charles, 60
Dinnerstein, Leonard, 162, 163
Disguises of Love, The (Macauley), 27, 119–24
Douglass, Frederick, 218, 226, 227
Drake, St Clair, 196
du Bois, W. E. B., 214, 226, 227

Ehrenreich, Barbara, 35, 40
Elkin, Henry, 149–50

Ellison, Ralph, 28, 196, 197, 201, 213–27, 235
Eros and Civilisation (Marcuse), 118
'Everybody's protest novel' (Baldwin), 200–1

family, nuclear, 5, 7, 9–10, 18–19, 22, 31, 34–5, 40, 115–16
Family: Socialization and Interaction Process (Parsons and Bales), 9–11; see also Zelditch
feminisation of American culture, 7, 12, 27, 31, 34, 44, 46, 49, 50, 68, 72, 107, 112, 165, 166, 167, 207
Ferber, Edna, 27, 30, 62–8
Fiedler, Leslie, 163
Focus (Miller), 27, 160, 162, 165–7, 193
Forth, Christopher, 21–2
Foucault, Michel, 112
Franklin, John Hope, 196, 197
Frazier, E. Franklin, 196
Freedman, Estelle, 131–2
'Freud and literature' (Trilling), 8
Freudian theory *see* psychoanalytical theory
From Behind the Veil (Stepto), 226
From Here to Eternity (Jones), 27, 72, 97–104, 107, 235
Fromm, Eric, 8
Frosh, Stephen, 21
Fuchs, Daniel, 172
Fussell, Paul, 155

Gallery, The (Burns), 1–2, 27, 111, 151–5, 156
Gardiner, Judith Kegan, 16–17, 18, 236–7
Garrett, Leah, 170–71
Gay Fictions (Summers), 137
gender
  and aggression, 76–7
  and the body, 11, 19, 21–3, 107
  and identity, 3–4, 15–16, 17–21, 48–9, 50, 61, 78, 118, 153, 155, 181, 200, 202, 228, 235–6, 238
  roles, 3, 4–7, 9–10, 56, 58, 65, 112, 114, 125–6
  transgressive, 65, 132, 134, 135, 138, 142, 189–92, 193

Generation of Vipers (Wylie), 59
Gerhard, Jane, 113, 122–3
Giant (Ferber), 27, 30, 62–8, 72
Gilbert, James, 6
Gilman, Sander, 164–5, 189
Ginzberg, E., Herma, L. and Ginzberg, Sol W., 83–4
Giovanni's Room (Baldwin), 1–3, 28, 227–32
Glory for Me (Kantor), 124–31
Goldstein, Eric L., 162, 163
Gorer, Geoffrey, 39, 54
'Gosh, Boy George' (Sedgewick), 24
Gothic (Botting), 138–9
Grant Study, 11
Grimshaw, Jean, 22–3

Hale, Nathan, 8, 79, 82
Handmaid's Tale, The (Atwood), 236
Hassan, Ihab, 119
Hearts of Men, The (Ehrenreich), 35, 40
Heath, Clark W., 85–6, 87
Heggarty, George, 142, 145
Herzog (Bellow), 183
Highsmith, Patricia, 27, 131, 138, 141–5, 155
Himes, Chester, 1–2, 28, 196, 200, 202–9, 219, 235
Hoffman, Warren, 189, 191
Holocaust, the, 3, 28, 163, 164, 168, 171, 192
Homeward Bound (May), 5, 31, 47
Homosexual in America, The (Cory), 141
homosexuality, 4, 12, 19, 33, 36, 42, 44, 112, 115, 131–45, 147, 149, 189–92, 228, 231
and inversion, 133–4, 189
hooks, bell, 202
Hoover, J. Edgar, 116
Howe, Irving, 213, 214

Ideal Marriage (van de Velde), 113
If He Hollers Let Him Go (Himes), 1–2, 28, 202–9, 219, 235
Immigration Act of 1924, 161
In the Name of National Security (Corber), 13

Intimate History of Killing, An (Bourke), 79
Invisible Man (Ellison), 28, 172, 213–27, 235, 236

Jacobson, Matthew Frye, 161
jazz, 15, 44, 45–6, 48
'Jazz America' (Malcolm), 45–6
Jefferson, Margot, 196
Jewish identity, 44, 161–3
and alienation, 165, 193
and assimilation, 163, 164–5, 187–9, 192
and passing, 188, 189
Jewish Self-Hatred (Gilman), 164–5
Jim Crow, 4, 196
Jones, James, 27, 72, 78, 97–104, 107, 235
Jones, James H., 121
Jurca, Catherine, 35

Kantor, MacKinley, 124–31
Kazin, Alfred, 163
Kerouac, Jack, 2, 3, 27, 30, 40–8, 68
Killer Inside Me, The (Thompson), 1–2, 25, 27, 72, 73–7, 143
Kimmel, Michael, 6, 16, 21, 237, 238
Kinsey, Alfred C., 4, 27, 60, 111, 112, 113–17, 119–20, 121, 131, 132–5, 140, 155
Kristeva, Julia, 105–6
Kristol, Irving, 163

Lacan, Jacques, 20
Leader, Zachary, 171
Life magazine, 97–8
Literary Situation, The (Cowley), 40
Lonely Crowd, The (Riesman), 31, 32, 34, 49
Lonely Crusade, The (Himes), 203
Look magazine, 3, 13–14, 190
Lundberg, Ferdinand and Farnham, Marynia, 59, 114

McCarthy, Barry, 77, 93–4, 101, 107
McCarthyism, 13, 112, 131, 140, 141
Macauley, Robie, 27, 119–24
and CIA, 121

McKinley, Maggie, 95–6, 224–5
MacShane, Frank, 98–9
Mailer, Norman, 1–2, 14–16, 27, 45, 72, 78, 87–97, 98, 107, 145–50, 162
Malcolm, Douglas, 45–6
Male and Female (Mead), 6–9, 11, 33, 55, 117–18
Male Sexuality under Surveillance (Thompson), 36–7
Malinowski, Bronislaw, 80
Man in the Gray Flannel Suit, The (Wilson), 27, 30–1, 34–9, 48, 68
Manhood and American Political Culture in the Cold War (Cuordileone), 13
Manhood in America (Kimmel), 6
'Mannish Boy' (Waters), 197, 199, 204
Marcuse, Herbert, 118, 152
Marked Men (Robinson), 25–6, 237
Marshall, S. L. A., 80–1
Martinez, Manuel, 40, 41, 45, 46
'Masculine protest in *The Catcher in the Rye*' (Robinson), 49–50
Masculinities (Connell), 19–20
Masculinities Reader, The (Whitehead and Barrett), 23
masculinity
　and abjection, 104–6
　African American, 15, 197–8, 201–2: rape myth, 205–6, 219–20
　and the body, 9–11, 21–3, 25–6, 64, 85–6, 103–4, 105–6, 126–7, 128–31, 135, 169
　and class, 13–14, 17, 19, 24, 35, 68, 80–1, 86, 99, 102, 107, 116–17
　construction of, 18–19, 22, 51–2
　and the cowboy, 41, 48, 63, 66, 73
　in crisis, 3, 6, 13, 16–17, 21, 25
　and effeminacy, 36, 39, 65, 126–7, 139, 170
　and fatherhood, 10, 18–19, 22, 34, 68
　and fear, 89, 90, 91–2
　and feminisation, 36, 92, 98, 104, 106, 193, 197, 214; *see also* gender
　hegemonic, 19–20, 63, 76, 78, 90, 92, 102, 104, 107, 136, 155–6, 202, 235, 238
　and homoeroticism, 44–5, 146, 149–50
　and homophobia, 20, 44, 208, 220
　and homosexuality, 36, 42, 131–45, 147–8, 150–1, 154–5, 228–9
　and the homosocial, 39, 43, 130–1, 146, 147, 148–50, 156
　and individualism, 12, 32–3, 34, 41, 68, 102, 214, 218
　Jewish American: the *mensch*, 173, 183–4; the *schlemiel*, 173–4, 182, 184–5
　and misogyny, 20, 42, 146, 148–50, 229
　and mothering, 58–60, 62
　and nostalgia, 18, 45, 49–50, 236–7
　and the Other, 91, 123–4, 152, 155, 166, 175, 183, 189
　and power, 25–6, 92–3, 94–5, 97
　and race, 14–15, 17, 19, 24, 63–4, 66–8, 213, 236
　and sexuality, 14–15, 36, 38, 42, 55–7, 62, 75, 123–4, 130–1, 131–45, 146, 153, 178, 180–1, 197–8, 205–6, 219–21
　toxic, 17
　and violence, 57–8, 72, 75–6, 79–81, 96, 102–4, 137, 143–4, 145, 167, 169, 213, 222–5
　and war, 37–8, 81–5
　and the 'warrior', 77–8, 90, 93–4, 100–1
　white, 7, 9, 12, 15–16, 25, 27, 28, 33, 34, 43, 52, 63, 64, 66, 67, 187, 200, 202, 220, 230, 231, 237–8; *see also* 'whiteness'
　see also conformity
Masculinity and the Paradox of Violence (McKinley), 95–6, 224
Masculinity in the West (Forth), 21–2
Masculinity Studies and Feminist Theory (Gardiner), 16–17
materialism, American, 177–9, 182–3
May, Elaine Tyler, 5, 31, 47, 65
Mead, Margaret, 6–9, 11, 33, 38–9, 55, 113, 116, 117–18

Men against Fire (Marshall), 80–1
Men in the Middle (Gilbert), 6
Men, Women, and Aggression (Campbell), 76
Mexicans, 45, 46, 66–8
middle classes, 5, 7, 9, 31, 34, 48, 55, 68
Miller, Arthur, 27, 160, 162, 165–7
Mills, C. Wright, 7, 8, 31, 33, 34
Mitchell, Juliet, 20
Mitchell-Peters, Brian, 137, 138
Modern Woman (Lundberg and Farnham), 59, 114
Modernization of Sex, The (Robinson), 112
Moi, Toril, 20
'momism', 59, 84
Moore-Gilbert, Bart, 154
Morrison, Toni, 199–200
Mumford, Lewis, 33–4, 35
Mutua, Athena D., 202, 209
Myrdal, Gunner, 197

Naked and the Dead, The (Mailer), 1–2, 27, 72, 87–97, 98, 145–50, 162
Narrative (Douglass), 226
Native Son (Wright), 200, 209, 213
Neal, Larry, 214
Needles, William, 83
'Negro writer, The' (Smith), 201
Negroes *see* African Americans
Negroland (Jefferson), 196
Noonan, Peggy, 17, 22
'Notes of a native son' (Baldwin), 198–9, 227

On the Road (Kerouac), 2, 3, 27, 30, 40–8, 68
Organization, the *see* conformity
Organization Man, The (Whyte), 31–5
Osgerby, Bill, 5
Other Voices, Other Rooms (Capote), 27, 131, 137–41
Ottley, Roi, 196, 197

Pareda, Prudencio de, 150–1
Park, Robert E., 197, 214

Parsons, Talcott and Bales, Robert F., 9–11
Partisan Review, 113, 163–4
Passing Game, The (Hoffman), 189
patriarchy, 3, 8, 19, 20, 22, 23, 39, 123, 147, 150, 188, 222, 237–8
Pearl Harbour attack, 27, 97, 99, 108, 162, 203
Pease, Bob, 238
Perfidious Man (Self and Gamble), 22
Peterson, Jordan, 18, 236
Petry, Ann, 28, 196, 200, 209–13
Phylon, 196, 201
Playboys in Paradise (Osgerby), 5
Playing in the Dark (Morrison), 199–200
Podhoretz, Norman, 172
Postcolonial Theory (Moore-Gilbert), 154
Powers of Horror (Kristeva), 105–6
'Preservation of innocence' (Baldwin), 228
Price of Whiteness, The (Goldstein), 162, 163
Prodigal Sons (Bloom), 163–4
Psychiatry, 83
Psychiatry and Military Manpower Policy (Ginzberg, E., Herma, J. L. and Ginzberg, S. W.), 83–4
Psychiatry in Modern Warfare (Strecker and Appel), 82
psychoanalytical theory, 120, 187–8
  in America, 4, 8, 118
  and desire, 115, 118
  and homosexuality, 132, 133, 142, 191
  and identity, 20–1, 49
  and the military, 78–81, 82–5
  and trauma, 73–4
  and women's sexuality, 59–60, 113–14, 117, 141–2, 186, 191–2
Psychology of Women (Deutsch), 114

Queer Gothic (Heggarty), 142
queerness, 15, 36–7, 39, 85, 132, 136–7, 138, 140, 142–3, 144–5, 189–92

Radical Innocence (Hassan), 119
Rado, Sandor, 132
Recreating Men (Pease), 238
Reumann, Miriam, 111–12, 115
Richardson, Dorothy, 24
Riesman, David, 7, 8, 31–4, 69, 166
riots, in Detroit and Harlem, 197, 198, 222, 223, 224
Rise and Crisis of Psychoanalysis in the United States, The (Hale), 8, 79
Rockefeller Foundation, 121, 140
Robinson, Paul, 112, 115
Robinson, Sally, 25–6, 49–50, 237
Room of His Own, A (Cronin), 174–5
Roosevelt, Franklin D., 13, 162, 197
Rose, Jacqueline, 20

Saad, Gad, 17
Salinger, J. D., 2, 24, 30, 48–62, 235
'Sanctimonius suburbanite, The' (Jurca), 35
Saunders, Frances, 120–1, 164
Savran, David, 40–1
Schaub, Thomas, 201
Schlemiel as Modern Hero, The (Wisse), 173–4
Schlesinger, Arthur, 12–13
Sedgewick, Eve, 24, 42, 131, 147
Segal, Lynne, 16–17, 138
Seid, Ruth *see* Sinclair, Jo
Self, Will and Gamble, David, 22
Seltzer, Carl C., 11
sex roles *see* gender
Sexual Behavior in the Human Female (Kinsey), 60, 113, 121
Sexual Behavior in the Human Male (Kinsey), 27, 111, 113, 114–17, 132–5
Sexuality (Weeks), 112
Shadow and Act (Ellison), 213
Shannon, Edward A., 142
Shaw, Irwin, 27, 81–2, 160, 163, 165, 167–71
Sinclair, Jo, 27, 160, 186–92, 193
Smith, Barbara, 209
Smith, Harrison, 49
Smith, William Gardner, 201
Souls of Black Folk, The (du Bois), 226

Soviet Union, 3, 5, 12, 13, 36, 121, 164, 201
Stepto, Robert B., 226, 227
Stowe, Harriet Beecher, 200–1
Strecker, Edward A., 59, 84–5, 87
Strecker, Edward A. and Appel, Kenneth, 82
Street, The (Petry), 28, 209–13, 219, 236
suburbia, 6, 31, 33–5, 40–1, 44
Summers, Claude J., 137

Taking It Like a Man (Savran), 40–1
Talented Mr Ripley, The (Highsmith), 27, 131, 138, 141–5, 155
Taylor, Harold, 33
Their Mother's Sons (Strecker), 59, 84–5
Thompson, Graham, 36–7
Thompson, Jim, 1–2, 25, 27, 72, 73–7, 143, 144
Trilling, Lionel, 8, 113, 115, 172
Truman, Harry S., 13, 163
Tuttle, William M., 125–6
12 Rules for Life (Peterson), 18

Uncle Tom's Cabin (Stowe), 200–1
Uncle Tom's Children (Wright), 199
'Uncontrolled desires' (Freedman), 132
Understanding Norman Mailer (McKinley), 95–6

van de Velde, Theodore H., 113
Victim, The (Bellow), 171
Vidal, Gore, 27, 131, 134–7, 140–1, 144, 155, 228, 235
Vital Center, The (Schlesinger), 12–13

Wagner, Philip S., 83
Wald, Alan, 165
Warren, Robert Penn, 171
'Warrior values' (McCarthy), 77–8, 93–4
Washington, Booker T., 216, 217, 227
Wasteland, The (Sinclair), 27, 160, 186–92, 193

Waters, Muddy, 197, 199, 204, 231
Weeks, Jeffrey, 112
What People Are (Heath), 85–6, 87
White Collar (Mills), 31
'White Negro, The' (Mailer), 14–16, 45
Whitehead, Stephen M. and Barrett, Frank J., 23
'whiteness' and American identity, 2, 3, 28, 48, 63, 161–2, 163, 164, 169, 188–9, 192, 196, 197, 199, 201, 203–4, 205–8, 209, 216–17, 219, 221, 227, 228, 236
Whiteness of a Different Colour (Jacobson), 161
Whiteness Visible (Babb), 161
Why Feminism? (Segal), 16–17
Whyte, William, 7, 8, 31–5, 36
Wiegman, Robyn, 18–19
Will to Knowledge, The (Foucault), 112
Williams, Sherley Anne, 201, 209, 222
Wilson, Andrew, 141
Wilson, Sloan, 27, 30–1, 34–9
Winnicott, D. W., 58, 62

Wisse, Ruth R., 160, 164, 165, 173–4
women
 and biological essentialism, 11–12, 113–14
 and morality, 38–9
 and mothering, 5, 9–10, 12, 34, 43, 49, 54–5, 58–60, 83, 84–5, 113–14, 122–3
 and sexualisation, 43, 75, 127–8, 210–11
 sexuality, 74, 113–14, 121–3, 127–9, 148, 152–4, 180–1, 189–92
Women, Race & Class (Davis), 205
Woolf, Virginia, 24–5
Wright, Richard, 199, 200, 201, 213, 214
Wylie, Philip, 59

Young Lions (Garrett), 170–1
Young Lions, The (Shaw), 27, 81–2, 160, 163, 165, 167–71, 193

Zelditch, Morris, 9–10
Zimmerman, Carle C., 116, 118
Žižek, Slavoj, 142

EU representative:
Easy Access System Europe
Mustamäe tee 50, 10621 Tallinn, Estonia
Gpsr.requests@easproject.com